FREE OFFER

If you want downloadable copies of the templates in this book, please go to my website at Montessorifamilies.com, or use the QR code below.

"Teresa's book is a dream come true for many parents interested in a little practical help implementing Maria Montessori's amazing insights in their homes. Her stories and information are spot on and come from many years as a parent, grandparent, Montessori teacher, and friend of parents. I wholeheartedly recommend this book to parents, grandparents, teachers, and friends of children everywhere."

–Mary Ellen Maunz, 50 years as a Montessori Teacher, Trainer, Consultant, Speaker, and Author

"I am truly inspired by the depth of knowledge and the sweetness of the words that carry this book into the hands of parents who can really make a difference in their children's lives. The book is a treasure chest of quality information expressed in clear and accessible language. That is why I highly recommend it."

–Philip Snow Gang, Ph.D., Montessori Graduate Educator

"As a Montessori infant-toddler teacher, teacher educator, and parent coach, parents often ask me what book they can read to incorporate Montessori principles into their homes. Teresa Angeles has now written it! Her enjoyable and easy-to-read book takes the essence of the brilliant work of Dr. Maria Montessori and weaves it into a practical guide for parents and others who want to implement the Montessori way of life into their home or school setting. The book shows you how to organize and prepare your space, skillfully present lessons, and talk to and gently guide your children to success. It describes how to give them a strong foundation for future learning and character development. If all parents read this book, the lives of parents, children, and the greater community would be changed."

–Nancy McNabb, Main Infant-Toddler Teacher Trainer, Authentic Institute of Montessori, AIM

"With warmth, expertise, and delightful stories of raising her six children, Teresa has written an inspiring book on ways to bring Montessori learning into your home. It reads as a friendly conversation over tea, parent-to-parent, respectful, practical, and kind. As a busy mom and child psychologist, I appreciate her attention to nurturing the heart and joy of the family, even while teaching the all-important Three R's and more. For educating children in today's world, her wholistic approach to learning wisely incorporates the vital brain health expertise of psychiatrist Daniel Siegel, M.D., and chemistry professor Edward Dratz, Ph.D. All-in-all, *The Montessori Home and Beyond* is a treasure, highly recommended for parents and all who care for children!"

–Joye Bennett, Psychologist

"Teresa Angeles' genius in this book is to take Italian educator Maria Montessori's key ideas for child development, along with other educators and psychologists who are compatible in thought, and find ways to integrate them into a practical vision of a loving, organic, and stimulating home environment. Where some parents try to "child-proof" their homes, this work will help you "learn proof" your home and nurture your children's gifts and hearts. Although Montessori gained worldwide fame at the start of the 20th century, her ideas to support and draw out children's creativity, self-discipline, inner wisdom, and compassion remain what the world continues to need. As evidence, many of today's most accomplished people in business, technology, the arts, leadership, and service attended Montessori schools. Lastly, the book summarizes Montessori's key ideas and follows Teresa's honest and down-to-earth personal journey, seeking to implement them for her own six children and home. Practical. Inspiring."

-James and Pamela Toole, Ph.D's, Educational Consultants

"The personal stories and gentle encouragement in this book make it so reader-friendly! There are many directions and options for parents to choose from. Most of all, it gives parents hope as they navigate the difficult world of parenting. Loved, loved, loved it."

–Carol Fisher, Owner, Saint Nicholas Montessori Preschool
and Elementary School, Federal Way, WA 1981-2012

"This is a very valuable resource for homeschooling families interested in the Montessori approach. It is thorough, in-depth, and very inspiring. The way the personal stories are woven into the book makes the whole book come alive."

–Marianne Molina is a Montessori Educator and past homeschooler.

"Great resource on how to apply Montessori principles in your everyday life. Teresa gives you the theory behind very practical applications. It doesn't have to be all or nothing. There are easy ways Teresa shows you how to start adding to your home life to give your children more independence. It also shows you how to follow your child to meet their needs. I would recommend this book to all families with young children."
–Hallie Lobaugh, Montessori Educator

"What an amazing book! I so love it! There is a lot of information nicely put together. It was more than just a book about Montessori learning and teaching. It is about a way of life that inspires and "creates" kids who are loving, nurturing leaders, self-sufficient, happy, and fulfilled. I honestly can't say enough about this book."
–Jaji Dhaliwal, Parent, Family Dentist, DDS

"What an incredible work you have created. What a wealth of information! You provide parents with a wide variety of resources for getting started. Indeed, a parent can set up a Montessori home and nurture the hearts of their children. It is indeed an asset to a parent serious about building a heart-based home. And the greatest asset of your book is your stories. They are so personable, but more importantly, enlightening for the reader to better understand your thoughts. I enjoyed that part of your book the best. I also think your stories lend credibility to you as an author, as you've been there, done that."
–Linda Cruce Robin, Educator and web designer

"*The Montessori Home and Beyond* is a very inspiring book that will help you understand your children's psychology and learning process, develop their full potential, and know and love them more."
–José Manuel González, Parent and Owner of a Manufacturing Co.

The
MONTESSORI HOME
and
BEYOND

The
MONTESSORI HOME
and
BEYOND

Nurture the Heart of
Your Child and Family

Teresa Angeles

Disclaimer: The author has sought to inform the reader and has shared personal stories about organizations that have given professional advice benefitting the parties involved. The ideas and suggestions contained in this book are not intended as a substitute for consulting with a physician. All matters regarding your health require medical supervision.

Copyright © 2024 by Teresa Angeles

All rights reserved. This book or any portion thereof may not be reproduced or used in any manner whatsoever without the express written permission of the author except for the use of brief quotations in a book review.

Published by Montessori Families

ISBN (paperback): 979-8-9919694-0-6
ISBN (ebook): 979-8-9919694-1-3

Book design and production by www.AuthorSuccess.com
Cover art by Maria Bano, Freelancer.com

Printed in the United States of America

Dedication

To my parents, who lovingly illustrated the beautiful image of family and home and etched it in my heart.

To my six children, who have inspired me to learn, grow, and love more than I could have imagined possible, and to their growing families, whose love touches and motivates me daily.

Contents

My Journey and Yours

It was 1989, and my family lived in a small town in Montana. My four-month-old son, Frederick, was asleep in my arms. His head grew heavy on my shoulder. His sparkling, dark eyes finally closed. I eased his tiny body onto the mattress gently so as not to awaken him. A few feet away, I could hear his two brothers, David and Francis, quietly breathing as they slept. I felt a special connection with these little boys who were so precious to me. They seemed peaceful in the small pine wooden beds my husband, Victor, had made.

"Ahhhh," I sighed as I fell into the soft blue rocking chair. They were asleep, and I could relax for the first time that day. I relished these moments to breathe and quietly watch our boys sleep.

"Soon, I will be on my way to bed," I thought. "I am so glad."

I walked by the bathroom and saw spills on the floor. "Oh, I'll just wipe these up and throw the towels in the washer quickly. It will only take a second, and I will be done."

Then, I noticed laundry on the floor. "Well, just a few pieces . . . I'll gather them and start the washer, and then I'll be done."

Minutes turned into hours, and before I knew it, it was very late. I knew I might be tired again tomorrow. Keeping a clean home while being a rested mom was a real challenge! I thought of the day when my friend, Annika, came to visit with her baby. My house was messy, with trucks and toys everywhere and the boys yelling and crashing into everything. Annika and I could not hear each other or feel at peace and had to go outside to visit. I was embarrassed and felt like a terrible mom and homemaker.

When I finally got to bed, I lay still. There was an uneasy feeling in my stomach. What was it? I was tired, and life was challenging. It was easy to feel like a failure and hard to know if I was making a difference. I loved caring for my family, but something was missing. My parents and relatives were in California. Was that it? I longed for more meaning and connection, especially with my children, and not just cooking and cleaning.

Like most parents, Victor and I had a dream to give our children the best life possible. We envisioned our children of the future facilitating creative projects and helping people all over the world. We hoped they would find their life callings and stay close to us. With so many children, life was challenging and not easy financially. We often felt afraid, but by putting one foot ahead of the other with faith, we kept moving forward. Families are so, so important.

I thought of how unlimited Victor and I were to raise and educate our children as we desired. I could see their intelligence and was inspired to teach them myself, but I didn't know how. They were getting older. We needed to do something. Feeling lost, I needed clarification on where to begin. We could educate them in religious, charter, public, or hybrid schools, or homeschool them ourselves. But, if we put them in a school, would the teachers, organization, and curriculum align with our philosophy for learning and life? Or, if we homeschooled, how would we find the right cooperative learning community and curriculum? Did I have enough patience and self-discipline to teach my children? If I did, I could teach them full-time. We could also supplement things we thought were important in the after-hours if they were in school. I would need some new skills. Whichever way we would choose, there were freedoms as well as responsibilities.

I sat up in bed. Victor heard me, sat up, and put his arms around me. We talked, and he understood my frustration. He asked what I wanted to do. I shared my thoughts with him. Although it was a stressful time for us financially, his openness toward me making whatever decision I thought would best serve our children touched and empowered me. We had faith that the resources would come if we did the right thing for our family. I was grateful for his love and support. It would take both of us to consider all the options and choose the best plan. I grabbed my journal and started writing, as I didn't want to lose the moment's clarity. I wrote for a long time, thinking and praying. I sensed that this was a peak moment in my life; one that would set the foundation for our future. We would determine a plan with God's help. Soon, I finally collapsed into sleep.

Moving forward began when I came across some articles about the Montessori method that I had read a few years earlier, and I recalled that I had attended a one-day Montessori seminar. I was deeply intrigued by Maria Montessori's educational philosophy and reputation for bringing out the best in children. She has impacted hundreds of thousands of people worldwide or more with her striking observations and unique recommendations for learning. She gave adults a new vision of embracing children. Her message was almost astonishing at the time, of love and respect for children, believing they had intelligence and wisdom all their own. And, this was at a time when society believed that children should be seen and not heard. The world was ready to accept her new ideas and recommendations.

I loved that Montessori taught that children's challenging behaviors disappear when they learn to concentrate on something they freely choose and love to work on. She said that concentration absorbs and focuses their energies. I thought about the beauty, order, and peace that were so tangible in my son's Montessori class. I wanted that at our home. I was busy and, at that point, was expecting our fourth child, so I questioned if it was practical for me to consider studying Montessori. I finally decided that having four children made knowing this philosophy vital.

At about this same time, we decided to move to Seattle for my husband's career. Coincidentally, Spring Valley Montessori was a wonderful school nearby, which was highly recommended for children's education and teacher training. The founder, Madeleine Justus, had met Maria Montessori and trained with one of Montessori's first students. A light bulb went off in my mind! I told Victor I had to take this training no matter what it took or how hard it was. He grew quiet, thinking of our responsibilities, but still supported me. I felt a surge of hope. My passion for loving and teaching this wonderful philosophy could come true.

My journey with Montessori education began at Spring Valley Montessori School in Federal Way, WA, where I gained knowledge and experience. Madeleine Justus, Founder and Head of School, and Gulsevin Kayihan, her associate director, gave me a fantastic orientation to the Montessori Method. Their love for European culture and their incorporation of history, botany, the sciences, art, and music into the curriculum inspired me more than I could ever say. With four young children, we had much to do to integrate this philosophy into our home. But we felt blessed to have found this program. The impact on our family life was profound.

I spent time at Saint Nicholas Montessori School in Federal Way, WA. Our young children came with me for a while, and we all flourished in the kind, nurturing environment. Later, my experience at Living Montessori Academy in Bellevue, WA, guided me to work with children and colleagues with compassion, collaboration, and professionalism. I grew in professional ways when I ordered new classroom furniture and materials, and mastered new online platforms. In all of these schools, I relished the emphasis on forested surroundings, beauty in the environment, gardening, and the spirit of gentleness, lovingly focused on children. These small communities of Montessori families deeply affected me and my family, impacted my teaching style, and played a significant role in shaping my vision for Montessori in the home.

The Montessori concept that most inspired my heart was the absorbent mind. I understood that children from conception to age six are in the most sensitive period of their lives. They learn effortlessly and absorb every detailed impression they take in from the people and environment around them. Further, Montessori described that children create themselves from these impressions, and the foundation of everything they will be is laid during this time. They need a kind, loving environment, excellent care, and growth opportunities. All four of my children were in this zero-to-six-year age range. My older children could learn to help the younger ones. It was ideal.

We found size-appropriate furniture at second-hand stores, garage sales, and many other places. We organized and put dishes in lower cupboards so our children could help themselves. We sorted closets and eliminated clutter. Routines gave our days a sense of structure. We gathered for meals, sang, and blessed our food. Celebrating holidays and traditions over the years enriched our family culture as we followed Montessori's lead. Little by little, our home felt more orderly and peaceful. We had found a plan for our family, although it was always a work in progress and never perfect.

I studied our children's developmental needs. As a family, we observed the seasons and life cycle of apples, and dissected flowers and fruit. We watched the moon and noted its phases. Life was beautiful even though we had much to do.

While planning and experimenting, I determinedly did my best to find what worked in our home. In those years, we discovered so many things! A learning process ultimately moved me to know my family more intimately and helped me see what we needed. Again, it was a continual growth journey, and I am still learning now. Ultimately, I believe it is the relationships that matter the most, and each family is unique. I hold sacred the message from Steven Covey, parenting expert, speaker, and author of *Seven Habits for Highly Successful Families*, who said that families can flourish when they do things right, even only *30* percent of the time. This thought always gave me hope. My dream is to give you hope for the dream you hold for your family, too.

An important thing I want to share is that having a Montessori home is not about being the perfect parent or having a perfect display of Montessori lessons, with everything in ideal order. It may not even mean that our houses are always clean and neat, even though we try. The heart of the Montessori home is love. It is a place where parents and children respect each other and communicate. It is about sensitive-hearted parents who watch to perceive their children's interests, contemplate how to share more about these, and then gently guide them. It isn't about being perfect, but about developing a special heart that follows the child. Montessori said that education should help life, whatever is needed.

As adults, we create the structure of the environment, set the boundaries and design it for their needs and interests, and then let them discover. There are certain ways to create order, but in that order is security. The order is for the child's development, and we encourage development by encouraging their participation in the environment.

As a parent, you are the most important person in your children's lives and their first teacher. In the very first years, the Montessori principles will help you develop relationships based on respect and an understanding of how children learn. They will guide you to nurture your children's strengths and develop an environment to inspire learning and critical thinking skills. From the gleanings I have made of Montessori's heart, I share a vision of what a Montessori home can be. I also share funny stories about my family. Applying the principles and using the resources here will help you structure your family life. And, when the time comes for academics, you will be a wise judge as to what environment will best suit them, whether it be formal schooling, homeschooling, religious, outdoor, or any other kind of educational experience. And, you can always keep a rich educational environment at home for your family, regardless of the type of schooling you ultimately choose, and that is the essence of what this book is about.

If your children are in a Montessori school, take advantage of the opportunity to learn more about the principles so you can support your children's development at home and coordinate with the school curriculum and activities. You can talk with teachers, volunteer, observe, and attend or request parent education events, which can be enriching for everyone.

We had our share of challenges as a family but also found the strength and faith to continue and not give up. Setting the foundation of a loving home environment that nurtures inner strength in our children is key to helping them learn to weather life's storms and come out shining, come what may. Every family will have challenges, which are opportunities to develop that spirit of overcoming.

With six children, I struggled with disorganization and choosing priorities. But, I found that there is a solution to a disorganized home. Order can be learned, especially if you start teaching your children to help when they are young. We could have done things earlier and had a neater home, but we did them when we learned how and benefitted. You can benefit, too. I have included templates based on Montessori and my own ideas for organizing the home and learning environment. These templates will make your path easier by teaching you to focus on the big picture first and then fill in the details.

Please understand that this book is primarily geared toward families with children ages zero to six. Yet, with the Montessori principles, it is foundational for families of all ages.

As I write, I use the words "children," "he," and "she" alternately to refer to children. If you are a primary caregiver, grandparent, family member, or friend who contributes significant time and energy to children, please know that I am speaking to you as I refer to "parents." You are vital in a child's life.

I respect each person's religious or spiritual orientation, what you believe of God, the Universe, or whatever you call the tremendous loving Presence of Life. If you believe in the greatness of the human heart as your life philosophy, I honor and appreciate that in you. Sometimes, I share my spiritual inspirations in this book because they flow from my heart to yours. Please translate these expressions into something helpful for your path and family.

I have tried to share the different aspects of the Montessori Method as it is related to families. Each chapter of this book has important keys. In the following chapters, I will share how you can cultivate your children's gifts, whether they are in school and you work with them for fifteen minutes every night or homeschool them full-time.

How This Book Unfolds

The organization of *The Montessori Home and Beyond* unfolds in the following order: In Chapter One, I briefly overview the Montessori Method with some practical recommendations. Chapter Two describes the principles of the Montessori environment that help you foster independence, order, and success in your children's worlds. Explore the potential of each room in your home as suggestions are made to enhance beauty and structure in your family's daily life.

Chapter Three defines the different Montessori materials and lists those most commonly recommended and why. Some lessons can be made at home following the concepts outlined here. This chapter also describes how to give lessons in a Montessori way. The remaining chapters will each focus on one concept, a story from our family, a description of a part of the philosophy, and activities you might try.

Chapters Four and Six provide information about right brain learning and multiple intelligences. In my mind, these are based on neuroscientific studies that confirm Montessori's findings decades later. They reveal her astute ability to understand the human psyche and character without technology and to design an approach to draw out potential. While these additional topics were developed outside of the Montessori discipline, I see them as extensions of Montessori's work and have found them to be truly helpful with children in my family and the classroom. I am excited to share what helped our family and what can inspire you. The title of my book includes the word *Beyond* because some parts of the information extend *beyond* the Montessori norm.

Chapter Five describes assessment and support for four aspects of our children: spiritual, mental, emotional, and physical. Observations noted in this assessment can sum up how well our children are doing as well-rounded individuals and will suggest how to help in areas of need. Keeping a notebook to journal what you observe can be a great help. Chapter Seven looks at bolstering family relationships as the foundational support for our children's lives. Here I share wisdom from Montessori and from doctors in the field of psychology. Chapter Eight depicts why traditions and celebrations are important for our families and how to make them events your children will cherish and remember always.

Benefits to the Reader

Using Montessori principles in your home, you will learn and grow with your children. There are many possible learning objectives, but nurturing your child's heart is the greatest. After reading this book, you will know how to:

- ✧ Recognize Dr. Montessori's approach of respect and unconditional love to draw out of your children the spark already there.

- ✧ Use timeless Montessori principles and templates to create a nurturing and successful home learning environment.

- ✧ Understand how right-brain learning can help your children use more of their whole brain.

- ✧ Encourage your young children's highly intuitive natures and bond with them.

- ✧ Take time for yourselves as a couple, and prioritize family relationships as foundational.

- ✧ Develop creative traditions that deepen your family culture with stories, music, and community.

In this book, I provide abundant information to encourage you to set up a learning environment in your home. If you choose to do this, I hope you will see it as an ongoing journey of evolution in which you can relax and enjoy the process. Because I know you are busy with a family, I encourage you to let your heart lead you. As you get ideas, do some now and a little more as you go. Keep asking yourself, "What is the next step I can take?" instead of allowing yourself to be stressed. If you keep doing that, magnificent things can happen.

Given the influences in the world today, raising children seems more challenging than when our children were small. More than ever, we need to draw our families together to nurture relationships that create a haven of love and community that supports them. They need to have those close to them that they can trust as they pass through the different stages of their lives. Let your family be a haven for them.

The best time to nurture your children is in the first six years when they live in the absorbent mind and the heart of a loving family and home. True intelligence and virtue begin there. The strength of your bond will foster their growth in every way and help them navigate life. Our world needs children balanced in body, mind, and soul to be tomorrow's leaders. They need homes where parents will care for them and recognize the opportunity to slow down and make life all it can be during this short period. When we provide this, our children will be whole. They will be the hope for the new world Montessori envisioned.

If you know what you want for your family, the Montessori principles can help you accomplish it. If you aren't sure what you want, this book will provide new ideas for you to contemplate. Be empowered and fulfilled as the parent you were meant to be, and make your dreams come true.

The Heart of the Montessori Method: Principles to Draw Out Your Child's Potential

> "If homes to nurture our children's hearts
> and souls do not exist, let us build them."
> –Teresa Angeles

Maria Montessori's passion and ideas about working with children spurred a revolution worldwide. Scientific and creative, her method was founded on the idea of "educaré," an Italian word that means to draw out what is within. She believed all children had gifts and strengths that only needed cultivation in an environment rich with opportunity and order. She saw that children's developmental needs were extremely important during each phase of life, and she sought to fulfill them innovatively. Her observations were the foundation of her method. The *Montessori Method* is a message of hope for our world and a heartwarming guide for families.

The principles discussed in this book will serve you well as you prepare an environment for your children and family. Implementing the principles is your home will be doable because they will be based on your family's interests and what works for you. You will grow as your children do. As you read this book, I hope your inspiration will lead you to new levels of understanding and excitement to embrace your children and experiment with new learning methods. There is a good amount of information here, but the heart of the Montessori message is love, sensitivity, and being present with children. Giving yourself permission to read and relax, not feeling that you must digest it and act on it all at once, will allow you to feel empowered rather than pressured. Since you are reading this book, you must already have a dream you are looking for ways to fulfill. I pray you will gain more vision about how to fulfill that dream. We incorporated the principles into our lives little by little, as you can see in the following story. We tried to provide opportunities to awaken our children's gifts and curiosity.

David, the Four-Year-Old Archeologist

One beautiful Montana morning, our smiling four-year-old son, David, tapped me on the back. He leaned up to whisper in my ear, "Mommy. I've decided I am going to become an archeologist! And I know where we can dig—in that hill over there. I want to see if there are treasures or gems in there."

He looked like he had the biggest secret in the whole world and showed me a book about archeology from our library basket. I knew he loved rocks. He also loved the crystals we had in our home. From our front door, you could see across the narrow road to the hill across the street. This was his target, and he wanted my help.

Knee deep in laundry, caring for our two-year-old son, Francis, and our new baby, Frederick, I paused. My initial thought was that I wondered how I would ever get everything done if I took an hour out of the day to go on this adventure with my son. I looked at his face, beaming joyfully at this newfound project, and took a deep breath. I would always have work to do and decided it was a priority to help make this a special event for the day. I believed in the Montessori philosophy that following a child's curiosity is a key to his developing genius. And this was the perfect opportunity. I loved David and wanted him to feel that, so I accepted his invitation.

With Francis in tow and Frederick in my snuggly, David and I went to his father's workbench and gathered essential tools into a plastic bin. We grabbed some screwdrivers and a hammer. Together, we crossed the road and set to work digging. He was the operator, and I was the assistant, nearby. We talked through it together as he searched. I offered guidance but let him take the lead. Something powerful inside of him was driving this project, and I respected it. The Montana soil was not easy to work with. After about half an hour, David had some gray and rough rocks, the fruit of his labor. He had worked hard and was tired now, but he had pushed through. Now, we would go home to clean and organize what he had found.

It was a time of happiness and warm bonding for David and me. As a parent, I had learned that my quiet presence while doing something was more powerful than talking. It communicated that I respected his thoughts and choices. I also found that being "present" was just as much my job as "doing," if not more important to his self-esteem and our connection. My presence communicated that I loved him, was happy with him, and wanted to be with him. What he believed about his attachment to me, his parent, and his thoughts about himself was crucial to his future confidence and peace. I didn't always know that, but I realized this more and more.

We carefully packed the precious rocks, washed them, and displayed them on our nature shelf in the living room. Later, when his daddy came home, David raced to the car, excited to show him. They sat down together to look at the rocks and try to identify them in David's book. He beamed with pride, knowing we could categorize stones by their patterns and colors. He enjoyed grouping those that were similar.

David had always loved rocks and minerals. When he was a little older, we took him and his siblings to a gem and minerals show in Tacoma, Washington, close to where we lived a few years later. We bought inexpensive strands of amethyst, lapis lazuli, and quartz. The kids loved looking at all of the many options and relished the chance to bring some home. Our older children strung the beads into necklaces and sold them at church or gave them away as gifts. They loved giving them but also enjoyed receiving some income for their work. David continues to appreciate stones and gems even today, at age thirty-seven. He remembers digging in that hill when he was four and enjoys the memory!

What the Montessori Approach Adds to This Story

The Montessori approach adds to this story by ordering the environment so that there is a place for these special items to be organized and displayed. Our nature shelf allowed our children to categorize objects from outside, such as stones, nests, and leaves. As they learned to sort these into categories, they translated the concepts into more abstract ideas and created an orderly mind. It doesn't have to be overwhelming or huge, but when we found a bug or a rock, we knew it went there on that shelf. We gathered books and other related things there, too, to learn more about them.

As you can see from this experience, one event can have many benefits. David enjoyed feeling respected and supported by his mom and dad. Our quiet presence nurtured his self-esteem. There was the memory of being curious and then getting support to explore. Building on his knowledge of identifying rocks and gems in books, he now could recognize some of the colors and markings of the stones to understand their makeup. This cultivated his scientific mind. When David got crystals and gems at a show years later, remembering this experience built on this positive memory as the spark of his interest continued to grow. This probably helped him connect later with the purchased gems he strung on necklaces. We can use the environment around us to nurture the curiosity in our children. It doesn't have to be expensive or complicated; instead, it takes a little ingenuity and resourcefulness. I learned this from my experience with the Montessori method and was inspired to use it with my children.

Who Was Maria Montessori?

I want to introduce you to the woman who started a worldwide educational movement at the beginning of the twentieth century. Maria Montessori was one of the first female doctors in Italy at a time when women rarely became physicians. Early in her career, she assisted surgeons and also worked in psychiatry. She visited mental institutions and was told that the children loved to pick up the crumbs from the floor after they ate. By observing this, she realized they were trying to satisfy a need for sensory experience in a hospital environment with little to stimulate their senses. She chose not to criticize them for acting like animals, as some others did. Montessori believed that the children needed physical movement and purposeful activity for their mental well-being and that the lack of activity was contributing to their mental illness. As she worked with children, her interest grew until she decided to pursue teacher training and became deeply engaged. Montessori questioned the approaches being used at the time to teach children with psychological and developmental challenges and was outspoken about her opinions.

Eventually, she became the co-director of a school to train teachers of special needs children. This was her chance to focus on a new way of teaching that could help the children. Using her medical background, she used precise methods to observe, assess, and create hands-on educational materials to fit the children's needs. She discovered how important it was for them to hold and manipulate physical objects in order to learn simple concepts. Using this approach, she saw they could later translate what they had learned through physical touch to an understanding of more abstract concepts. She was very careful to introduce and use only the materials the children showed satisfaction with, which she believed met their developmental needs.

Later, when she helped open a school in a poor area of Rome called San Lorenzo, she also found that these same materials were key for working with children without special needs. These children were home alone all day while their parents worked. She jumped at the opportunity to try her method with children without mental and developmental challenges. At first, they were not well-behaved, but their cooperation and attention improved when they learned to focus on interesting activities. Montessori observed that when children had materials that nurtured their development, they could actually teach and discipline themselves and were happy.

All around the world, people began to hear about the children in Montessori's classes who flourished with self-discipline and concentration. Newswriters, administrators from famous educational institutions, and even royalty came to observe her students and classrooms. They wanted to understand how this seemingly miraculous change was possible. This went on for the rest of her life.

Maria Montessori, World Renowned Speaker

Montessori developed a curriculum and began training teachers to use her educational method with two-and-a-half- to six-year-olds. Teachers who came from many different countries took her training and returned to set up classrooms in their towns and cities. Classrooms designed with Montessori principles give children a strong foundation for developing their senses. They learned to choose work, concentrate, and experience joyful independence. In 1909, she authored her first book and many more after that. Soon, she developed an elementary program, began holding classes, and trained teachers. The environment she created for the elementary children differed from that of the zero-to-six-year-old children because she saw that their needs differed.

After some time, Montessori also lectured at length about her vision of an adolescent program where youth would be empowered by the work of their hands. Her entire process of education became a revolution that changed the image of the child for all humanity.

A New Education to Embrace the Whole Child

Montessori had a burning desire to improve children's lives, which led her to abandon the lucrative medical field. Instead, she created a kind of education that nurtured the "whole child." This new education cultivated the qualities of compassion and sensitivity *for* children and *within* the children. The children came to love and care for themselves, others, and their environment.

Montessori realized the importance of the parent regarding the child's development and future. She clarified the vital role of the environment in the child's development, which this book will go into in more detail, and based much of her observation and teaching on it. She also talked about the need for adults to prepare to love unconditionally to overcome tendencies toward anger and pride, which children's innocent emotions can easily trigger, but also addressed the adult's need to establish structure or boundaries. She advocated for children to have freedom within these boundaries.

This information has been taken from the *American Montessori International* website, https://montessori-ami.org, which has a wealth of information. You can find much more about the details of Montessori's life, and I encourage you to visit their website to learn more about Montessori's history, valuable information about Montessori concepts that can be implemented in your home, and facts about Montessori schools and training programs worldwide.

Montessori's Principles and Message to the World

The key concepts of the Montessori method inspired me. I loved how they made me think and feel about my children and suddenly saw them in a different light. They were beings on a spiritual journey with me, with wisdom and depth in their souls that would unfold naturally if the correct elements were in place. I could look into their eyes, even as tiny babies, and see their wisdom.

One of the most profound inspirations came to Montessori after she had worked with children for some time and had become well known. She shared her observation of the "inner teacher." This concept resulted from her experience with how children choose their work. Her perception was that each child had an inner sense of what they needed, including direction in the classroom to satisfy developmental needs. She saw this as an inner sense, an inner direction she called the "inner teacher," like the voice of conscience. It also helped them to know right from wrong. Since every child is born with an "inner teacher," it is within all of us for all of our lives. Mary Ellen Maunz, mother of three, internationally known speaker, teacher educator, and author, says that parents also have an "inner teacher" who directs and helps them do their best. It is the part of us that is authentic, wise, and kind, and it helps us honor and respect our children and do what is best for them. She says, Montessori is really a message, . . . not a method. And that message is the respect for the inner teacher within yourself and within the child, and that message calls for a whole new way of behaving with children.

The Absorbent Mind

Montessori observed that children from zero to six years old have a different way of interacting with their surroundings and an absorbent mind that allows them to absorb knowledge and teach themselves without being taught. She saw that children learn effortlessly when the environment is set up for them with attractive learning opportunities and things they can touch and work with. Their absorbent minds take in information and, especially in the earliest years, do not filter it. They absorb everything they see and experience like sponges. Children see, hear, and remember things, incorporating these images into their souls. Everything that touches them influences what and who they will be. Montessori's book, *The*

The Beautiful Absorbent Mind of a Child

Absorbent Mind, expounds profoundly on these concepts. We realize what an amazing and active mind works in the two-year-old child who can recognize all the persons and things in his environment without being taught. With this revelation, we are also faced with the tremendous opportunity and responsibility to care for our children intentionally by giving them every opportunity to learn, grow, and thrive. With awe, we understand that we were also created by the children we once were and that our most essential faculties were built in the first years of our lives.

A Child's Sensitive Periods

Table 1.1 Sensitive Periods – Birth to Age 6

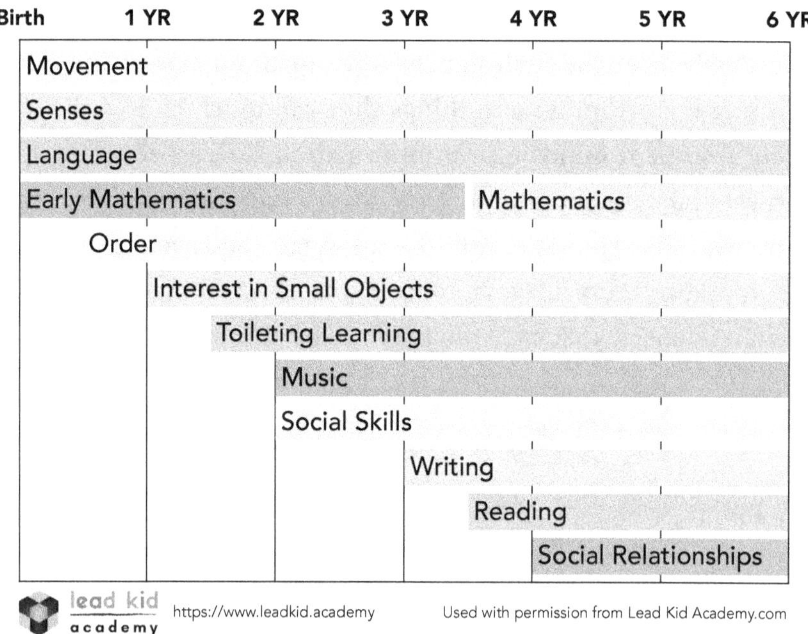

We may notice our children's desire to work on a particular kind of skill with intense interest and focus. They may pick up tiny specs of dust or repeat the counting of beans from one to ten, or any other skill, over and over every day for some time. Suddenly, another activity may come into their awareness, such as spooning beans or washing tables, and they switch their focus again for a prolonged time. With this hyper-focus, children work in what Montessori called the "Sensitive Periods." The different areas of the brain are developing and inviting almost exclusive attention to one type of activity. These sensitive periods identified by Montessori in the three-to-six-year-old child make learning new concepts and skills much easier. In fact, they are drawn to develop specific skills more than at any other time. For example, reading is much more appealing to the three-to-five-year-old than an older child. Montessori said that providing the stimulation the child seeks at that particular time will maximize development opportunities.

Confirming this theory of Montessori, the University of Maine published an article entitled "Children and Brain Development: What We Know About How Children Learn." This article explains, "There are sensitive periods in children's lives when specific types of learning take place." This article also shares observations about how children focus on these sensitive periods. Some of the main sensitive periods that Montessori identified include movement, order, spatial relations, language, small objects, music, math, writing, reading, and grace and courtesy. This information will be extremely helpful to you.

These sensitive periods are unique for each child and can last for different amounts of time. Children don't necessarily complete their learning in these areas in this time frame or reach an abstract understanding, but this time helps them in concrete and sensorial ways. It sets the foundation with building blocks for later learning.

At home, we tried to be aware of these cycles in our children's lives. We read about and watched for their sensitive periods and tried to consciously supply what was needed. For example, from the earliest years, reading was essential in our minds. We read with our children and also taught them to read, which still are my favorite memories of spending time with them. When we realized one of our children was in a sensitive period, we could better meet their needs.

Normalization

Montessori said that normalization was her most important discovery. With this word, *normalization,* she described the behavior young children exhibit when with short attention spans, they learn to focus and concentrate for sustained periods on hands-on work they have freely chosen. In this way, self-discipline and calmness appear; from this work, they often emerge refreshed and contented. For children under six, work may be washing a window, counting beads, or cutting a banana to share with siblings or friends. Their "work" may look like a frivolous activity to us, such as picking up tiny pieces of fuzz in the carpet, but be assured that it is purposeful work, building the brain and heart. Normalization occurs when children, because of sustained concentration, develop normally or become normal and calm. **Because it is so important for normalization, we try to train ourselves not to interrupt children as much as possible even if we think we have something more valuable for them to do.**

In his article, "Motivated to Grow: The Child's Passion for Work," Paul Epstein, Ph.D., Montessori teacher and head of school, talks about how children love to work and how their work helps them to develop concentration and normalization. He shares that it is the work itself that they love and not the result. They see their mistakes as part of the learning process and, remarkably, do not tire from work. Instead, they become energized from working on tasks they have chosen, whether it is for a two and a half to six year old, washing a window, writing a numeral, cutting an apple to share with others, or tracing a geometric shape. This experience would seem to set children up to meet life confidently and enthusiastically.

In our home, we encouraged normalization by involving the children in our usual household routines and by trying to find activities that would attract their attention. Some examples of activities that helped our children concentrate included practical life activities such as cooking and cleaning. We raked yards together in the fall when the leaves were abundant and planted gardens in the spring. Spooning beans from one bowl to another or pouring sand or rice from pitcher to pitcher developed fine motor skills and helped with concentration. Discovering nature helped their budding curiosity and sense of order because the beautiful seasons are cyclical, and nature follows this order. We tried to create exciting activities to attract them, such as learning to fish, which led to practical life skills in food preparation and nutrition. It also showed them how they could contribute to the family, and they learned so much.

The Four Planes of Development

Table 1.2 The Four Planes of Development

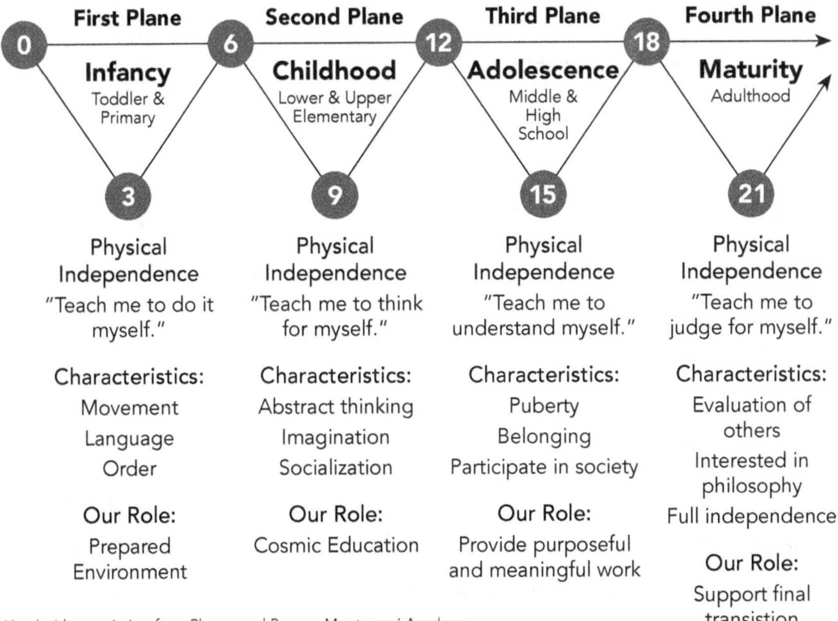

Used with permission from Rhyme and Reason Montessori Academy.

Montessori talked about the *Planes of Development,* describing four periods children and youth go through. She felt that each lasted for about six years, and led to maturity at about age twenty-four. She believed that the child had an inner blueprint to attain specific developmental milestones during each period and that these built upon the previous development. The above chart reflects these developmental stages. Children are internally driven to accomplish these, with the most potent time being at the beginning of each period, peaking sometime during those six years, and then gradually leveling off until the beginning of the next period. In her book, *The Absorbent Mind,* Montessori said that personalities change from plane to plane. We realize what powerful and vast transformations occur if we compare newborn children to six-year-olds. If we understand the developmental stages of our children, it is easier to identify and meet their needs. We can prepare the right environment to nurture potential. Without understanding, we are like sailors at sea without a rudder.

The four time periods or planes mentioned by Montessori include the years:

1. Birth to Six Years Old
2. Six to Twelve Years Old
3. Twelve to Eighteen Years Old
4. Eighteen to Twenty-Four Years Old

Parents need to understand the continuum of this long cycle, where their children are at any particular time, and their future development goals.

The First Plane

In the first period, from birth to age six, Montessori identified the goal of adaptation and saw that young children have a miraculous and special kind of mind that can adapt to their surroundings effortlessly. She spoke about children from infancy to three years old, describing the *unconscious absorbent mind*, when children absorb everything without a filter and, like a sponge, take in the mindset, postures, and ways of their families and cultures. To do this, they have no lessons or teachers, but just naturally integrate these impressions into themselves. This fantastic quality of the absorbent mind allows children to merge into their circumstances.

According to Montessori, this first three-year period is the most critical stage for children because they are developing their personal selves, both physically and mentally. She saw this period as foundational for who they would become. They are sensitive and vulnerable, needing love, attachment to a primary caregiver, respect, and protection. They also need to move freely without being constrained to develop coordination and flexibility. They need to learn to communicate and interact on many levels. They learn their complete mother language with all its syntax, grammar, and intricacy, and this alone is an achievement that would take an adult decades to accomplish. When a child is three years old, the foundation of who they will be is established.

The second half of this first period or plane, from three to six, is that of the *conscious absorbent mind*. During this time, a child begins to act on the foundation he has laid in his mind and body, making decisions about what he will focus on and do. The absorbent mind also continues to learn effortlessly at this time, but in a slightly different way, with *conscious* determination. Montessori saw how children teach themselves if the environment is set up for them with appropriate materials and supportive adults standing by to help when needed. I have personally observed this over and over again when things are attractive and interesting. Three to six-year-olds are ready to start acting decisively, to calculate, and to explore. They are more physically skilled than younger children at manipulating materials to process and learn. Seeing how the absorbent mind teaches and leads the child in their discovery process is wonderful. Now, I will discuss the future planes in more detail, although birth through six is the main subject of this book.

The Second Plane

The second period of six-to-twelve-year-old children involves a time of great intellectual potential. Children of this age tend to be balanced and healthy, with curiosity and a tremendous drive to learn. My observation of this time from working with my children and others is that they love interacting with others, working on group projects, searching for information, and using their imaginations. They move from concrete understanding to more abstract thinking, using what they have gleaned from the first plane of the absorbent mind and employing it now in the next, more complex development phase. There is often a sense of natural happiness and calmness during this time.

The Third Plane

The third period of adolescence, from twelve to eighteen years old, is when youth are idealistic and seek to establish an identity and explore careers. They need respect and a nurturing environment for their sensitive spirits. Montessori felt that adolescence was not a time for intense intellectual pressures and studies. She recommended adolescents work with their hands, using practical experiences to comprehend complex concepts. She suggested they learn science and finance by growing vegetables and selling them, or by operating a small hotel or business. She lectured and wrote about these ideas of working with adolescents and called it "*Erdkinder*," meaning "children of the earth." I believe that her recommendations have and will continue to impact the way our society approaches adolescents in schools. Since Montessori's time, many schools have created alternative programs where students can focus more on projects.

Montessori was not able to develop these programs for youth before her passing, but her book entitled *From Childhood to Adolescence*, published in 1987, is a wonderful reference to her revolutionary ideas. This book paints a beautiful picture of cultivating practical idealism in adolescents and empowering them to build strong identities during this unique time. Parents and families can find a new vision and inspiration for cultivating a happy, satisfying life for youth. The *NAMTA Journals* also provide a treasure trove of innovative ideas from Montessori's lectures about living and working with adolescents. These wonderful journals will fill you with a whole new way of thinking about life with adolescents.

A Teen Works at Farming

The Fourth Plane

Finally, from eighteen to twenty-four, young adults consider their spiritual, physical, and social life, establishing their place in society and determining how they will contribute. During this time, they will consider what they want to do for a career, whether they will have a family, and what personal interests and responsibilities they will evolve. They will aim for independence spiritually and emotionally. It is a time to complete the foundation of their lives.

During these four planes, the goal is for the individual to gain the skills and strengths needed to fulfill their life purposes. With this valuable information, we parents, have a magnificent opportunity to help our children set the foundation for a successful life. We do this by understanding their needs at each developmental stage and by then preparing environments that offer rich opportunities and experiences to satisfy these developmental needs. Each period or plane offers opportunities to nurture their innate interests, strengths, and gifts.

Our Family and the Planes of Development

We believed that young children have deep emotional sensitivity and treated them with tenderness. We tried to keep things as calm as possible, knowing babies were intuitive with their mother and father and receptive to everything touching their lives. We realized how careful we needed to be about their care, so we tried to handle and speak to them gently and were conscious of what they saw and heard. We wanted them to have a loving, positive, and peaceful experience because we understood that these impressions would impact their minds and nervous systems. This is all because of the fantastic absorbent mind of a child under six years old.

We became observers of their needs and interests. I loved to find activities they enjoyed that helped to enhance their focus. Their thirst for knowledge and adventure was very apparent, even as toddlers. "Where were they curious? What did they want to learn?" For example, I remember seeing my eighteen-month-old son consistently peering into one kitchen cupboard and reaching in to handle the lids and pot holders, so I made it safely accessible. I often asked myself what they needed and what I could do, even when they were tiny. My husband and I often worked with them in the evenings when they were curious about books. We used simple early reading materials that were like games. These hours stand out as some of the most cherished times and became the backdrop of our lives, a time of closeness and love.

Dr. Montessori recognized that human development is not perfectly linear but occurs in cycles and grows in holistic ways. Our goal is for our children to develop into the authentic persons they were meant to be and to have the foundation needed for that development.

Qualities of the Montessori Environment

There is a growing movement to use Montessori concepts in the home to recreate the successful environments that Montessori schools have enjoyed for decades. This section presents some of these elements so you can be conscious of them as you set up your home and a learning environment.

Freedom and Self Discipline

Montessori believed that children are on a mission to be independent from birth and want to do things by themselves as soon as possible. Parents often hear this when children say they want to do things by themselves, especially as toddlers. Children need the freedom to respond to their developmental needs for movement and timing. They are also eager to fulfill their inner desire to understand and be understood as a part of their social environment. Encouraging independence allows children to do things by themselves and facilitates spontaneous self-discipline because they feel free and empowered. If we provide interesting opportunities for them to freely choose to work on, they will also feel satisfied. We can hinder them at home by doing everything for them, not letting them participate in caring for themselves and their environments, thinking we are helping. Even from the earliest months, we might avoid doing for the child what the child can do alone. This may include giving them a chance to try to turn over before we rush over and do it for them.

Working with children to provide an environment of love and boundaries was not easy for me, and it was a puzzle at first. I understood how important it was to have balanced boundaries and how it helped children direct themselves, but I kept running into my own psychology and frustration. I really had to work on learning how to discipline in a firm but loving way. We had very strong-willed children. I wanted to respect them as well as myself. My husband came from a very authoritarian background, and I came from one that was a little bit more relaxed, so our expectations were different. This is something I believe many couples experience. We went to classes and worked hard together to communicate, and we learned so much over the years. Our children taught us so much about love and patience. Gradually, I found that creating boundaries that allowed our children to have certain freedoms worked the best, as Montessori described, so it wasn't so top-heavy. It was freeing for our children as well as for us. I saw that it invited children to trust themselves, to explore confidently, and to trust us as parents who believed in them. This nurtured loving relationships among us all.

Montessori claimed that the children in her program were unruly at first. However, after a few months, they developed self-control, moving and choosing their work quietly, putting it back on the shelves when they finished, and being careful not to disturb their peers. They had freedom of choice and became independent, kind, and joyful through their inner motivation. These became some of her most important findings and later a part of the foundation of her classrooms everywhere. She said that freedom and discipline can coexist and that self-discipline comes naturally when the child feels respected and free to follow his heart's inner promptings.

Structure and Order

Structure and order help children feel secure as they sense rhythm in their lives. They can learn to trust that things will be predictable when there are routines, such as regular mealtimes and naptime, though we were flexible when needed. We can organize learning materials and toys in baskets or on shelves so children know where they go and can put them away as they get older, sometimes with help. Doing our best to see that beds are made daily helps children with their sense of order. It's also important to be balanced and gentle, not striving for perfection but doing our best and adjusting as needed. Between one and three years old is the sensitive period for order.

Beauty

A Montessori environment should be beautiful and preferably simple. Even though things are simple we can add tasteful nature pictures, hang a rug or macrame, or place calming pastel-colored pillows. Our home can be lovely, whether it is a house, a trailer, or a mansion. The structure of a home is not as important as the feelings and intentions within it. Where you gather to nurture your family is a very special place. Important things happen there. Order in the environment makes beauty more apparent. Eliminating excess can be really helpful. Your family may feel a sense of peace and tranquility when there is beauty.

Nature and Reality

Montessori had a reverence for nature, and she felt it was important for children. Her writings often reference children exercising outside or working in gardens. They did different kinds of work outside in the fresh air, including math and language activities, rather than staying inside all day. She shared that it is not the outside work that enhances the children's development, but the idea of *living naturally*. She discussed ideas of planting, gardening, and knowing nature, but the most important objective was to free the children from the isolated and artificial confinements of life in the city. To expand on this idea, she recommended that children wear simpler, lighter clothing and sandals or go barefoot so they could feel nature. She described how our current way of life has caused us to have given up freedom in exchange for a prison house that we have grown to love and have passed on to our children. She described how we have come to be restricted to the growing of flowers and caring for domestic animals as our source of nature, which she believes has caused our souls to shrink and develop internal "contradictions."

Montessori encouraged adults to let the children be free to run outside in the rain, to remove their shoes and jump in puddles, and walk in the meadow with bare feet when the dew is wet. Her vision for children was so beautiful, encouraging them to rest peacefully under trees and shout and laugh when the sun awakens them in the morning, as it does every living creature. Montessori discouraged the habit of pushing children in a stroller who were old enough to walk, keeping them in the shade when the sun was out and bright. At these times, she invited them to activities. Her image of immersing children in nature warms the heart!

Nature Montessori Rope Bridge

A Place to Be Social

In the Montessori environment, children are encouraged to be gracious and courteous contributors socially. They learn to give, receive, and work conflicts out with others. As parents help guide them through challenges, children can learn compassion in their communication. In the traditional Montessori environment, children can be of different ages, between two and a half and six. The older children in this group learn to introduce concepts and lessons to the younger ones once they master them. Younger children also play a role as they are mentored, giving the older ones a chance to lead and themselves a chance to follow. In a Montessori home, children often have siblings and can work with this idea. There is an emphasis on sharing what one has learned so children can learn different roles and grow in love and closeness with each other. It seems that the home can be the ideal place for this sharing and mentoring, increasing family bonding.

There is also the opportunity to resolve conflicts at a peace table at home, where children and families can talk things out and try to hear each other. They learn a specific process of taking turns to listen and hear everyone's point of view. It is a transformative place where they can independently look at problems and resolve disagreements. A peaceful symbol, such as a talking stick or an artificial

Siblings Brushing Teeth

flower, is passed back and forth between the two speakers, who have identified a conflict. Two chairs or pillows allow them to sit comfortably, facing each other. We can follow this format to model kind communication and even sit at the peace table to discuss an issue and ask questions to better understand a situation. Children learn early on how to empathize and express their hearts. Our family struggled with this concept of working things out, and I learned more about using a peace table when I started working in a classroom in my later years. It is an empowering format for children to learn to work things out with others.

The following is a sequence of steps to take as children use the peace table in your home. You can print one out, Google similar templates, or design your own booklet and keep it at your home peace table to guide discussions. Your children can follow this when they want to resolve an issue with someone. At first, they will need your help, but gradually, they will do it independently.

Peace Table Work

1. Keep a hand on your heart

2. Hold the talking stick to speak

3. Tell the truth

4. Use kind words

5. Use "I observe, I need, I feel, I would like it if you … or I can…."

6. Listen silently

7. Seek to understand and be understood

8. Resolve

Intellectual Opportunities

The Montessori curriculum has five learning areas where lessons are organized and introduced: Practical Life, Sensorial, Language, Math, and Cosmic/Cultural. Children can develop many skills by engaging in carefully prepared lessons in these areas. Lessons can be very simple and even homemade, yet collectively, they have a profound impact on their lives.

Simply put, we tried to make our home an environment created with consideration for our children. We allowed them to explore, investigate, and question. They also learned to use common tools found in everyday life, even in the preschool years, including such items as safe kitchen utensils and materials for cleaning. They learned to help load the dishwasher and wipe the table. The younger ones learned many skills from their older siblings, while the older ones learned what it was like to lead and help others. We also did simple service projects for neighbors and the food bank, using this vision to help us create a family mission of service. Our home involved our children and was a place where we tried to kindle respect and compassion for each other.

Learn to Observe Your Children

Maria Montessori's observations led her to discover what children need to develop naturally. Observing our children is equally important. Observation allows us to see them without judgment and let go of our biases or opinions of what we think they *should* be doing. Instead, knowing that all children are different and learn at different rates, we can see and accept what they do and love. Being able to step back from the situation to watch our children allows us to know what they need so we can support them. We can be responsive rather than reactive. We can understand their limits and help them before they get overwhelmed. Learning to hold back when we see our children struggling to accomplish something that is within their reach, rather than rescuing them, will support their growth. We may give them a little more time before we offer help, though always compassionately and in balance. It is best if your children will allow you to sit in a corner where you can quietly watch and hear them without interaction. Remaining as quiet and still as possible allows you and your children to concentrate better—them on their activities and you on your observation. It is usually easier not to draw attention to what you are doing by explaining. If your children do not allow you to watch for a few minutes, you can say you are just being quiet and would appreciate them letting you do it. A specific notebook that you keep just for observation can be a great tool. Over time, you can look back and see how things have changed and what you have learned about your child.

The list of what you can observe is endless, and often you will notice things that you have not seen before. When you follow up on these little things week after week, you may get insights that will be very valuable.

Learn to Observe Yourself in Interaction with Your Child

In a different kind of observation, we can watch our own interactions with our children. Finding out how we interface with them can greatly help us. We may observe our impatience or anger when they do certain things, and we can note these without self-judgment. Later, we can reflect and try to understand why we felt and acted the way we did. We can think about how we might approach the situation differently, reach out for support and talk with a friend or therapist, or read a book and refresh our approach. We can realize that it is up to us to create a supportive environment. Children can help us see what is not the best in us and help us to change. And we change because we love them so much. This is one of the greatest benefits of having children. Love makes us change for the better.

Because observation is so important, there will be a box called "Observation Practice" at the end of every chapter. Each box will have just a few questions you may choose to answer. As you learn more about the Montessori message, you may find observing and reflecting on these ideas easier. Understanding your children's needs will also help you envision how to teach them.

If we observe weekly for fifteen minutes, we will learn many things. Sometimes, I have asked myself a question that I will try to answer while I am observing. We might see changes in our children or ourselves from the week before. If we run on auto-pilot non-stop, we may miss amazing details that can help us understand ourselves or our children, that might help life flow better. Observation is a key Montessori principle upon which everything else is based. It sounds simple, and it is, but it takes self-discipline and focus. It is also extremely valuable.

Embracing the Montessori Way

Embracing the Montessori way as a parent is a magnificent journey of discovery about our children, our environment, and ourselves. It will make us stretch, grow, and change in unimaginable ways. Taking one step at a time, remembering to breathe, and love are essential keys. We can relax if we strive to be helpful instead of perfect or important. This was something my Montessori teacher said to me that left a lasting impact.

We will reflect on the concepts discussed in this chapter as we go on to the next chapter on setting up your physical Montessori home. Because our children are so sensorial, the quality of the physical home is vital. The journey continues!

T1.1 My Observation Practice One: Sample Template
Child: Gina   Age: Eleven Months   Date: Jan. Third

Things to Observe	Things I see
Does my child seem at ease and empowered in her environment? Can she do things for herself? How can I help her be more independent?	She seems empowered in her environment, can reach her toys and activities, may like to sit at a weaning table and chair.
What kind of fine motor activities does he like? (Drawing, writing, cutting, coloring, pincher grip activities such picking up small specs of dust or crumbs?) What does he need?	She loves putting geometric shapes into the posting holes, making things work, and seeing cause and effect.
What kind of gross motor activity does she like to do with her whole body? Crawl, climb, run, jump? What is she not doing and how can I help her in that direction? (Do jump with her...)	Gina is crawling and loving to explore the whole house. I can get down on the floor and crawl with her? I can play with her and do exercises on the floor that increase her comfortability.
How does he best communicate? • With words? What words? • Without words: Smiling, crying (How? Can you read his facial expression?) How can I reciprocate with the same and slow down to show him I am Present?	She is very interactive with her smiles and is making lots of first sounds and starting to say Dada, and first sounds of some words. I want to stop and listen when she makes an effort to communicate. I want to give her space to fully express. I can try to express what I think she is saying and then wait for her response.
What makes him feel emotional and out of control? How can I help him express these and resolve any fears?	When she gets frustrated because she can't make things work, I will sit beside her to lend a quiet presence. When I do, she calms down.
Does he enjoy being with other people? With peers? Does he have stranger anxiety?	Gina loves to be with people and interacts with smiles and body language.
What kind of gross motor activity does she like to do with her whole body? Crawl, climb, run, jump? What is she not doing and how can I help her in that direction? (Do jump with her...)	Gina is crawling and loving to explore the whole house. I can get down on the floor and crawl with her? I can play with her and do exercises on the floor

You will find a blank version of this template as part of a downloadable set of templates on my website. See the QR code on the inside covers of this book, front and back.

Table 1.3 Chapter One Takeaways

Chapter One Takeaways
• In the first six years, through the absorbent mind, children take in impressions from the environment that they use to construct themselves.
• The inner teacher is the heart's inner voice that quietly guides children.
• Normalization is the process children go through to be capable of concentration.
• Sensitive Periods are the different periods occurring from birth through age six when children are extremely attracted to certain activities and can learn easily because of this focus.

Creating Your Montessori Home and Learning Environment

"I love Montessori's teaching that children's challenging behaviors disappear when they have an environment where they can freely choose something they would love to work on."
—TERESA ANGELES

Our home is where our children's minds and hearts develop. Its structure can pave the way for a wonderful family life. It's helpful to observe and assess our children's developmental needs to set up our house for our family. When we know these, we can provide what will fulfill them and support a happy, productive future. This home can have special places where children feel comfortable.

In this chapter, you will learn about setting up the rooms of your home with inspired Montessori principles. Your children's confidence and independence will grow when they feel encouraged to explore and when they feel the home is set up for them. They will find things that excite them and will look for more. Interacting with you will be a joy because they will feel your support, enthusiasm, and desire to learn with them. Childproofing the environment will help you relax so you can be fully present. If you do this, you will be giving your children the gift of yourself—your observation, time, and love.

You will kindle a fire of enthusiasm for learning that will not stop because they will forever know that learning is fun. The Montessori approach also encourages families to set up a Learning Area, which will be discussed later in this chapter.

Determining your children's developmental stages is important so you can provide child-sized furniture, supplies, and common items that fit their hands. You can help them understand how to use these items for their success. The following story is about my family as we worked to understand our son's needs and motivations to be independent and capable. Children gain confidence working in a home that is set up for them.

Creating a Space for Tools with Our Children

We had moved from a very large two-floor, four-bedroom home in Montana to a three-bedroom home in a suburb of Seattle. We had three little boys aged six, four, and two. I was pregnant with our fourth child, and we had a garage full of boxes and tools that took some time to get organized.

Our four-year-old Francis was not only curious but intensely fascinated by these tools. He watched his daddy work on the car at any chance. He loved to touch these tools and play with them. One day, he secretly lifted some tools out of a box and took them apart. We found the pieces piled up behind the house.

At first, his daddy was angry and sat down to talk with me about it before approaching Francis. After thinking this over, Victor was the first to say, "Maybe Francis really just wants to learn about these tools and work with them. He is so attracted to them. Maybe working with them will teach him to take care of them and teach him skills, too. Let's turn lemons into lemonade. Let's talk with him."

So, Victor brought Francis to the pile of pieces. "Francis," he said, "Do you know anything about these tools? Your mommy and I found them here in pieces."

Francis looked sheepishly at his dad. "Yeah, I just wanted to look at them."

"I can understand your interest in them. If we want to keep our tools to use them, we have to take care of them. If you want to learn, I will teach you."

Francis nodded and said, "Yes, I would like that." And he dove into his Daddy's arms, hiding in his shoulder, sad and happy at the same time. After that, Victor took time to show his boys how he used the tools, and then let them take turns. Francis developed a real skill using them. Victor and I always said that those broken tools would be worth their weight in gold when Francis got older, and they were, as they helped him develop great mechanic skills.

What I would do differently now with Montessori understanding is place a large pegboard on a wall in the garage where we could hang all the tools. Outlining the tools on the pegboard would help us all know where to return them. Drawers with small labeled containers for small pieces would work great. This would be a true Montessori environment. Helping children learn how to keep things organized enhances their sense of order and helps them learn to live that way. It helps them create an orderly world and thrive.

Montessori Described a Relationship Triangle That Impacts Children

Montessori's *relationship triangle* is a great image to remember as we develop our home. The *environment* is one side of the triangle that impacts our children. The *adult* and the *child* herself are the other elements. As an adult, you can positively support your children by keeping them in mind as you structure your home and help them build good habits and self-discipline. The environment holds all the

Table 2.1 Triangle

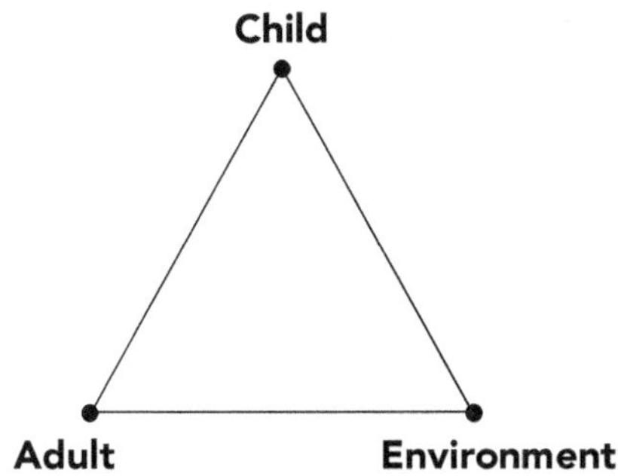

beauty and ideas we bring to it, and the child brings her own interests, enthusiasm, and energy to synergize with us and the environment. All parts work together to draw out your children's potential.

Designing your home in this way will bring many benefits. Whatever sensitive period or developmental level your children may be going through, your home will support them. Your furniture and materials will change as your children grow. The principles of the Montessori environment can guide you.

Here is a chart of some of the principles of the Montessori environment you can use, and it is also included in the set of templates on my website. See the QR code on the inside cover of this book, both front and back, to download the PDF set from my website.

Table 2.2 Principles of the Montessori Environment

Principles of the Montessori Environment
• Freedom and Discipline – develop spontaneously as children move and choose their work.
• Structure and Order – in the environment helps children develop confidence and security
• Beauty – in the environment inspires the heart and soul, and relaxes the mind.
• Social Environment – allows interaction and compassionate connection with family and others.
• Intellectual Environment – nurtures curiosity and interest, and stimulates the brain and heart.
• Nature and Reality – refreshes, inspires, and grounds our children.

Room-by-Room in the Montessori Home

In the following sections, we will walk through the different rooms of our house, making suggestions for a setup based on these principles. I also include tips from my own experience.

The Kitchen

The kitchen has been called the "heart of the home," with the hearth as a place of connection, warmth, and comfort. Many beautiful meals, rituals, discussions, and projects take place here. A kitchen is a place where everyone can pitch in and work together.

Creating a place in your kitchen where your children can access child-sized utensils on a low shelf or storage area is ideal, as well as having a small table with chairs where they can work. They can learn to prepare food with you, which helps them get involved. They can also eat snacks there or do other work, like coloring, while others cook. This way, they are still a part of things and feel included. Having a handy stepstool so your children can reach the table or counter to work with you will facilitate this. There are items now called toddler or child towers where they can safely stand next to you as you are standing but where they are safe from falling. Some children as young as two are capable of making a salad, gathering and arranging flowers, washing dishes, and helping with cleanup. You can also organize a place in your kitchen for recipes you can use with children and collaborate on a meal prep checklist for rotating jobs at mealtime. It might take a lot of patience to teach them how to help, but over time, they'll become self-sufficient and will help you! It is so fun for kids to do dishes and other jobs together, and they enjoy contributing, especially if you empower them with skills early. Working together with parents is the best. Our children often cooked with us and watched us cook, even as infants.

Foundational Kitchen Needs

Table 2.3 Child's Cooking and Baking Equipment

Child's Cooking and Baking Equipment			
low cupboard or shelf accessible to child with backup storage	measuring cups, spoons	small butter spreader	water filter dispenser
small mixing bowls of various sizes	scale for weighing is helpful	crinkle cutter	
child-size plates, bowls, cups	pitchers, scoops, small tongs	stepladder, if older	wooden spoons and spatulas

Table 2.4 Child-Size Cleaning Supplies

Child-Size Cleaning Supplies			
small broom, dustpan	dust cloth	child-size apron	dishwashing area: low sink or basins
mop	squeegee and spray bottle	step stool to the sink	child-size apron
cloths for spills	access to a faucet for cleaning	access to a faucet for cleaning	two small brushes: · for table · for floor

Table 2.5 The Dining Room or Eating Area

The Dining Room or Eating Area			
chairs children can access alone	cleanup materials accessible: sponge, small crumb set (brush)	table-setting items on a tray	stepstool for setting the table

In the dining area of your home, arranging a family dinner table with chairs children can climb in and out of by themselves is helpful. Everyone being together bonds and strengthens your family culture, which is a great need for families in our world today. Beauty in your kitchen will nurture your family, such as a bouquet on the table, warm pictures on the wall, or pretty curtains.

Dishwashing Station

The Bathroom

Structure the bathroom environment to create independence. Your children will use the sink, toilet, and bathtub here. Freedom means having a way for them to use these by themselves. Certain practical, chemical-free materials can simplify your life with your children in the bathroom. The following list may be helpful.

Table 2.6 Bathroom Furniture and Organizational Materials

Bathroom Furniture and Organizational Materials			
low towel hangers	low bathrobe hooks	potty chair over the toilet / or self-standing	sturdy, gripping stepstool
open cubicle shelves with cubby for each person to hold baskets	or easy open cupboards or drawers	chair or stool for adult to sit with child	smaller containers for: · teeth brushing · comb and brush · small shampoo
containers (baskets/ bins) for items belonging to all	container with washcloths	container with squeeze bottle/ small amount soap	container diapers/ pullups/sleep underwear/wipes
spray bottle: baking soda, soap, water for child to use to clean	scrubbers, sponges, paper towels/rags	small plastic bin for bath toys -may hook over bathtub	

The Bedroom

The bedroom should be a place of peace and relaxation. Parents and children need time for rest and a quiet atmosphere. Soft colors, lamps, and plants are calming and can help everyone.

Many opinions and options exist about where children should sleep in the early years. Parents juggle concerns about infant and child safety and emotional security while also wanting them to develop healthy independence. I have chosen to focus on the Montessori suggestions in this chapter. Please feel free to decide for yourself what is best for your family.

Considerations for Sleeping Arrangements for Infants and Toddlers

When setting up a nursery, it is good to consider our baby's needs rather than our own. Their needs are for safety, closeness, and responsive adults nearby. They also need movement. Even newborns move around as they sleep, and this movement helps their bodies and brains develop. In her books, Montessori shared her view that life for babies is challenging because they cannot move or function for many months. I have observed this in my infants. By setting up an environment with options inviting movement and safe exploration, they could evolve out of this stage of helplessness faster and seem happier.

Montessori has recommended floor beds or very thin mattresses on the floor to allow for freedom of movement for infants after about two months. Floor beds allow infants and toddlers to move in and out by themselves and access what learning opportunities are around them. This idea of the floor bed may be foreign, but it makes sense when we look at it in the light of development. In an effort to be child-centered, we are willing to look at their needs and respond to create an environment that will help them. Read on to understand what else might be helpful in such an environment.

Parents who choose the floor bed option for their children must ensure the room is completely safe and warm, whether in their own room or another. Complete childproofing is essential. If your older child can go outside the room, there must be a plan for how to keep him safe. Can he open doors, drawers, and cupboards? It is essential to consider and plan for all of these possibilities.

A baby monitor is also highly recommended if children sleep in a separate room so parents can always see and hear them. Having said that, it is also vital that parent use all their senses to follow up with regular physical checks to make sure all is safe.

As parents, we tried many different sleep options at different times for our family, with pros and cons for each. The most important thing is establishing an arrangement that feels comfortable and supportive for everyone. We never used floor beds for our infants because I did not know about them then, but we did use them for our toddlers. I like the idea of floor beds for children because they can freely move and occupy themselves. Our children were almost always with siblings in their bedrooms, which, for the most part, was comforting to them.

Mastering Self-Care Needs in the Bedroom

There are many ways to help your children learn to master dressing and undressing and caring for their clothes and belongings. You can create a system that will help them manage it. A low rod in the closet lets children get their clothes and put them away. Some parents have hangers that are hooks for easy use. A small wardrobe or dresser with easy-sliding drawers at your children's height also works well. A shelf with transparent baskets or boxes allows clothes to be visible and easily accessible. A small hamper or basket near the clean clothes lets children put dirty clothes away, and even toddlers enjoy doing this if you help them learn how. A few toys or activities on a small shelf that change frequently enable children to be constructive if they are alone in their rooms after waking. If you place a few books in a basket, you can rotate them weekly. A special basket just for library books can be useful, and your children can learn to read right near the basket so they can keep them safe.

Full-length mirrors help children see their reflections. A little bed that allows the sheets to be tucked in easily is also helpful. I think struggling to tuck sheets in can lead to frustration and often results in beds that never get made. Sewing string to the corners of small quilts can allow them to be tied onto the end of the bed so the child just needs to pull the top of the quilt to the top to make the bed.

Keeping the bedroom relaxing and not visually stimulating is essential for rest. Restful pictures on the wall that comfort your child may be helpful, such as images of your family or nature, or those that reflect your spiritual faith. Just a few are best to keep it calming and peaceful.

Montessori suggestions are listed here for your child's bedroom.

Table 2.7 Sleep Area

Children's Materials in the Sleep Area			
floor bed or mattress	a baby monitor	door-knob covers	four-inch guard rail for changing area
a bed that allows easy making	outlet covers	electrical outlet covers	hazards are identified easily
complete childproofing	a secure gate or door at the room entrance	cabinet safety locks	window cord / blind hiders safety wraps

Table 2.8 Bedroom Storage Area for Clothes and Belongings

Bedroom Storage Area for Clothes and Belongings			
low rod in the closet	shelf with baskets or boxes	special library basket	a small shelf for a few activities
small wardrobe		full-length mirror	a book basket
dresser at the child's height/ easy drawers	a small shelf for a few activities		small hamper/ basket

The Living Room

This room is where everyone can relax together. You can enjoy visiting, studying, playing games or music, and being a family. You can include the following or design your own:

Table 2.9 Materials for the Living Room

Materials for the Living Room			
comfortable couches	musical instruments	art on walls	a small pitcher for watering
relaxing chairs	yoga mat, Pilate balls	pastel colors for walls and decor	fun, relaxing exercise materials
shelves for books, games, entertainment	beautiful plants	moveable, big pillows piled on the floor	

Setting up Our Family Home Together

One Sunday afternoon, we took our children, David, Francis, and Frederick, to Home Depot, a construction store. At this time, they were five, three, and one. We wanted our older boys to have a chance to contribute to our home design. Together, we picked out some beautiful pastel wall paint colors that we thought would be nice and decided on a light peach color. We purchased two plants for the corners and some new aqua pillows and throws for our couches. Lastly, we picked out soft lamps and a new shelf. The children helped us choose everything, and it was fun.

Dad did the painting. Our three-year-old helped a little, and our five-year-old helped a lot. They loved helping. It took more work to include them, but it was fulfilling for everyone. Later, I was able to pitch in after the kids were asleep. We added new low shelves for our children's books and some musical instruments. This room turned out to be beautiful and comfortable. When everything was in place, we loved spending time there. Sometimes, I played the guitar. Our children played rhythm instruments, and we sang. The natural elegance of this room gave us a peaceful feeling about our home. And it belonged to all of us.

An Outdoor Area

A child's ideal world would have woods, fields, and gardens. It would have places to build forts, climb trees, and explore. Fruits, vegetables, and herbs would be readily available. Children could eat what they feel attracted to and would see beauty everywhere. An outdoor area can have many different parts to it. There can be a yard for chickens, goats, and other animals. Even if you don't have land or space for gardens or animals, installing small garden planters on a balcony or in a small yard can be very fruitful and exciting for children. Many cities have classes to support a family's set-up of a small urban or rural farm, or have community plots to garden in. If you do this at home, ensure that your outdoor area is safe with even ground and healthy soil. If you have space, you can organize a shed or garage to store tools on a pegboard and where you can work on family projects and activities. Even in an apartment, you can find a bin or box to organize tools. A small farm-like environment can give children wonderful experiences with plants and animals. Being set up simply can support your family's intention to keep it in order and be successful in caring for life.

Table 2.10 Your Family Outdoor Area

Your Family Outdoor Area			
outdoor game area	trees for climbing, if appropriate	a natural or man-made hill for climbing/sledding	a place to care for animals
covered areas for play	a secure tree swing	Carpentry area	Plant care area

Our Family's Learning Area: Thoughts from Marie

My grown daughter, Marie, recently told me that her friends always felt our home was cozy because we had a little "classroom." We used our small dining room as our learning area to organize materials, engage in discussions, and work with Montessori activities. We had a large couch and replaced the dining table with small tables and chairs. We used rugs for floor work and the kitchen table if we needed more project space. Often, we spread out throughout the house. Half of our kitchen pantry stored maps, activities, and materials. A map of the world and one of Washington state was posted on the front of the pantry door. These maps were adjacent to our family dinner table, so we could refer to them as we ate dinner. We had discussions there and sometimes planned our trips, too. 

Create Learning Areas for Your Children

Your Learning Area is often the heart of your Montessori home; a heartwarming place for exploring, finding out information, and bonding with family. Your children can learn a lot from the activities you provide there, especially if your library is rich with a variety of topics. You will find them there quietly purusing the shelves in their free moments, and this will inspire them to become voracious readers.. You can set up the Learning Area as you set up your home. Chapter Three will share information about the activities and lessons that will be provided there. Having a Learning Area may be a new idea for you, and if you want to focus only on setting up the home, that is okay and will be a great help to your family. If you choose to set up this special area to work with your children, it will benefit you in a different way. This book has ideas for you to reflect on and choose from. It is all up to you. If setting up the home is your first step, I encourage you to read on so you will have an overview from which to make educated choices now and in the future.

The Five Learning Areas

When we approach the idea of facilitating learning at home, Montessori gives us a wonderful structure for organizing and creating predictability. This very clear system uses the five areas of the Montessori curriculum: Practical Life, Sensorial, Math, Language, and Cosmic/Cultural. Creating a special place for all the practical life materials for the present, the math materials, all the language materials, and so forth, will help your whole family focus. It is also a really fun way to organize your learning. You will use shelves to identify each subject's area and the materials that will go there. It is up to you to have one separate shelf for each subject, or two subjects on a shelf, with one subject on the upper layers and one below, or something different. I will give some examples, and ultimately, it is up to you.

Your children will naturally be attracted to certain activities and areas based on their interests, such as a love of math or science, and they will be guided by their inner teacher on what to choose to work with. Working with the beads in the Math area, our children will automatically associate these with counting, even if they don't realize it at first. They will learn that letters and reading work go in the Language area and that learning to sweep or wash a table is an activity introduced in the Practical Life area, and so forth. Creating your Learning Area will be a joyous journey. The following shelf has mostly practical life and language materials which I started with at one time with my grandchild. You can designate what goes where and even label the areas.

A Learning Area

A cubicle shelf is a nice layout for a very simple learning area. You can label one cubicle for each area. If you use an eight-cubicle shelf, you will have three cabicles left over. Using the extras for library books or art supplies helped me. But it will be up to you. Cubicles are great for helping us get a visual of the different areas so we can learn to work with them. There is also no reason that you could not use more than one cublicle shelf and identify the areas as you would like them.

A Cubicle Shelf Works for Five Areas +

You may find having a small table with chairs of your children's sizes helpful in the area. Rugs that they can spread out on the floor are also helpful. Your whole house can be their learning environment, including the kitchen sink, the garden, the sewing machine, the workbench in the garage, the office, the front porch, and so on. It is all up to you. As you will learn in the next chapter, there is also a very helpful structure to presenting information to children that helps them learn, as well as a way to lay out the materials so that it is easy for them to follow and understand.

Table 2.11 The Five Areas of the Montessori Learning Environment

The Five Areas of the Montessori Learning Environment
• Practical Life – activities teach skills for self-care and care of their surroundings
• Sensorial – activities refine the senses: color, shape, texture, smell, sound, weight, and temperature
• Mathematical – activities cultivate mathematical awareness
• Language – activities nurture reading and writing processes
• Cultural – activities cultivate your child's sense of science, history, culture, music, and art

The Practical Life Area

The Practical Life Area is about purposeful activity and developing children's fine and gross motor control and coordination. The exercises in this area focus on two fundamental areas of development: care of self, and care for the environment.

The Sensorial Area

Providing children from two and a half to six years old with sensory activities helps them obtain information about their surroundings, and classify and refine their senses. These senses include taste, smell, sound, touch, and sight.

The Language Area

A Language Area exposes your children to communication through writing and reading. The richness of this area can inspire them to develop skills and use our language for communication in many forms, adding wealth to every area of their lives.

The Math Area

This area is where children can learn math concepts such as counting and measuring. Montessori saw that young children could understand mathematical principles in a concrete way when they were free to manipulate objects, and she often used color, as well.

The Cosmic/Cultural Studies Area

The Cosmic/Cultural Studies Area is where your children will learn about life related to history, geography, science, art, and music. Studies in the history area help children understand how the events of the past shape the world today and the social and cultural aspects of how civilizations developed. In geography, they will perceive the structural formation of the earth, and in science, the characteristics and behavior of the physical/natural world, including physics, astronomy and space, botany (plants), and zoology (animals). Art and music encourage them to express themselves creatively with different media and instruments.

Conclusion of the Five Learning Areas

Materials can stay in order when the environment is set up with the five areas as a structure. Helping your children understand the design of the areas by talking about the Language area, the Practical Life area, and so on will help them know how to find and return materials to their place. This way, the environment stays organized. Shelves are usually arranged from top left to right and from easiest to hardest.

Some parents will read this chapter about setting up the home and will be content to make the setup of the basic rooms of the house their goal for now, returning later to add new dimensions to their activities with their children. Some will do a little more and set up learning areas and create a little routine. Others will decide to go full steam ahead and homeschool. You get to decide what you want to do, how to do it, and how to incorporate any ideas presented here. And, whatever you do, it will benefit your family. Regardless of your plan, I encourage you to continue reading to understand what is possible.

Create Your Family Circle Area

In a traditional Montessori environment, a teacher will create a circle on the floor with colored tape or use a round or oblong rug to represent a gathering place. Your family can also have a gathering circle to discuss, share presentations, read books, and learn together. It should be big enough for your family members to sit around, plus a few extra guests. You may want to include a device to play music on and a calendar to keep track of the days with your children. Having these handy sets up good routines.

Here is a sample template I created for you to organize your family learning area. You can access a blank version of this and all the templates as a downloadable PDF series from my website. Use the QR code on the inside cover of this book, front and back.

T2.1 Five Learning Areas Defined in My Home:
Sample Template

Area Name	Structure
Practical Life	One four-tiered shelf. Basket to hold lesson rugs. Space for one to two lessons per tier.
Sensorial	One four-tiered shelf. Space for one to two lessons per tier.
Language	One four-tiered shelf. Space for one to two lessons per tier.
Math	One four-tiered shelf. Space for one to two lessons per tier.
Cultural	One four-tiered shelf with a shelf each for: • History • Science • Music • Geography • Extra four-tiered shelf for art supplies, resources, and artwork • Another small shelf and table for botany and zoology and what we find in nature (Nature Spot)
Circle Gathering Area	Large circular or oval rug on the floor Small shelf to hold a device to play music and other items Large pillows
Outdoor Practical Life Extension	Playground: sandbox (five' sq.) rope/tire swing in tree, handmade obstacle course, swings/ slide Collection of stumps (six" to eight") for children to move to build and design structures Shed: (seven' x five') with five-tier shelf (30-depth x 70-width) for bins and handheld equip Five' square pegboard on wall for tools & workbench for repairing and building Work table and chairs for children and adults for planting, transplanting, and artwork Garden (twenty' x ten') and fruit trees (twenty various native types)

Safe Learning Areas for Infants and Toddlers

Somewhere near the hub of your family life, you will want to create a safe learning space for your infants and toddlers. (In this book, we define an infant as zero to twelve months old and a toddler as one year to two and a half years old.) Both need a carefully considered environment as they absorb everything and feel deeply. You may ask why you would provide a learning area for your babies or toddlers. They are the most sensitive and capable learners of all our children because of the unconscious absorbent mind discussed in Chapter One. The following information applies to setting up both the baby's and the toddler's learning area or safe space. Then, we will look at each learning space separately.

Peace is essential for infants and toddlers. Soft pastel fabrics and rugs create a calm, soothing atmosphere in which our children may feel confident and free to explore. They learn through discovery. A device to play beautiful music will add to a feeling of harmony. A few beautiful pictures on the wall promotes a sense of beauty, and having them down low allows your children to see them. You can lie on the floor to look at the wall from your infant's and toddler's angle and view the shelf, materials, and room. Ensure that the area is clean and safe. Sometimes, things need to be repaired, and if so, this angle will show us. Because infants and toddlers are in a sensitive period for order, keeping their spaces especially clean is essential. It is important that a responsible person is always close to your infants and toddlers.

An Infant Area for Children
(Approximately Zero to Twelve Months)

A large blanket on the floor can frame this area, and your baby can spend much of her time there. The environment can have things for her to focus on, such as a mobile hanging on the wall to stimulate the visual pathway in her brain. Babies will move more and more, encouraging the development of muscles, the convergence of their eyes, and the organization of the brain. A small floor gym is great. A one-tiered shelf for your baby's toys and activities encourages movement. She may stretch to reach the materials on the shelf and will enjoy rolling and eventually crawling and creeping in this area.

Infants Thrive and Develop Well on the Floor

Because movement helps to organize the brain, we wanted to give our babies a warm, clean, and flat place to move. We also found the infant crawl track ideal, described in more detail in Chapter Five. It supports the building of their muscles and can be comfortably moved to any part of your home throughout the day. Chapters Four and Five discuss more about the baby and toddler.

A Learning Space for Your Toddler
(Approximately Twelve to Thirty Months)

Your toddler can concentrate more if this area is outside of the house's busiest area and yet nearby. There needs to be consistency in where things are put for daily activities. Because our toddlers are still small, a two-tiered shelf, low to the floor, can allow them access to materials they may enjoy touching and playing with. We want to provide only a small number of activities so that they can focus. The floor is the main workplace for toddlers. As they get older, they may learn to lay out a small rug (about two feet by three feet) to put their work on, keeping their activities contained and helps them stay focused. We can teach our children to use a rug and our family members to respect and walk around these rugs instead of stepping on them. The children can learn to sit at a rug instead of on it, so their work is protected.

A tiny weaning table (about twenty inches by thirty inches) and a small chair are options to have available for working and playing. A size-appropriate larger table can be helpful as children age. A toddler can climb in and out of such a chair without help and sit upright at the table. They enjoy this independence and gain confidence to strive in other areas. Having the option of the floor and a table is ideal.

Toddler Weaning Table

Toddlers love to use their bodies to do all kinds of balance activities. Realizing that movement organizes the brain, we can provide physical gross motor opportunities, such as a traditional balance beam or a board on the floor that they can walk on. Any kind of climbing equipment, swing, or other play structure that stimulates movement is good for them. Nearby parks can be a great resource. More about activities will be discussed in Chapter Three.

The following story indicates an event that shows how very young children can organize their lives when the environment reflects the Montessori principles and is set up for them. Their absorbent minds can perceive the order of a task if we structure it for them, and then they can do it themselves. Here is a story about how we helped our toddler, Clare, develop her skills.

Sorting Clothes with Clare

Our petite twenty-three-month-old daughter, Clare, was happily playing outside on her teeter-totter. The big, beautiful apple trees were gorgeous, reaching about forty feet into the air. I enjoyed spending some time with Clare. She was so peaceful. I was seven months pregnant and happy to relax for a few minutes in the sunshine. After a little while, I said, "Let's go inside, Clare."

Slowing down her teeter-totter, she said, "Okay, Mommy." And, then, she quickly climbed down and ran to put her hand in mine.

Together, we sauntered into the house. I sat down on the couch to begin folding a big pile of laundry. I was prepared to stay there long, thinking I would tackle this myself. Three little boys, one little girl, and parents make a lot of laundry! I placed the boys' three laundry baskets in front of me, each with the name of one of the boys printed on it. Clare came to sit by me, her big dark eyes watching intently. I started sorting the boys' clothes and pointing to the different baskets, and said, "David's green plaid shirt goes here in his basket." "Here is Francis's blue t-shirt, and it can go in his basket." Seeing her interest and concentration, I asked, "Clare, would you like to help me?"

"Yes," she said, as she jumped up to help.

She followed all of my directions. Quietly observing, she had understood which basket belonged to which of her three older brothers. After responding to my directions like this a few more times, she started sorting them by herself, to my amazement. Piece after piece went into the baskets. She knew which piece belonged to who and into which basket it should go. She was a definite help, keeping me from having to lean over so much at that point in my pregnancy.

"Clare, you are doing this all by yourself. How exciting that you know how to sort your brothers' clothes. You are such a big help to Mommy!" I leaned over and gave her a hug. She loved to help and take care of people. Her sweet face lit up in a big smile of pride and happiness. And, she hugged me back.

We folded the clothes together, with me doing the majority of the work. Later, she attempted to help me put the folded clothes into the drawers. I told her daddy what had happened when he came home, and we both marveled at it. Clare has always been a helper at home to her family, especially later when she had younger sisters. Her sweet heart has continued to care for and serve. This story created such an aha moment for me, as I realized her capability when she was not yet even two years old. From the beginning, she was a natural mommy, and she still likes to keep her children's clothes orderly.

So, the idea in the story that each child would have their own laundry basket helped Clare to know how to work in this situation. It helped her organize her thinking, understand the sequence of the process, and do it successfully.

Envision Your Dream Home

Imagining the beautiful home you would like is important. Write down these ideas, and the plans you can accomplish now. If obtaining some elements for your dream home and learning areas is not possible right now, tuck them away in a journal. You might create a vision board to attract them, including sketches or photos. At one time my vision included such things as flowering wisteria on the front porch with a swinging couch bench and my home painted a certain beautiful peach color. Keeping your visions high is an important creative process and this helped me.

Here is a sample template I created for you to use for organizing your home's rooms and noting down new ideas. You can find it as part of a downloadable set of templates on my website. See the QR code on the inside cover of this book, front and back, to download the set from my website.

T2.2 Design your Home with the Principles of the Montessori Environment: Sample Template

Room or Space	Furniture	Pictures	Other	Paint/Other
Jen's Bedroom	Floor bed 2-tier shelf Rocking chair Wardrobe	Cascade Range Angel	Soft Lamp Cotton blankets	Peach color
Joey's Bedroom 2	Twin bed 3-tier shelves Stepstool for closet Dresser	Images of Frogs The World map	Soft Lamp Cotton blankets	Aqua color
Dad & Mom's Bedroom	King Size Bed Dresser Cozy chairs Book Shelf	Forests Flowers Angeles	Cotton Blankets Beautiful Pink/green quilt	Pink
Bathroom	Shelf Baskets for each one's self-care Step-stool	Peaceful sea	Checklist with pictures for Jen and Joey	Light green
Living Room	Curved couches Stack of pretty floor pillows	Family Pictures Holidays and Celebrations	Baskets of nature items: Shells, rocks, live plants Basket music instruments	Cream color
Learning Area	5 Two-Tiered shelves 1 cabinet to hold supplies Child-size table/chairs Piano	Children reading or doing other learning with parents	Oval circle rug on top of carpet Big floor pillows Beautiful plant Learning Materials	
Outdoor Learning Area	Picnic and other tables and chairs Swings/other Workbench Pegboard for tools		Small garden/ orchard Adult/Child Tools Garden/repair/wood/mechanics Children's paint Storage/ trays/baskets	Children's paint to help paint house Storage Area

T2.3 Chapter Two Observation Practice: Sample Template

<table>
<tr><td>

- Describe ideas about changing anything in your home to better support your family?

  I want to create greater independence for my kids in the kitchen with a small shelf for all their baking and food prep. A small table there would be awesome too, so they can work there. I'd even have extra small chairs so we can join them there, too.

- How can you make your infant or toddler area safer or more interesting?

  I would like to lay out a big blanket and a one-layer shelf to create more of a learning area for my baby. I am looking for wooden and cloth toys that are really clean and enticing. I will do this between the kitchen and the living room, where she can see us all as she is playing.

- Are there any new outdoor area designs that excite you that you might want to use for your home?

  I want to create a safer and more exciting outdoor learning environment with a workshop, covered area for weather, play equipment, and tools my kids can learn to use.

</td></tr>
</table>

Table 2.12 Chapter Two Takeaways

Chapter Two Takeaways
• Montessori encouraged adults to design an environment around children's developmental needs.
• The environment of your home can be set up according to the five Montessori areas, Practical Life, Sensorial, Math, Language, and Cultural.
• Infants and toddlers also need a learning space, according to their development.
• Create an outdoor learning area to encourage your children to spend an extended period of time outside for health and connection with nature.

Selecting the Right Montessori Lessons and Materials for Your Child

"Children need to touch, handle, and manipulate objects to gain experience. In this way, the hand becomes the key to intelligence."
–Teresa Angeles

In the last chapter, I talked about how to set up the rooms of your home and a learning environment with the five learning areas. In this chapter, I will talk about how to create and find learning activities for your children two and a half to six years old that will go into these specific learning areas, by category. The true Montessori way is a mindset of respect and love. It is also an awareness that our children crave learning. Their lives are all about exploration and discovery. For us, teaching and sharing the world with them is a form of love.

In this chapter, I will take a more in-depth look at how the Montessori parent can approach teaching, which is very different from the role of the traditional teacher. I will explain the ways the Montessori Method can help your children learn, and encourage you to decide how it applies to your family and home. There may be a good deal of information that you are not familiar with, or that you will need to think about and digest. It is okay to realize that you have a learning curve and need to take time. See what will work for you and your family. There is no right or wrong way. But, I do encourage you to keep reading to learn what concepts are here for you when you are ready for them. You can start with a few ideas and later do more. This chapter will teach you about incorporating Montessori activities into your home.

Maria Montessori had deep insights into the developmental needs of the children in her care. She saw that children three-to six-years-old live in the **conscious** absorbent mind and are ready to **consciously** engage in work and choose their own activities. It is a wonderful, industrious time. Her observation of infants and toddlers is that they live in the **unconscious** absorbent mind and their needs are very different. I have designed a separate section for them at the end of this chapter. How we approach them and set up their environments is very important, also.

Montessori also realized that children remember what they do through physical activity. For this reason, she made it the foundation of her work to provide hands-on, concrete materials for them to work with. As they manipulated these and understood concrete concepts, their experiences were later translated into more complex concepts.

Montessori materials take complex concepts and simplify them. Each lesson is designed to help children discover specific learning outcomes. The curriculum presents lessons in sequence, from easiest to hardest, promoting a layering of knowledge, gathered gradually. Children naturally are drawn to practice and repeat tasks, often focusing on one skill at a time.

For families learning at home, it is helpful to establish a routine that can help consistency. Daily learning times can be planned with flexibility.

Lessons in a Montessori Environment

In her book, *The Montessori Method*, Dr. Montessori defined what she believed were the three most important characteristics of giving a child an individual lesson. These are conciseness, simplicity, and objectivity. When we think of presenting lessons to young children, we realize that it makes sense to be concise and short, using as few words as possible. We want to help our children understand a specific concept. Montessori's guidelines can be incredibly helpful to parents at these times.

How to Give Your Child a Lesson the Montessori Way

When you are ready to start teaching your children, there are Montessori manuals that give clear instructions on how to do so. Please see my recommendations later in this chapter about this topic in more detail. Here are some more general tips to help you with giving lessons.

If you are going to demonstrate spooning beans from one bowl to another, first of all, ensure that all the parts of the lesson are there and in good condition: the tray, two bowls, a deep spoon, and some beans. Be mindful of how you will model the lesson because your children will copy your movements, posture, and attitude.

1. Prepare an attractive presentation on a tray, and make sure it is precise and neat.

2. Put the tray on the shelf related to the subject area (math, language, etc.)

3. Know your plan clearly in mind.

4. Practice beforehand, pretending your child is there for best results.

5. Relax. Envision a strong connection with your child's heart.

6. Enthusiastically invite your child to do a lesson with you.

7. Go to the shelf with him to choose the lesson.

8. Slowly and gracefully carry the tray with two hands to a table or a rug on the floor. Know ahead of time where you will work (typically at a table or on a special rug laid out on the floor).

9. If you are right-handed, sit on your child's right side and model how to use the material. Montessori guidelines suggest you sit with your dominant hand away from your child so it does not get in the way of your child seeing your presentation.

10. Show your child how to do the work gracefully and precisely, with few words.

11. Clean up the material and put it back on the shelf when you are finished and ask if he would like to do the lesson alone. If so, he can pick it up by himself.

12. You can stay available and quiet while he works on the lesson.

13. Say little to him after you have presented a lesson and your child is working on this lesson, or possibly another that he has chosen. You will want to ensure that his attention stays on his work and not on your approval of his performance. For example, instead of praising him, we can share a loving smile or, "You finished!"

14. When he is finished, ask him to put it back on the right shelf. If he uses a rug, ask him to roll it up and put it away.

At the end of this chapter, you will find templates for planning lessons for your child.

Montessori Three-Period Lesson

Teaching vocabulary in a simple three-part lesson helps

children become familiar with and learn new words. With the Three-Period Lesson, we can present up to three new vocabulary words at a time, usually connected to objects or images, such as geometric shapes, farm animals, or something else.

1. You name it, saying, "This is . . ." We generally ask the child to *repeat* the word and touch or hold the object or the image.

2. When you are sure the child knows what it is, you may ask, "Show me . . ." "Give me..." "Put the ... in your lap." Many Montessori teachers will spend most of their effort emphasizing this. The whole point of the lesson is to teach the child about this vocabulary. It is good here to emphasize the second period's importance and find ways to extend it.

3. Finally, when you are sure your child can recall it independently, you may ask, "What is this?" But you want to be sure they can answer before you ask them. You can also ask them to show you what they know and join them in identifying various answers or items in a category and playing the game. You will understand what they are familiar with without pressuring them.

Helping your children to identify something can be empowering for them. They should feel happy to show you what they have learned rather than being afraid of correction. If they can show you that they have mastered this part of a lesson, you can move on to working with other vocabulary, objects, or images soon. If they need correction, you can help them identify what they did know and stay positive while helping them figure out what might need to be corrected. You may not even want to mention what they did *not* know. You can quietly put it away for another time if it seems that they don't understand something and be at peace knowing that children learn at their own rates.

Sometimes, when I wanted to review letters or numbers and didn't want the children to feel that I was testing them, I played a game like Bingo. We took turns calling out the sounds or numbers that we knew and put our own colored markers on them. They always loved showing me what they knew without feeling stressed about what they did not know. And, by watching me, they observed and learned more.

The following story exemplifies how the Montessori approach can help children develop. We set up our home environment so that Clare could be independent, and we communicated this to her. We helped her understand how to do things by herself and showed her that we respected her. She really liked that and developed skills that made her feel confident. This story highlights how to give a lesson by demonstrating a very specific activity, with very specific materials. At the same time, the greatest beauty of the Montessori approach is our ability to be present with our children. As the following story highlights, our presence is shown in our quietness and respectfulness. Using few words as Montessori recommended, we allow our children to engage fully with the materials. We give them space to focus on the lesson and absorb the concepts. Our attention is on our children and the lesson we are sharing. We have a plan, and we listen to our children's interests and needs with flexibility.

Giving a Lesson—A Story

When Clare was four years old, I prepared a lesson on autumn leaves. I demonstrated to her how to write her name. Then we wrote her name on all her papers so she could identify what work was hers and not her brother's. Calmly and simply, I demonstrated how to hold a pencil, use glue, and sharpen colored pencils with only a few words.

Then, I showed her how to carry the tray to a mat on the floor. I said, "This is your workspace, Clare. I will show you how to do this work, and then you can do it by yourself if you want. When you finish, you can put it back on the shelf. I will help you, if you need it."

The colors of the different leaves attracted her. I affirmed her joy and commented on how beautiful nature is.

She was eager to work, but I asked her calmly and with a smile if she would be willing to watch me first and then try. Clare agreed. I asked her to sit cross-legged and put her hands in her lap, which would make it easier for her to watch. Clare was at my side, watching.

I took the fall leaves off the tray and gently laid them across the mat. I said, "Clare, I am so happy to sit with you. Since today is the first day of autumn, I thought it would be fun to look at some colorful fall leaves together and do an activity. I will show you how."

I took the glass which held the colored pencils and placed it on the far corner of the mat, so it was reachable. Then, I placed a writing board and a piece of paper on the mat in front of me. I chose a maple leaf, picked it up, and placed it upside down on my board. I told Clare, "Here, we can do a leaf rubbing using colored pencils and paper. We choose the leaf we like and turn it over like this, so the veins on the back of the leaf face up. Can you see the veins on this leaf?"

She nodded, "Yes."

With her bright eyes watching me closely, I said, "Clare, now we take a small piece of white paper I have on the tray and lay it on top of the leaf. Then we choose a colored pencil and rub it on the white paper, over the leaf. At first, I rub gently to see how much pressure is needed to show the lines of the veins coming through. As I keep rubbing carefully, a beautiful pattern emerges from the leaf onto the paper. Do you see it?"

"Yes, I see it," she said.

"It is beautiful, and I will put this work back on the shelf so you can get it when you are ready." After I had collected the materials and returned the tray to the shelf, I asked, "Clare would you like to choose a leaf and do this work yourself?"

"Yes, I want to do it, Mommy," she said.

So, I stepped back and gave her space to do it. It was hers to do now. As much as possible, I stayed quiet and cheerful and would only intervene to protect her or the environment from damage. She rubbed and some veins showed, and she stayed with it for several minutes. Sometimes children concentrate for a long time, and sometimes choose not to, and instead choose to return to the activity later. My experience has been that if we are unattached to how perfect their work appears and do not make positive or negative comments about it, they will own the experience of working and be happy. They won't need us to reward them with lots of praise or be fearful of judgment.

If she hadn't been interested, I would have left it on the shelf for her to choose at a different time. She was learning to concentrate and was now peaceful. I was, too. It is essential to realize that children will only some-times be this calm and attentive. They will be more likely to sit and watch if the theme is something they enjoy. We do our best to be in our hearts and not be attached to the outcome. Our children feel when we love interacting with them and don't worry about the results. This approach to presenting lessons is how we introduce materials in all the subject areas. If our children feel at peace and inspired, they will love to learn and look forward to more. 🖎

Using Materials in the Five Areas of the Montessori Learning Environment

We reviewed the Five Areas in Chapter Two and will do a more in-depth review in this chapter of the traditional Montessori learning environment, which can be duplicated in your home. The five areas, Practical Life, Sensorial, Language, Math, and Cosmic/Cultural, all have activities and lessons specific to each area. These areas are where we invite our children to use these activities. You will learn about lessons in these areas to attract and inspire your children's curios-ity. A table at the end of this section will provide a list of suggested lessons for each area.

Using Materials in the Practical Life Area

In the Montessori philosophy, the Practical Life area is often where we begin with our children. Our goal is to help our children feel comfortable and capable in their environment for them, not for us. Learning to comb their hair, sweep the floor, or help make their beds are examples of activities that can make our children's daily routines meaningful. Developing muscles during these activities also prepares your children to work in all Montessori curriculum areas and to better enjoy life. These exercises also build self-esteem and a sense of responsibility for the environment. The prospect of learning new skills is wondrous and engaging for young children. These activities are also very calming.

Practical Life Lessons

The five areas of the Practical Life curriculum include Preliminary (preparatory) Exercises, Care of the Self, Care of the Environment, Grace and Courtesy, and the Control of Movement. There are specific lessons in each category. The *Preliminary Exercises* help a child learn to move with grace and balance as they carry a chair, fold a cloth, or pour a liquid. The *Care of the Self* activities helps children learn to care for their personal physical needs, washing, dressing, caring for their clothes, and some food needs. The *Care of the Environment* is also essential. Exercises in this area teach children to respect their environment. Examples include watering a plant, wiping the floor, or washing a table. *Grace and Courtesy* exercises teach children social interactions, such as shaking hands. *Control of Movement* is about teaching children to be aware of their bodies, refine their control, and coordinate their movements. For example, they can walk on your family circle line that you made with tape on the floor. They will put one foot ahead of the other around the line, stepping gracefully one at a time, while you play music and lead. After a little bit of practice, a child can try having a beanbag on their heads as they step around the circle. This increases the complexity and helps them gain better coordination. They can also try spooning lessons to transfer beans from one bowl to another.

Sponging Water   Cutting Bread   Picking Tomatoes

Pulling Grapes off the Vine   Children Making Dumplings in China   Scooping Veggie Burgers

Younger children will respond best to one-step activities such as wiping up a spill with a sponge, pushing in a chair, or getting a spoon for lunch. As children mature, they can handle more steps in a sequence. Children two and a half through six can practice putting on their clothes, sharpening pencils, rolling and unrolling mats, and washing windows. They can help clean. Providing child-sized equipment such as feather dusters, window washing squeegees, and brooms will allow your children to work more easily and have more fun. Smaller items also seem to attract them. The Practical Life exercises are often the first lessons presented to young children.

Using Materials in the Sensorial Area

In the Sensorial area, lessons encourage experimentation with differences in size, form, color, touch, taste, and smell. These aim to refine your children's senses to obtain information about their surroundings. Montessori lessons have an element of self-correction, allowing children to independently correct their work.

Sensorial Size Category

In this area, children develop discrimination of size, length, width, and breadth of objects, separating and clarifying their differences. Many of these size lessons involve the orderly layout of different wooden blocks. They work from left to right and then from top to bottom as they develop coordination, independence, and concentration. The pink tower, as an example, comprises ten pink cube-shaped blocks, each larger than the one that sits upon it, building upward in consecutive order. The Cylinder Blocks are a material that children are introduced to, with pegs that fit into the blocks with differing

Child Using the Cylinder Blocks   Boy with the Red Rods

heights and diameters. The blocks look the same at first glance, but they are subtly different from one block to another, and the child must sort and fit the pegs in the appropriate holes. The red rods, also pictured below, allow children to differentiate length.

Sensorial Form Category

Geometric shapes help children develop visual discrimination. They learn the various shape names and differences, such as square, rectangle, and circle, and can hold concrete geometric solids. The four to five constructive triangle boxes contain different wooden triangles, which the children are invited to combine to form other kinds of rectilinear or right-angled figures. The name "constructive" refers to the idea that these shapes can be combined to form other shapes.

Child Working with Constructive Triangles

Sensorial Color Materials and Lessons

There are Montessori lessons to help children recognize color similarities and differences. Using the words "darker" and "lighter" can allow them to apply vocabulary to gradations of color. After working with color activities, children can watch for variations of colors in the environment. For instance, they might notice different shades of green in a forest or shades of pink in a garden.

Tactile Sensorial Materials and Lessons

Through tactile lessons, children learn to understand the world through touch, developing discrimination among textures. In one lesson, they feel different grades of sandpaper and match similar pieces, identifying rough to smooth. They can also distinguish various textures of fabric.

Deciphering and Matching Textures
of Foil, Cardstock, and Fabric

Gustatory and Olfactory Materials and Lessons

These lessons stimulate children's abilities to sense different tastes and smells and develop their gustatory and olfactory senses. Examples include smelling and tasting foods. You can ask, "Which herb smells the best or sourest?" Your kitchen and garden work well for lessons here.

Using Materials in the Language Area

A Language area exposes your children to writing and reading. Here you can set up materials to help them understand the foundations of language. Dr. Montessori believed that children should write before they read. Sandpaper letters allow children to trace the shapes of letters before they start using them in writing and reading. She also said that putting physical letters together to form words is a form of writing, for example, using letters of the moveable alphabet. One of the benefits of a strong language program is that children develop excellent vocabulary and communication.

Teach Your Child to Read

I always felt that teaching our children to read was important because once they could read, they could learn about their worlds and soar in knowledge and imagination. When children are confident readers early on, they expect to be successful in life. My children loved reading to their siblings when they were young. They could occupy themselves, entertain each other, learn about so many things, including jokes, and let their imaginations soar with interesting stories. We had books about many different subjects, especially about animals, which our boys devoured. We also had more than one set of colorful, picturesque children's encyclopedias, which were well-loved. Having a wealth of books available to your children is a great resource that will change their lives. They don't have to be brand new, but you want them to have a quality of content. That is what is most important. Give them stories about real heroes; virtuous people who will impact their minds and protect their innocence.

To Be Able to Read is True Freedom

Children can easily learn to read with the Montessori approach and the right materials. I provide resources for recommended materials on my website, montessorifamilies.com, which are fun for children, as well as for you. And they are tried and true. You can teach your child to read if you can spend ten to fifteen minutes a day working with them on these specific activities. I have done this and have seen it work repeatedly. The consistency, not the amount of time, makes the difference. Working with these materials five days a week can help you create an amazing foundation for your child. For any learning goal you have for your child, consistency is key.

Learning about Sounds and Letters

Randall Klein, Montessori Master Teacher and author of *The Klein Method of Early Reading Mastery*, says that children begin to read by isolating the first sounds of words. Next, they associate those sounds with printed letters. When they can hear the first sound of "duck," they can associate the /d/ sound with the printed letter "d," and understand that abstract symbols represent sounds of spoken language we call letters. His book and printable educational materials at earlyreadingmastery. com will be very helpful for parents learning to help their children learn to read. There are many games, and the following one shows a child matching the first sounds of pictures to letters with the same sound.

When you first teach your children to read using the Montessori approach, it is important to emphasize the SOUNDS of the letters

Matching Pictures to First Sounds

and not the NAMES of the letters, as this will expedite their reading. For example, in Montessori reading, we call a 'k' a /k/, calling it by its sound. Children don't need to know the names of the letters to read, but they do need to know the sounds. If your children have already learned the names of the letters, no worries. You can tell them they will learn the letter sounds in a new way now. You will see how easily they will read this way.

I encourage you to use the tables included here to ensure the right pronunciation. If English is your second language and pronunciation is challenging, seek help from a friend, librarian, or tutor. Often, the library will have helpful resources. Vowel sounds can be especially troublesome as they change subtly from one language to another. I encourage parents dealing with this situation not to feel burdened; instead, they should know that their ability to teach their children another language is a great gift. Be determined to give them the proper English sounds so they can thrive. Getting help to ensure that your child learns these sounds clearly at the beginning will be very helpful for your whole family, and successive children will build upon this success.

The beginning of the Montessori reading sequence emphasizes using only the short vowel sounds and teaches the long and other vowel sounds much later. Below is a table with words containing the alphabet's beginning sounds. It will be so helpfu if you can help your children learn these beginning sounds of the letters.

When your children have a solid grasp of the letter sounds and their symbols (printed letters), they can begin building words with 3-D letters. The Montessori movable alphabet is a wooden box with compartments that hold physical letters. Children can hold the letters and form words. Any foam or magnetic letters will work. Letters that are red or pink, with blue vowels will be especially helpful. You can buy these online.

Table 3.1 Sound Key to the Alphabet with Only Short Vowels

Sound Key to the Alphabet with Only Short Vowels					
a as in ant	b as in bat	c as in cat	d as in dot	e as in elk	f as in fox
g as in gas	h as in hug	i as in igloo	j as in jam	k as in kit	l as in lip
m as in man	n as in nap	o as in ox	m as in man	n as in nap	o as in ox
s as in sun	t as in tin	u as in us	v as in van	w as in wax	x as in tax
y as in yak	z as in zap				

Three-Letter Short Vowel Word Reading

Montessori created her reading sequence so that once children have learned the sounds of letters, they can start putting letters together to build short vowel words.

Randall Klein says building words this way is the best way to prepare a child to sound out (or decode) and read words. Building them first allows them to be intimately connected with letters and sounds so they can read them. Some examples of three-letter short-vowel words include hop, tip, sun, map, pup, and ran. A game from Randall's book uses moveable letters to build words. Once children know the letter sounds, help them build words with the letters, remembering to call letters by their sounds instead of their names. And then, when they show you they are ready, let them do it independently.

Segmentation and Blending

While children learn to read short-vowel three-letter words, they will segment the individual sounds of letters in a word. Segmentation is the ability to hear and identify the separate sounds in a word. This is the most important skill for learning to read. We segment when we come to the word "van," and say, "/v/ /a/ /n/." We say just the individual sounds. After we segment and identify each sound in a word, we blend the sounds together to read the word. The sounds we segmented are /v/ /a/ /n/, and we blend them together and say, "van." Blending is the putting together of sounds to say a word. Klein discusses how segmenting words and breaking them into their separate sounds is the most important skill and predictor of a child's success as a reader. Other doors will open once you have accomplished this with short vowel words.

Longer Short Vowel Words

With your help, children can learn step-by-step how to read. The next step is gradually working with words with more letters but still only short vowels. These longer short-vowel words may include bags, sled, gift, drop, and picnic, and are sometimes also called "phonetic."

The full reading sequence unfolds from here.

Finding Materials to Help You Teach Your Children to Read

If you want to find materials to teach your children, please see a list of resources on my website, montessorifamilies.com.

Only Give Your Child Reading Material They Understand

Your children's reading material, such as little readers and books, must be diligently reviewed to make sure that these books have only what your child can read at their current ability. This review is vital at every level and can be challenging when you, the parent, are just learning about phonics. If this is challenging, take heart. You will learn with your children, and it will work if you keep on striving. Children must have learned the phonics to sound out words. If they are working on three-letter short vowel words, make sure that every book they read has only three-letter words, except for some small inevitable sight words such as "is," "the," and "are." Do your best to see that there are only three-letter short vowel words. Another important element is to see that the size of the print is large. Some doctors believe that children's eyesight doesn't fully develop until they are seven to eight years old and so to err on the side of caution, I try to provide materials that have a large font. Please see my website Montessorifamilies.com for recommended materials in this and other reading-level categories.

Writing

Being able to write involves many different elements. It is a multi-dimensional activity that helps us communicate our ideas and is a vital skill for every vocation in life. When your children are two and a half or developmentally ready, they can trace sandpaper letters with their fingers and use the moveable alphabet to identify letters and practice their sounds. Children can start using a pencil or other writing implements to draw shapes and then letters, building on these activities. They can trace metal insets with various colored pencils using metal frames to draw beautiful geometric shapes. This is one of the first activities for young children. They can also trace shapes in the geometric and botany cabinets with their fingers, which allows them to prepare for writing. Your children can gradually write words, sentences, and possibly even paragraphs between three and six years old. Writing simple sentences in a journal and drawing pictures is a wonderful activity, even at four years old. An adult can help the child to write an entry, forming the words on the page as the child speaks or letting the child copy their writing. This helps them to realize that their words can become symbols on the page. If you try this, you can gradually write less and your child, more.

Developing the muscles in their hands is the biggest step toward helping your children to write. They can use pencils, markers, crayons, and scissors. They can also strengthen their muscles as they work with playdough and do any kind of work with their hands. You can start when they are very young helping them hang from bars, even when they are infants to hang. If you keep it up, their hands and grip will be strong.

Writing is such an important skill. Always observing that your children are holding the pencil correctly from the start will make a difference later. Holding a pencil correctly helps them to relax and write easily and fluidly. You can buy **pencil grips** from educational stores and online, showing the child where to place each finger to develop the proper hold. Helping your children ease into writing will be a great gift as they gradually develop skills.

Using Materials in the Math Area

Counting Numbers to Ten

Children must be able to manipulate the objects they are counting to understand the quantity and assimilate the basic mathematics facts. For example, a child can hold a bead and feel its weight and size. They can start to discern one bead as different from ten beads. This sensorial experience impacts their understanding of quantity, weight, and size. They can name the different material quantities and their "kind" (units, tens, hundreds, or thousands) and see the outcome when they combine bead quantities, count, separate, and compare. Children who learn math with physical manipulatives, such as beads, cubes, rocks, beans, or any kind of counters, often connect deeply with math principles as they mature. They can demonstrate this depth through their advancing years.

In the Montessori environment, putting a number to a quantity, or counting, is first, and often accomplished through activities with the number rods, the spindle box, and sandpaper numbers. Each of the Montessori number rods has sections of ten-centimeter lengths. Each of the ten rods progresses from ten centimeters to one meter in ten equal parts, each part alternating blue and red. The number rods help children understand quantities of one to ten and the corresponding number symbols. The spindle box is another early math material that helps to teach counting. It allows children to visually identify printed numbers in each of the nine-box sections and gather a loose quantity of wooden spindles to match each number. Finally, the sandpaper numbers give children a sensorial connection with the quantity as they trace and say the number images on the cards.

Introduction to the Decimal System

When children can confidently and consistently count to ten, they can move on to work with the golden beads. Montessori wanted to give children a concrete experience of the decimal system and chose these particular beads because of their soft golden color and pleasant glass texture. They were pleasing to the eye and a favorite of children. The golden beads work is based on ten numerals: zero, one, two, three, four, five, six, seven, eight, and nine, with all numbers built with these ten digits. Your children will learn about place value using this material. They will identify the value a digit represents in a number *based on its position.* For example, understand that the place value of six in sixty-three is six tens or sixty. The place value of six in thirty-six is six units.

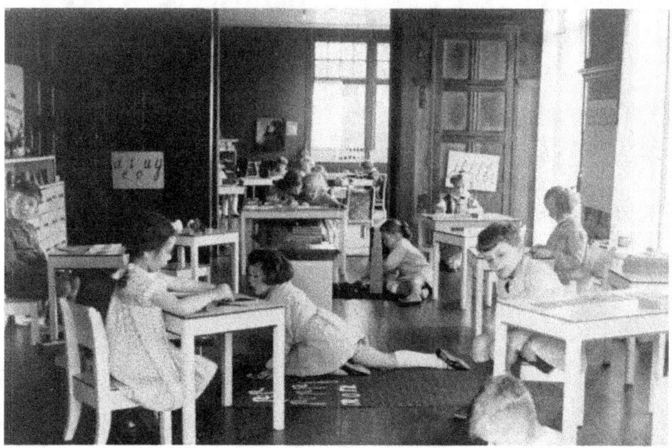

Children Working with Math Materials

The Four Operations

Other skills your children will learn include the four operations, which are working with numbers and computing answers in addition, subtraction, multiplication, and division. The children understand that addition means combining things, and this is accomplished using beads or other objects. The idea of subtraction is to take something away. Multiplication means counting something a number of times. Division means to share equally, and that the quotient or answer is always what one person receives.   As they manipulate the materials, they see clearly what the terms mean. In the same way, they understand what borrowing or carrying might mean. Children start calculating with larger numbers up to nine-thousand, nine-hundred, ninety-nine. These large computations are called operations in the Montessori curriculum. The operations may also be done with the Stamp Game, the Dot Game, and the Bead Frame.

Girl Working with the Stamp Game

Children learn advanced math concepts in Montessori two-and-a-half to six-year-old curriculums. These may be whole numbers, fraction names and shapes, telling time, and measurement. In Montessori education, both the metric system and imperial systems are taught. The metric system is used throughout the world and is easy to understand as it is based on the number ten and is measured in millimeters, centimeters, and meters to measure length and grams, and kilograms to measure weight, and as milliliters and liters to measure capacity. The imperial system, which is used in the United States, is measured in inches, feet, yards, ounces, cups, quarts, and gallons. These lessons are not included in the table of lessons, but you may choose to add them.

Teens, Tens, and Hundreds

The first set of Seguin boards demonstrates tens and the building of teens. A series of nine tens is printed on the board in a column. The children work to transform the numbers by adding numerals to the tens, thereby building teens. The work is used with golden beads. The second set of Seguin boards introduces numbers twenty-one to ninety-nine in the same manner, allowing the child to lay and count golden beads alongside the board and to manipulate and replace number cards as they do so, gradually building larger and larger numbers. Other materials used for counting, skip counting, and ultimately multiplying, squaring, and cubing are the colored bead chains.

Memorization

Children in the Montessori environment follow up their hands-on work with materials that help with memorization. These include the strip boards and many other charts and boards used for simple addition, subtraction, multiplication, and division facts. The math materials contribute to a valuable learning experience.

Using Materials in the Cosmic/Cultural Studies Area

The Cosmic/Cultural Area is where your children will learn about their world related to history, science, geography, art, music, and your family's cultural heritage. You can adjust things to the current time. The world's geography and history have evolved greatly since Montessori's time. Even science is different. Montessori classified living things into plants and animals. Today, life is classified into five kingdoms: plants, animals, fungi, protists (micro-organisms), and Monera (another type of micro-organism). We can teach this to our children.

History

Studying history, such as the calendar, the days of the week, and the months of the year, helps children understand the passage of time. They can learn about ancient mythology, religion, and rituals and how songs and artwork accompanied them. Montessori curriculums often include timelines of ancient history. They can be purchased online from the *Montessori Services* catalog. These can be hung on the walls of your home, and your children can color and cut out pictures, hanging them underneath the appropriate places/dates on the timeline. Integrated with geography, history presentations and activities like this can inform your children about how people adapted to climates and designed their homes, customs, food, and clothing to survive through the ages. Children love to learn about the interconnectedness of all life and appreciate how people have evolved.

Botany and Zoology as Nature and General Science

Focusing on nature combines the scientific studies of plants (botany) and animals (zoology). If you have a garden or outdoor environment, spending time there is a natural entry into these studies. Children can recognize the shapes of leaves and trees, even as toddlers. They will look for beauty in nature if you marvel at the unique designs. Children can learn about the five types of life: plants, animals, fungi, protists, and Monera, in-depth, such as learning the five types of animals as fish, birds, amphibians, reptiles, and mammals. Understanding about animal body parts, life cycles, and habitats is valuable. A nature shelf can allow for dissecting a flower to label its parts. Children can explore and learn about the physical properties of matter as experiments related to gas, liquid, and solids, about sinking and floating, and develop curiosity about the world.

Geography

Your children can learn about the continents with the sandpaper globe and the beautiful wooden Montessori puzzle maps. These are a favorite of mine as they nurture in children a very intimate connection with the whole world, including its flags and languages. Learning about the weather, land and water forms, the moon, and the solar system are fantastic studies. The Montessori Birthday Ritual where a child carries a globe and walks around the sun (a lit candle) for each year of life is so special.

The Arts

Encouraging your children to use music, art, and dance to express themselves helps them develop social and emotional skills and creative and cognitive abilities. You can set up a music area with rhythm instruments, a device to play music, and stories of great composers, artists, and dancers. Your family may play music together or dance. You might study art and engage in artistic projects such as drawing, creating a nature journal with pictures, and writing. Having supplies of pencils, lined and unlined paper, colored pencils, glue, and paints appropriate for your children, that they can access themselves, can be helpful. Studying art history by finding beautiful pictures of paintings and other artwork can be educational. You can share stories and information about art and artists with your children. You can also visit an art museum and study artists and their artwork online.

Music

Incorporating songs into your day can make your learning time enjoyable and mark the sections of time. You can use your voices, online digital recordings, or instruments. You can help your children identify musical instruments by studying the symphony orchestra. Books, pictures, videos, and visits to children's programs at a city symphony or youth music school can be enjoyable family activities. Young children can also learn to play musical instruments at an early age.

A cubicle shelf works well for your five learning areas if your child is young and you want to keep it simple to start. You can put one lesson in each area and change the lessons each week. It is an easy way to get started. You can also label the areas (math, language, sensorial…), which will also help you learn. Here is an example.

After you have set up your five learning areas as defined in Chapter Two, you can find a curriculum and materials if you plan to homeschool or get ideas for supplementing their schooling to meet your family's needs. Once again, remind yourself not to feel overwhelmed or pressured. This whole journey is up to you and your creative genius. Everything you need can unfold as you hold a positive vision and believe in yourself and your dream. Little by little, it is a great way to go; remember to stop and breathe! You can remember that it is love that will show you the way, as it was for Maria Montessori, at every point in her life.

A Cubicle Shelf with One Lesson for Each Learning Area +

Maria Montessori Loving the Children

Montessori Lessons

Here is a brief list of some of the most important lessons in the Montessori early childhood curriculum.

Table 3.2 Some Key Montessori Early Childhood Lessons

Please note that the following is an overview of lessons and not a complete list of Montessori lessons.

List of Some of the Main Montessori Early Childhood (Preschool) Lessons				
Practical Life	**Sensorial**	**Language/ Reading**	**Math**	**Cultural**
Preliminary Exercises	*Size* Category	*Pre-reading:* Matching Cards:	*Numbers to Ten*	*Botany*
How to Roll a Rug	Pink Tower	Sand Tray	Number Rods	Parts of the Plant
How to Sit Down or Stand up from a Chair	Brown (or Broad) Stair	Mystery Bag	Sandpaper Numbers	Parts of the Root
Carry a Tray	Knobbed Cylinders	Language Objects	Spindle Boxes	Parts of the Stem
Sponge Water Bowl to Bowl	*Form* Category	Nomenclature cards	Zero Game	Parts of the Leaf
Spoon Rice or beans	Geometric Solids & Bases	Rhyming objects	Numbers & Counters Short bead stair	Parts of the Flower
Pour Rice or water	Binomial Cube	Matching rhyming objects	Short Bead Stair	Parts of the Fruit
Care of the Self	Trinomial Cube	Sequence Picture cards	*Intro to Decimal System: The Golden beads*	Parts of the Seed
Wash Hands	Knobbed Cylinders	Metal Insets Develop the Hand	Large/Small Number Cards	*Geography*
Dressing Frames	*Constructive Triangles:*	Three-part Cards	Counting Golden Beads	The Continents
Wash Face	Blue Triangle Box	*Beginning Letter Sound Skills*	The Bank Game of Change	The Oceans
Polish Shoes	Rectangle Box	Listen for Sounds in the environment	*The Four Operations*	Land & Water forms
Comb Hair	Triangle Box	Beginning sound isolation	Golden Bead Addition	Wooden Puzzle Maps

Table 3.2 Some Key Montessori Early Childhood Lessons, *continued*

Prepare Snack	Large Hexagon Box	Beginning sound-letter association	Golden Bead Subtraction	Flags of the Nations
Blow One's Nose	Small Hexagon Box	Match sound with object	Golden Bead Multiplication	Your Heritage and Geography Study
Care of Environment	Large Hexagon Box	Match sound with pictures	Golden Bead Division	*Zoology – The Five Categories Animals*
Wash a Table	Small Hexagon Box	Sandpaper Letters	The Stamp Game	Parts of the amphibian
Dusting	*Color Category*	*The Letter – Short Vowel Words*	The Dot Game	Parts of the mammal
Arrange Flowers	Primary Colors Box	Build 3 letter words	Solving Word Problems	Parts of the reptile
Wash a Window	Primary Colors Box 2	Decode 3 letter words	*Teens, Tens, and Hundreds*	Parts of the bird
Set a Table	Secondary Color Wheel	3 letter word pictures and labels	Short bead stair	Parts of the fish
Sweep	Value (Black, White, Gray) Color Tablets	Practice 3 letter word lists	Seguin Teens Board	*Earth Science*
Grace and Courtesy	Mix Black and White	Reading words, phrases, sentences and books	Seguin Tens Board	Earth's Rotation around the Sun
Greet Someone	Color Gradation Color Box 3	Build 4+ phonetic letter words	Hundred Chain	Seasons
Introduce Oneself	Tactile Category	Decode 4+ letter words	Hundred Board	Months of the Year
Offer Help	Mystery Bag	Practice 4+ letter word lists	*Memorization*	Calendar
Excuse Yourself	Matching Mystery Bag	Reading 4+ letter, phrases, sentences and books	Addition Snake Game	Days of the Week

Table 3.2 Some Key Montessori Early Childhood Lessons, *continued*

Cough Politely	Fabric Box	*Final Silent "E"*	Addition Strip Board and Charts	Stories of Greek Gods related to Names of Days
Interrupt Politely	Baric Tablets (weight)	Final Silent "E" word building	Subtraction Snake Game	*Science*
The Control of Movement	*Gustatory/ Olfactory*	Final Silent "E" decoding: Words, phrases, sentences & books	Subtraction Strip Board	Magnetism
Walk on the Line	Smelling jars	*Multi-Letter Phonograms*	Multiplication Bead Board	Buoyancy
Walk on the Line with a Bell	Tasting jars	Introduction	Multiplication with the Colored Bead Bars	Density & Volume
Silence Game: Listen to Sounds in Environment/ Share	Grate Different Fruits and Tasting the Differences	Word Building and ID multi-letter Phonograms in words	Multiplication Strip Board and charts	Evaporation
Carry an Unlit Candle Across the Room	Gather Herbs and Smelling the Differences	Phrases, Sentences, & Books	Division Board & Charts	Science of Light

Note: In the cultural area, lessons can be given in any order, depending on your child's readiness.

Plan Your Week with Your Children

It is helpful to plan out your lessons before the week starts so that you will be prepared when your children are ready. Being prepared is a reward in itself, will remove stress, and give you confidence. I eventually found a rhythm of planning that worked for our family. I would start planning a month ahead with an overall brief plan, and then during the week previous to the lessons, in more detail. This way, I was prepared to teach a lesson before the week started and had time to gather last-minute materials. You can note the lessons you will present, make a detailed plan, and list any needed materials. Keep the past lessons and store them in a binder for the year so that you can review what you did or even use them for another child later.

T3.1 Weekly Lesson Plan for Two-and-a-Half to Six-Year-olds: Sample Template

A Summary of the Multiple Intelligences					
Topic	Language	Math	Sensorial	Practical LIfe	Cultural
Monday	Match Pictures and Initial Sounds (Cluster One: a, b, c, d, e)	Fetch (Get quantities of beads or other items): ex.: Request three units or two tens		Sweeping (child broom and dustpan) Sweep into a corner on the floor.	How to water a plant (Check soil, pour carefully while putting two fingers under spout)
Tuesday	Matching Pictures/ Initial Sounds (Cluster Two: f, g, h, i, j, k)		Eye Patch Feel and identify objects on a tray with eyes shut)	Pouring rice (one pitcher to another)	
Wednesday	Matching Pictures/ Initial Sounds (Cluster Three: l, m, n, o, p)	Counting one to twenty with cards			Flower arranging
Thursday	Matching Pictures/ Initial Sounds (Cluster Four: q, r, s, t, u)	Counting and matching with twelve and twenty (two cards and twenty pennies		Spooning beans from one bowl to another	Rhythm Instruments: Sing a song and keep rhythm
Friday	Pictures/ Initial Sounds (Cluster Five: v, w, x, y, z)		Sorting colors of puffs into a sixsection cupcake tin		

You can find a blank version of this template as part of a downloadable set of templates on my website. See the QR code on the inside cover of this book, front and back, to download the set from my website.

Here is a sample of a lesson plan you can use to help you design individual lessons which you will want to write out. Doing this helps you think in detail about what you will do and how you will introduce the concepts. You can find a blank version of this template as part of a downloadable set of templates on my website. See the QR code on the inside cover of this book, front and back, to download the set from my website.

T3.2 Plan an Individual Lesson: Sample Template

Lesson Plan: Practical Life Spooning Beans Plan:	Materials Needed:	Resources/ Notes
1. Go to the shelf with Marie and find the bean spooning lesson on a tray	1. Two bowls	
2. Gracefully carry the tray to a table	2. 1.5 cups red beans	
3. Ask Marie to watch with her hands in her lap. Pick up the spoon with thumb and forefinger	3. Large Serving Spoon	
4. Identify the objects on the tray	4. Tray	
5. Say, "This is a bowl, beans, and a spoon"		
6. "This bowl is empty." "This bowl has beans."		
7. "I will spoon the beans from the left bowl to the right bowl."		
8. Slowly and carefully, spoon beans from the left bowl to the right bowl, using thumb and forefinger with spoon.		
9. When finished, spoon beans back into left bowl and place the spoon on the tray.		
10. Take the tray back to the shelf and invite Marie to take it.		

Montessori Curriculum

A Montessori curriculum is a wonderful tool. Training helps tremendously, as well. Official training and manuals will give you a broader scope and understanding of the approach and lessons in a more comprehensive way than trying to gather information on your own from various sources. If you plan to homeschool, I suggest you find a professional training program with a parent component. Usually, a training program will have its own curriculum manuals. Participating in Montessori training will also give you a community, and it will be worth investing time and money for the benefit your children will receive. The Authentic Institute of Montessori, https:// aimmontessoriteachertraining.org, is my recommendation. They have a comprehensive in-depth training program with great options for parents with manuals and resources. This parent program gives the full training, such as a teacher would receive but does not require a practicum, testing, or the expense of the total teacher certification. For this reason, it is perfect for parents. Please see my website, Montessorifamilies.com, for information on Montessori training, materials, and resources.

Further Thoughts About Materials and Lessons in Your Home

The structure of the Montessori environment is brilliant and can be created in your home. The materials are ingenious and worthwhile, but I do not believe you must have all professionally-made materials to teach. Yes, do your best to find, purchase, or make materials, but also know that when you focus on learning with your children and seek authentic connection with them, you experience a certain peace that helps you feel that "right now, I am fulfilling my children's needs, no matter what." It is fulfilling for them and you. There is a certain balance between acquiring what we need and keeping our children as the focal point so that your work with them grows over time. The true Montessori way is a mindset of respect and love that connects with the child and follows their needs. The materials are important, but they can be provided in different ways.

How to Find or Make Your Materials

You can purchase professionally-made materials, or you can make your own. You can **find them used, borrow them, or combine them all.** There is no one way to secure materials. If you understand the purpose of each material and where it comes in the sequence, you may figure out inexpensive ways to produce it yourself.

There is a wide range of quality and prices in the products from different Montessori material companies. So, you need to be wise and observant. There are now many online sites where you can buy secondhand Montessori materials that are like new. Making your own will require a little more out-of-the-box thinking and a reasonable amount of time, but it could also inspire great creativity. Many beautiful online Montessori home-oriented websites have been developed, offering nice examples and resources. Getting some professionally made materials can help you establish a certain quality and expectation for your environment.

If you choose to make materials, they can be simple but should be neat and realistic. If there is the wording, it should be neat and accurately spelled, and consistent lettering should be used with the same font or handwriting that looks the same from material to material. Handmade things can be beautiful and can contain all of these elements. Children are often endeared to well-done work of our hands.

By being aware, you can expose your children to many things in your home and environment that can help them become aware, logical, and perceptive people, even apart from using actual Montessori materials. You can be attentive to teachable moments and ask your child how many rectangles they can see on a certain building (point to the doors and windows) or how many circles they see on the tires of cars in a parking lot. This is Montessori!

Infants & Toddler Learning Materials

Montessori Infant Area (Birth to Twelve Months)

The Montessori infant curriculum unfolds spontaneously with each child's unique interests and skills. Dr. Montessori did not develop educational materials and a curriculum for infants but talked about an environment for them. Based on her words, we can use daily observations of our infants to guide what activities and materials we offer to stimulate learning and pique curiosity. We can watch for what they look at, what they reach for, and what seems to excite them. This chapter approaches infant learning both directly and indirectly.

Arranging low shelves with materials your baby can reach may not seem like giving lessons, but you can see that they learn about the physical world as they touch, listen, taste, smell, and see. They are taking in everything sensorially. Babies also build their bodies and muscle memory by picking up toys, stretching, and transferring them hand to hand. Reaching for toys across the blanket will motivate them to move. You can be creative and find things your baby might enjoy by observing them. One teacher I knew in a Montessori infant program where I worked made a simple activity. She saw babies love to play with fabric, so she cut colorful twelve-inch cloth squares and laid them on the blankets around them. The colorful and patterned squares were set up in peaks, attracting the babies' attention. They naturally wanted to grab, suck on, and wave them. These were simple and basic items, but they led the babies to experiment and explore. These were invented by caring, observant adults who watched what their babies enjoyed. Wooden toys and natural fiber materials are helpful.

Babies develop concentration, language, and problem-solving skills as they interact with materials within their reach. Physical coordination and visual discrimination are their learning objectives.

Infant learning materials have been recently made in the spirit of Montessori's work with babies. You can demonstrate to your baby how to use them and then move away and let her try. It will take time for her to master their use, but children are naturally attracted to practicing what they are in the process of mastering.

The Object Permanence Box is a material that allows older infants to explore hand-eye coordination and become familiar with object permanence. Babies can learn that even when the ball goes behind a wooden wall and out of sight, it is still present and That objects can exist even when they can't be seen. You can make an Object Permanence Box with a square box, a lid that can open, and a ball. You must put a hole in the top and the side big enough for a ball.

Object Permanence Box

Another material for a baby who can stand is called the Ball Tracker. They can place a ball in the Tracker, watching it slowly move down a ramp from left to right to left again. When they follow the ball back and forth with their eyes, they track it, strengthening their eyes for writing and reading later.

The Imbucare boxes assist children in recognizing different shapes of the same size. They work to fit the pieces into the holes and learn to identify what shapes fit and which do not. This activity also strengthens their eye-hand coordination and fine motor control.

We can make materials that develop needed skills. For example, you can put clothespins in a small, wide basket and find a wide-mouth jar. With a little practice, your older infant may drop the clothespins into the jar. The pincer grip of the thumb and forefinger used to hold the clothespins will develop writing muscles.

Babies need an environment that encourages movement. This develops the baby's muscles and organizes the brain for learning, as you will read more about in Chapter Five.

Building your children's lives around the Montessori principles discussed in Chapter One will be valuable. We will make our baby feel respected by being soft-spoken, using eye contact, and kneeling at our baby's level. When we are responsive to her needs and patient and tell her what we will do before touching or moving her, she will trust us and be more readily receptive to learning. Most importantly, infants need a secure attachment to their parents. Carrying your baby in your arms or a sling or a wrap frequently in the first few months facilitates bonding. Move with her. Talk and sing! Tell her about everything around her. Your interaction with her and others stimulates learning indirectly. It is also helpful for her to spend time on the floor where she can move independently. I recently realized again how much babies move if they are on a flat surface, as I spent time sitting and watching my grandsons when they were four months old. They continuously moved their arms and legs up and down for thirty minutes or more, almost like they were marching. Imagine how adults would feel if we did the same for more than thirty minutes daily. It was amazing to comprehend. No wonder they sleep so much—they work so hard! It also highlights why it is recommended for parents to put their babies on flat surfaces as much as possible. Chapter Four will discuss working with infants with the right brain learning approach.

Take Time to Interact with Your Baby

When my babies were little, I learned that our time together could happen haphazardly, or I could be intentional. Planning my time with my baby made me feel closer to them and more satisfied at the end of each day. It helped me to think ahead about what she might need, what I wanted to do with her, and when things would work best. Forethought can help a lot. In the following chart, I have created a template for you to fill out for your time with your baby, considering the information in this section. Feel free to change any of the categories so they work for you.

T3.3 Weekly Infant Care and Learning Plan: Sample Template
Child's Name: Joshua   Age: 4 Months

Respectful Approach	I will take time to observe and connect with Joshua each day. I will try to slow down and quiet my mind in order to sense his moods and needs. I will communicate respect by my calm, still presence.
Communication	I will look at Joshua and tell him what I will do before I touch or move him. I will talk to him, looking right into his eyes, and wait for his response. I know he will have something to communicate.
Movement	Joshua is not crawling but kicks and stretches for hours every day. He spends time on a soft blanket spread on the floor. This week I will change his position often so he can see and hear new things and spend lots of time on the floor. I will walk and dance while holding him so he feels different kinds of movement.
Sensorial	I will use different essential oils lightly in our home, and cook delicious smelling food to stimulate his sense of smell. I will bring different fabrics for him to touch and feel, putting them in his hands as well as softly stroking his arm, leg, or face with them.
Toys	He cannot grasp anything yet, but does like to bat at things and see them move. I will attach a bell to the string to the arch over his playmat on the floor so he can bat it. I will provide a mirror and black-and-white visualization charts where he can see them.
Music	I want to provide different kinds of music that calm as well as liven Joshua's mood, such as Mozart and Bach which can be lively as well as relaxing to stimulate the brain and increase his mathematical sense.

Montessori Toddler Lessons and Activities
(Twelve Months to Two and a Half Years)

The first three years are the ones that lay the foundation for later learning, neurologically and in every way—and the stronger the foundation, the more the child will be able to build upon it. The toddler stage is exciting because they change almost daily. Their observations, skills, and vocabulary are growing, and their communication with us is endearing. They are highly active and impressionable. They are open to all we want to do with them and are often excited about life. It is irresistible! It is also mind-blowing to watch how every effort we make to support them results in their growth. For example, if we make them a bottle/clothespin lesson, if it's developmentally right, they will work at it continuously until they have it. Our routines in everyday living with them can provide learning opportunities for independence, coordination, order, and concentration and encourage social, emotional, cognitive, and physical growth.

T3.4 Early Practical Life Optional Activities Chart for Growing Toddlers

Self-care:	dressing, washing, eating, and toileting according to each child's individual ability
Care of the environment:	cleaning, sorting, plant and animal care, simple food preparation
Large-motor activities	(outside/inside) walking, running, jumping, climbing steps, balancing
Fine motor skills:	using tools and utensils, a paintbrush, pencil, crayons, doing artwork
Language:	naming objects, talking about intentions and feelings, describing actions
Social Skills:	using manners with family members, saying and meaning, please and thank you, and small group games

Choose one or any number of the activities in the above chart to help your child develop practical life skills this week. You can review the previous section to refresh your image about these lessons.

Keeping the environment simple will leave you less stressed, allowing you to focus more on your constantly moving toddler. You can prepare beautiful, practical life activities. Lessons can increase in complexity as children grow older. Follow your child's interests and abilities. Watch and listen. Since the Learning Areas are in our homes where our children live twenty-four hours a day, we need a way to keep our spaces and our little ones safe. We can have materials on the lower shelves for easy and safe use every day and keep activities or lessons that have small pieces or don't clean up easily in an out-of-the-way place, like a high shelf, mantle, or closet. Then, we can access these to work individually with our children, introducing lessons at their developmental level. Ten to fifteen minutes with each child four to five times a week is wonderful. This allows us to let them explore throughout the day without our concern about a choking hazard or creating a difficult-to-clean-up situation and still provide challenging opportunities.

Montessori Recommended Toys

The best toys that fit the Montessori theme require action or effort from your children. They will encourage physical and cognitive development. Those with big sounds and lights may not inspire your child to think, explore, or move, which is important. When children interact with toys, they often learn skills. When looking for toys for your child, ask yourself these questions:

1. Is it age-appropriate for my child? (If so, there will be less concern about choking hazards, which is something we must constantly watch for.)
2. Does it stimulate learning?
3. Is it realistic? (When picking stuffed animals, choose real over make-believe, such as a fox over a cartoon character.)
4. Does it interest your child?

5. Does it encourage exploration or problem-solving?

6. Does it motivate your child to move and develop muscles?

You will want to look for toys made of natural materials such as wood, cotton, silk, natural rubber, and other natural fabrics. Having natural fabrics may reduce the possibility of allergic reactions or chemical impacts. Silicone teethers are good. You will want to check over all toys to ensure that no parts are unstable or sharp.

Some toy suggestions reflecting Montessori principles:

- ✧ **Birth to one year**—wooden rattles, plush sensory balls, wooden blocks, stacking toys, twelve-inch square sample fabrics with different textures/patterns, silicone teethers, sensory color rings

- ✧ **Two to three years old**—large piece puzzles, matching cards, big trucks, play tools, kids picture charades, play kitchen, lacing material, fairy garden, magnifying glass, doll houses

- ✧ **Three to four years old**—magnetic tiles, blocks, playdough, train sets, play scarves, climbing and balance toys, tying toys, jigsaw and matching puzzles, sensory toys, musical instruments

- ✧ **Four to five years old**—screwdrivers and screws on a board, pattern blocks, realistic figurines, workbench, puzzles, climbing toy, balance beam, small broom, rake, shovel

- ✧ **Five to six years old**—scissors, playdough tools, ribbon wand, cooking and baking utensils kit, scooter board, child microscope and slides, magnet and metal filings, butterfly grow kits

Maintain the Learning Environment

The learning environment retains a cozy feeling that invites participation when it is well-maintained. I truly understand the challenge of keeping your environment clean when you are busy with children twenty-four hours a day or if you work and have little time to plan and clean. Yet, it can be our aspiration to maintain the learning area as well as possible. Your children can help you as they grow. What is most important is that our children feel our love and support. We want to strive to do our best, yet the environment doesn't have to be perfect, and we don't need to stress. What is most important is that our children feel our love and support. As balanced parents, we will inspire and motivate our children to learn.

How to Organize Your Belongings

You can organize objects and materials for your home and learning areas in a storage location. This might be in a garage, extra room, or a closet, or you could get an extra outdoor container. Some people have built rafters in their garage. We found very tall metal shelves with six three-foot-wide shelf layers on each. You can use boxes or bins to hold clothing, belongings, or lesson materials. The lesson materials can be categorized for each of the five learning areas. Including a bin for a small collection of trays, baskets, or containers to use with your lessons will also be super helpful. You can use my following template to organize your plan for storage, or you can sketch a picture or type a list of how this storage area will be organized instead. Use whatever format works best for you. Post this plan in a prominent place in your storage area as a handy reference.

Here is a sample template I created for you to use for organizing your storage details. Feel free to use it however you wish, recreate it, or make your own. You can find this template,as part of a downloadable set of templates, on my website. See the QR code on the inside cover of this book, front and back, to download the set from my website.

You can find a blank version of this template as part of a down-loadable set of templates on my website.

T3.5 Home Storage Area Organization: Sample Template

Category: Clothes	Language, Sensorial, & Practical Life	Math and Cultural
1. Joey's shirts and sweaters	9. Language: Sounds and Letters	17. Math: Counting
2. Joey's pants, shorts	10. Language: Short Vowel	18. Math: Addition/ Subtraction
3. Jasmine's tops and sweaters	11. Language: Silent E	19. Math: Multiplication
4. Jasmine's pants, skirts, dresses	12. Multi-Letter Phonograms	20. Math: Division
5. Children's clothes ten to twelve	13. Sensorial	21. Zoology/Botany/ Seeds
6. Children's boots /snow gear	14. Sensorial	22. Music/History
7. Mom and Dad's Seasonal	15. Practical Life Supplies: trays, etc.	23. Geography
8. Mom and Dad's Snow Gear	16. Practical Life: Cleaning Supplies	24. Science/Art

Set Up a Workspace for Yourself

Organizing one place where you will make materials and create lessons can help you focus and be efficient. You will need a table or desk, shelves or drawers, a printer, markers, pens, paper, and a paper cutter. Having all of these in one place will help you so you don't spend time looking for things. As we did in our home, you may need stackable plastic drawers for the small and large items described above. A paper cutter is optional but highly recommended; it is an inexpensive purchase that will save you hours of time. A paper cutter will also make your materials neat with straight edges and convey a quality of excellence to your children. See what a Montessori home can do for your family.

You can find a blank version of this template as part of a downloadable set of templates on my website. See the QR code on the inside cover of this book, front and back, to download the set from my website.

T3.6 Observation Practice Three: Sample Template
Child: Henry   Age: 30 Months   Date: Oct. 4, 2019

Observation Practice
• What materials in the different areas of learning does your child seem attracted to? Henry loves the math beads. He wants to count them over and over. The colors and texture really appeal to him. I want to make or find more math materials for him.
• What practical life skills does my child need to develop? Henry is good at pouring and posting. He could use practice with pouring water accurately and refining his pincer grasp for writing.
• How can you stimulate his taste buds to help him grow sensorially? Henry loves to grow peas and string beans. We can introduce some new vegetables for growing this year. I would like to do a taste test and have her taste a few different vegetables and see if she can taste the difference.

Table 3.3 Chapter Three Takeaways

Chapter Three Takeaways
• Observation will help you perceive your child's interests in order to prepare lessons to inspire them.
• There are five areas of learning areas of the Montessori environment: Practical Life, Sensorial, Math, Language, and Cultural.
• Prepare your lessons ahead of time and practice before giving them.
• The three-period lesson will help you present information to your child in the Montessori way.

Enhancing the Montessori Method with Right Brain Learning Techniques

"Stimulating your children's right brain wonder and dynamic creativity early will propel them to develop more of the whole brain as they grow and engage in our left brain world and its linear expectations. Nurturing the right brain will give them more life resources and greater joy."
–TERESA ANGELES

When my first baby, David, was about eight months old, we visited an acquaintance who had a library of pictures and flashcards. The whole room had shelves labeled with different categories. These categories of pictures included language, math, music, botany (plants), zoology (animals), geometry, space, earth science, and more. I was intrigued and started showing flashcards to David regularly. He really seemed to enjoy watching them, as did my other children, later on. I didn't realize that I was stimulating the fantastic potential of the right brain and didn't even know what the right brain was at that time. This chapter is about the scientific findings regarding the brain, especially in young children. I want you to understand the incredible opportunity to embrace the right brain in the earliest part of your children's lives and know about valuable resources to help you do so. Montessori led the way, and later neuroscientific studies revealed more.

Dr. Montessori was a pioneer who advocated following the child and drawing out the child's innate abilities. Science has shown that there are many different parts of the brain, and her method seeks to nurture them. This chapter will share valuable discoveries about the two sides of the brain, focusing on cultivating the creative, feeling power of your child's right brain and why this is important. It will be beneficial for you. As in the previous chapters, I encourage you to read on with an open mind and an intention to enjoy this fascinating information so you can use it when you are ready.   Relaxing and enjoying life allows our right brain to be highly creative. This is one of the secrets to creative living!

Experts in the field of right brain learning believe that before birth and through age six, a child's right brain is predominant, allowing her to learn effortlessly by simply absorbing what is in her environment. This description matches what Montessori described as the child's absorbent mind in the first six years of life. In fact, it is amazing to realize how Montessori's discoveries compare so closely to the findings of neuroscientists one hundred years later. She arrived at these conclusions, describing the young child's development in detail with similar observations, but without the scientists' technology, testing, and data. She taught about this special time in the first six years when children are in an absorbent state of mind and move from an unconscious to a more conscious absorbent mind by the age of six. When Montessori first began to observe children, scientists had not yet identified the right brain. The children she wrote about exhibited unique creativity, problem-solving abilities, patience, and sensitivity to the spirit, all now associated with the right brain.

Both right brain learning theories and Montessori focus on education to develop children's innate intelligence and abilities, and not just to put knowledge into the mind. The more I have learned about them, I believe both are vital. Right brain learning compliments Montessori, and vice versa. Explore right brain learning concepts in this chapter and see if you agree with me.

It is so valuable to know that love is the greatest key to the child's wholeness, regardless of the approach. And, because love is mostly recognized in the right brain, love will open the door for the cultivation of right brain skills in our children. Love opens the way to security and, therefore, learning.

Taking the time now to understand why and how to give your children right brain activities will open doors you may have never imagined. My recommended resources are in this chapter. I encourage you to consider new ideas about nurturing your child.

Understanding the Two Sides of Your Child's Brain

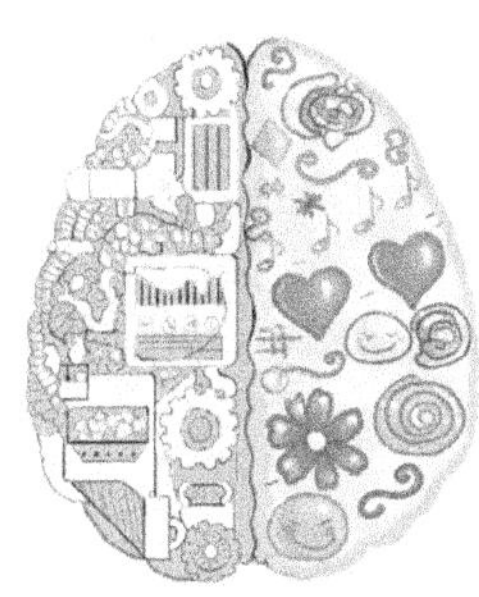

A medical science revolution, spearheaded by neuropsychologist Dr. Roger Sperry, occurred in the second half of the twentieth century. It was related to psychology, infant education, and the brain. The results of these neuroscientists' studies determined that the human brain's left and right hemispheres have different qualities, process information differently, and represent different modes of thinking and acting. Our children learn, feel, and act in ways that reveal what side of the brain they are living from. Strengthening our children's gifts in both hemispheres will help them to fulfill their potential, but right brain visualization, with its optimism that makes life wonderful and believes that all things are possible, will most of all help accomplish this.

The left brain represents conscious awareness. The left brain is more about thinking and analyzing, taking in information, and making lists rather than feeling. Some examples of left brain activities include using the conscious mind for drilling math facts, like one plus two, and writing letters, words, and sentences. It may mean writing down notes of music theory. The left brain can have a more serious nature.

Our children's right brains are creative and use out-of-the-box thinking, with curiosity that soaks up information like sponges. The right brain in our children is hopeful and positive. It seeks out joyful play and interaction, asking questions and discovering answers about life. The right brain in our children is open to spirituality and seeks to find meaning, purpose, and connection with life.

The following table helps us understand the two sides of the brain. The table is used with permission and taken from the tenth-anniversary version of Pamela Hickein's book *Right Brain Education: Changing the World One Heart at a Time*. Hickein has over thirty years of experience teaching right brain learning and founded RightBrainKids.com, an online right-brain learning program. Her programs help parents create experiences that cultivate their children's right brains.

Logic	**＋**	**Creativity**	**＝**	**Balanced Whole Brain Learning**
(Left Brain Skills)		(Right Brain Skills)		(EN4.3)

Table 4.2 The Two Sides of the Brain

Left Brain	Right Brain
Conscious awareness	Subconscious awareness
Short term memory	Long term memory
Slow input	Fast input
Detail analysis	Gestalt (whole picture)
Linear, sequential, reason	Creative, imaginative
Relies on physical senses (sight, sound, taste, touch, smell)	Relies on intuition (resonance with subtle frequencies)
Likes repetitive input	Soaks up information like a sponge
Uses words, lists and numbers	Uses rhythm, shapes and picture images
Processes one data at a time	Processes data all at once
Practical, works well under stress	Emotional, works well when fully relaxed

(EN4.4) Used with permission from Pamela Sue Hickein

Why Emphasize Right Brain Learning?

Studies reveal that having skills in both hemispheres of the brain allows children to use their whole brain. By integrating both sides of the brain, whole brain learning is the ultimate goal. *So, why, then, is this chapter about right brain learning? Because we live in a world that emphasizes developing the left brain with more linear, data-driven expectations, we need to employ significant effort to produce right brain skills to balance this. This is the core of what right brain learning is all about. It is also because right brain abilities being discovered can make life so much better than we have known. Your child needs a strong right brain with creative problem-solving and other right brain abilities to partner with the left brain's strong,*

logical, disciplined thinking. The magnificent abilities of the right brain have only recently been discovered, giving our children new opportunities for heightened creativity. If the right hemisphere is left uncultivated or unused, or a child is in a predominately left brain learning environment, the left hemisphere will dominate. The best time to use right brain learning techniques is before the left brain becomes predominant (before age six)—and, if possible, throughout life for whole brain balance. It is also never too late to cultivate right brain skills.

We can observe a possible example of right- and left-brain integration in Mozart's musical compositions. He heard beautiful musical melodies in his mind and envisioned when different instruments, such as the flute or oboe, would enter the pieces. This was his creative right brain working. He must have had a strong and well-developed right brain, able to visualize and imagine whole symphonies in his head, possibly from having beautiful classical music all around him from before birth. From early music training, he also knew how to do the tedious work of writing down the symphonies' musical notes and details. This was his left brain working. In doing so, the integration of the two sides of his brain allowed him to create masterpieces, making it possible for others to play them. With these integrated abilities of the right and left brain, he enriched the cultural climate of the world. The real key here is that he had a magnificent right brain that was able to hear beautiful symphonies, and then he also had left brain skills and training to match. Since the world will mostly likely see to much of the left brain development of our children, it's in our hands to see to their right brain development. Ensuring this will allow them to maximize their gifts and opportunities.

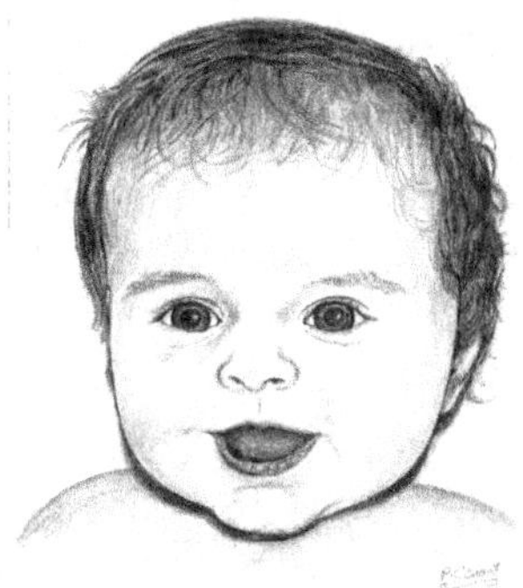

The Right Brain Window of Children from Conception to Three Years Old

The developing brain grows from the right hemisphere to the left hemisphere. The outer cortex, or outer layer of the brain, develops first. The first three years are the time when the right brain pre-dominates. It is like a window of opportunity when the child, first in the womb and then for three years after, functions completely in the right brain. This phenomenon also describes the unconscious absorbent mind spoken about by Montessori, referenced in Chapter One. It seems that surely they must correlate, as they are described almost identically. Hickein and right brain philosophy claim that during this three-year time frame, the child is most receptive to learning, is inspired, and filled with insatiable curiosity. This is a time of great opportunity to ignite the right brain's creativity, a potential that families can work with to shape a child's future.

Other experts have discussed this right brain window in their work using other terms to describe children from zero to three. Dr. Thomas Verny, M.D., author of *The Secret Life of the Unborn Child*, wrote about how the baby can see and sense on many levels and learn in the womb. Science has shown us that even unborn babies can communicate and learn. In these three years, their experiences shape their character, beliefs, confidence, and subconscious mind. Infants and toddlers up to three years old can absorb an amazing amount of life and a wide variety of information through all of the senses. For example, children absorb their culture and can participate appropriately in family and social gatherings by the age of three or four. They are also deeply affected by the quality of their mother's love. If the mother uses relaxation and visualization, two important right brain approaches, these can help her feel peaceful so she can easily connect with her baby. She can visualize happiness and health in her child, born or unborn, and feel the emotional results in her child's peace. This also can promote emotional security.

Three to Six Years Old is When the Right Brain Integrates with the Left Brain

From three to six years old is the period Montessori called the *conscious absorbent mind*. There is a bundle of sensitive nerve fibers between the left and right brain called the corpus callosum. This is the bridge over which the left hemisphere gradually moves to integrate with the right hemisphere. Hickein calls it "bridging," when the left brain comes into play with its cognitive approach to life between four and six years old. Your children will start to consciously make decisions about their learning. You know this is happening when your child starts speaking in complete sentences and begins reading, writing, and counting. They will start understanding linear concepts, like time. Introducing patterns, matching games, and memory games helps to foster cognitive thinking while you continue to nurture the right brain. Until about six, they will still be in the absorbent mind, soaking up all learning opportunities, but they will also start thinking more logically.

Cultivate your child's right brain with activities at home. There is a wonderful program online that I recommend in the next section. You can also make or buy physical flashcards and do them at home with your children, though it seems that with the speed of life, the

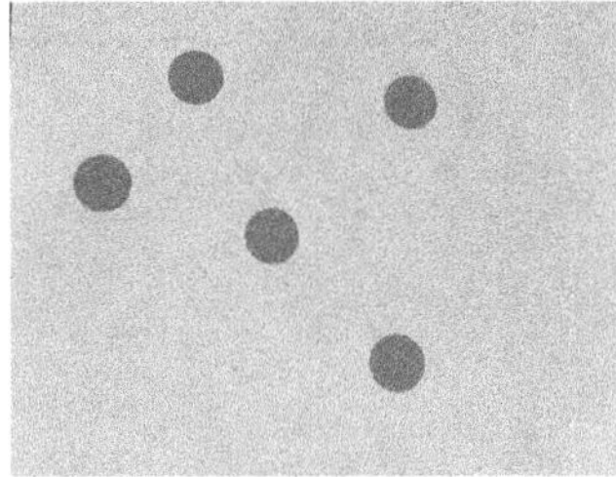

Flashcard with Five Dots
to Show Quantity

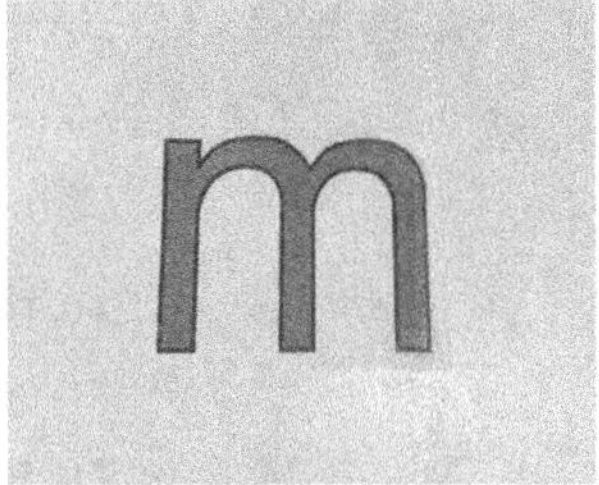

Flashcard of Letter Sound m

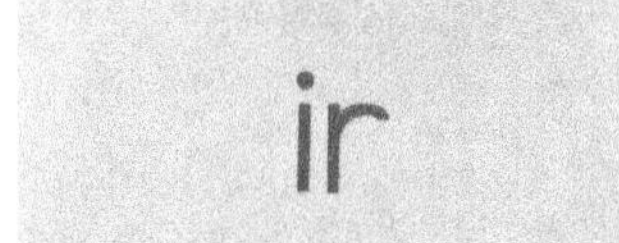

Flashcard of Multi-letter
Phonogram ir

Word Card Nana

Flashcard of the
Flower Columbine

Flashcard of Alaska

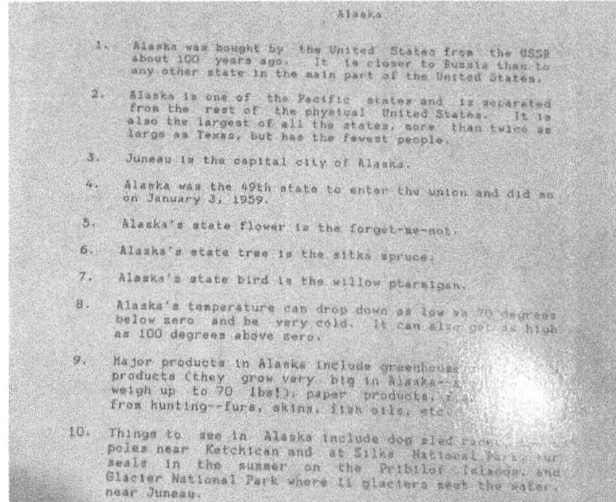

Alaska

1. Alaska was bought by the United States from the USSR about 100 years ago. It is closer to Russia than to any other state in the main part of the United States.

2. Alaska is one of the Pacific states and is separated from the rest of the physical United States. It is also the largest of all the states, more than twice as large as Texas, but has the fewest people.

3. Juneau is the capital city of Alaska.

4. Alaska was the 49th state to enter the union and did so on January 3, 1959.

5. Alaska's state flower is the forget-me-not.

6. Alaska's state tree is the sitka spruce.

7. Alaska's state bird is the willow ptarmigan.

8. Alaska's temperature can drop down as low as 70 degrees below zero and be very cold. It can also get as high as 100 degrees above zero.

9. Major products in Alaska include greenhouse products (they grow very big in Alaska—a weigh up to 70 lbs!), paper products, from hunting—furs, skins, fish oils, etc.

10. Things to see in Alaska include dog sled races, poles near Ketchican and at Silka National Park, fur seals in the summer on the Pribilof Islands, and Glacier National Park where 11 glaciers meet the water, near Juneau.

Information on the back of Alaska Flashcard

online program is more doable. I will share more about the physical flashcard option later in this chapter.

Right Brain Kids

Their Tweedlewink program offers high-quality online lessons for children from two months to six years. The eight-minute videos in their Flashcards to Go program or the enhanced versions with downloadable follow-up activities, are ideal. The curriculum, which covers math, science, world languages, culture, music, and art, ensures a holistic development for your child. Engaging in these presentations increases neuron activity in the brain and develops neural pathways that grow by use. It is recommended that online lessons be shown three to four times a week. Hickein says, "Small amounts of time, even ten to fifteen minutes daily of giving the right brain lessons, can be invaluable for your child." I now use these programs with my grandchildren and follow up with hands-on activities. My grandchildren love the videos and the activities. Right Brain Kids products have been a dream come true for me and have saved me a lot of time and work.

Six Stages of Development in Young Children

Hickein designed her programs based on six stages of development, which she saw in children between conception and age six. At certain points, there were indications that the children were ready for new levels of learning. Below is a list of characteristics that guided Right Brain Kids' program development and can help you assess where your children might be.

*It is important to note that the developmental chart is meant to adapt to your child's developmental abilities. Right Brain Kids views "being behind" as a time of great opportunity because your child still lives in the right brain window. This time allows for connections to be made deep within the brain. If your child seems "ahead," you are encouraged to follow the guidelines recommended in the program so you can keep the right brain pathway functioning along with all other development.

Table 4.3 Right Brain Kids' Characteristics of the Six Stages (EN4.6)

Right Brain Kids' Characteristics of the Six Stages	
Stage	**Approximate Age Range**
1. Prenatal: Zero to Nine Months in Utero	• developing in the womb • intimately linked to mother's thoughts/ feelings • hears sounds from outside the womb at 5 months • brain development is rapid
2. Newborn: Zero – Nine Months	• dependent upon the mother • highly sensitive to the emotional and physical environment • developing outer senses • brain developing quickly, absorbing all information • preparing for mobility
3. Infant: Ten to Eighteen Months	• developing fine and gross motor skills—actively mobile! • imitating sounds and actions • beginning independence, curious, eager to explore environment • building communication skills
4. Infant-Toddler: Nineteen to Twenty-Seven Months	• moving and communicating • craving exploration and independence • responds to instructions • able to match • able to hold a pencil • has limited ability to focus (up to fifteen minutes) • enjoys pretend play
5. Toddler: Twenty-Eight to Thirty-Six Months	• speaks and understands well • beginning to count • beginning to read letters using basic phonics sounds • shapes, pictures • able to sequence and classify objects and events • able to focus up to 20 minutes at a time
6. Preschooler: Three to Six Years Old	• reads letters (and possibly words, sentences, books) • understands basic math concepts (add/subtract) • organizes material mentally (match/sequence/classify) • expresses imagination • expresses independent ideas • able to focus up to thirty minutes at a time

(EN4.6) Used with permission

Our Children's Right Brain Abilities

Our children have right brain abilities that can be developed, including photographic memory, visualization, creative problem-solving, speed reading, instant math calculation, multiple language acquisition, and perfect pitch. These may seem almost too good to be true, but they are real. Right brain abilities seem to manifest effortlessly when they have the right stimulation, which you will learn about in the next sections. They can manifest in subtle or pronounced ways. Hickein says they tend to unfold according to the child's own inner timetable and unique passions.

Children may be able to play a musical instrument, dance at a very early age, acquire perfect pitch, or sing beautifully. Some children enjoy investigation, hypothesis, and experimentation, desiring to understand how things work and being driven by curiosity and imagination. Others may feel driven to communicate ideas about any topic, enjoy writing and speaking, and greatly impact others.

Children can develop creative problem-solving abilities, even at four and five years old, which is more about perception than hard work. I have observed this in certain families where parents discuss problems with their children, prompting them to verbalize different elements of a problem and suggest solutions.

Hickein mentioned that having a right brain ability of photographic memory may mean your children can look at something once and recall the original picture or image in vivid detail. She saw that some children applied right brain speed reading activities to read the things they were most passionate about, while others developed speed reading to specialize in it. They could glance at a page, take in all the information without much effort, and retain the information for future use.

Children can also learn visualization. For example, you might work together with your children before going on a family outing to enhance the family experience with positive thoughts. You might think together how it will feel to be in the fresh mountain air, enjoy the sun's warmth, and smell the evergreen trees. You may envision everyone smiling, being harmonious, and saying kind words to one another. Later, you can see how this right brain visualization impacted your family experience, and that the day was happy and enjoyable.

If your children have intuition, they may sense what other family members need without being told. If they have computer-like math calculation abilities, they might be able to glance at a simple math problem and quickly see the answer. Multiple language acquisition means that some children can easily and quickly learn to speak to people of other languages and understand them by immersion and association. This is a right brain ability. If they have learned a second language, then mastering multiple languages can follow with even greater ease.

These right brain abilities can be cultivated in everyone, but most easily when children are very young. Children manifest abilities in the area of learning that they most resonate with.

The Twelve Tweedlewink Right Brain Learning Techniques

Hickein's program started in a Montessori school with children as young as three months old. These children absorbed the flashcards, foreign languages, and classical music. They had eye exercises, lots of physical exercise, and right brain lessons. They also had various hands-on activities on shelves that they could freely choose, sparking interest and curiosity. The infants and toddlers seemed happy and appeared to enjoy circle time.

The following twelve techniques are purposeful and, most importantly, fun! They contribute to a beautiful developmental plan for your child, zero-six years old. Parents use these techniques to help their children develop the right brain, and the fun element ensures that both you and your child enjoy the learning process. The choice of which techniques to use is based on their current developmental needs rather than age, trusting in her body's wisdom and inner time-table. These techniques can be used with any curriculum, although Right Brain Kids has a specific curriculum, which you will find in the following pages. You can use Right Brain Kids' online programs, create your own, or do both. Activities can begin in the prenatal period, and you can add more as the child ages. You will find a blank template on my website, using the QR code in the book cover to assess and plan for your child's learning.

There is a sample template I created for you to use to note your children's ages and developmental stages when planning which techniques you want to use.

T4.1 Right Brain Learning Techniques

Techniques	Developmental Age	Child: Tiana, 18 mos.	Blank: Child
Right Brain Builders # One-Four	For all children through age six, and for anyone doing the right brain lessons	How I will use this information with my child:	How I will use this information with my child:
Technique One: Love	Create a loving connection with your child. Parents can take time to show children how much they are loved and place a priority on expressing it. Tweedlewink encourages parents to listen carefully, make eye contact, and have loving interactions with their children. Our children will feel our thoughts and feelings and will be supported by the quality and strength of our love. This love will facilitate your children's ability to learn	Sing the "I Love You" Song to Tiana. Talk to her and hug her before we start. Ask her how she is, and take a moment to breathe together.	
Technique Two: Image	Imagine health, success, and happiness for your children. We can create vision boards with words and images of our hopes and dreams for them. With our help, they can envision their goals and dreams as becoming reality and imagine journeys to faraway places. This increases their ability to visualize and use their imaginations.	I will hold pictures of Louise and envision her feeling happy and peaceful. I see her doing things that make her feel empowered and contented. I see our relationship blessed with joy and care.	
Technique Three: Flash	Show high-quality flashcards at a one-second-per-card rate, and you will cultivate the imaging potential of your child's right brain. Flash information about unlimited subjects, which may include nature, science, music, culture, math quantities, symbols, words, and patterns. Flashcards affect the passive right brain's reception of information. Tweedlewink online programs include many flashcards for each lesson.	I will show her beautiful images of different kinds of flowers and ladybugs, which she loves, and say the names of each one.	
Technique Four: Listen	Play a variety of high-quality audio such as classical music to help develop the right brain and establish a foundation for composition, rhythm, and tone skills. Choose musical pieces from international composers featuring different rhythms and instruments. We can also help develop perfect pitch in our children by using musical tuning forks and humming with notes played on a well-tuned instrument.	We will listen to Mozart music and tap the rhythm as we listen. We will march around the room, and hop to the music. We will hum the notes we are familiar with.	

Corpus Collasum Bridge Builders # Five-Seven	Newborns – six years old (when the left brain starts awakening)		
Technique Five: Talk	Surround your children with multiple languages that nurture their right brain ability to speak fluently. "Talk" plays with sound by repeating, speaking, singing, and humming, including musical notes, bird calls, and rhymes. Our children can learn from us how to enunciate, use good vocabulary, and speak with excellence, by absorption. We can use puppets, songs, rhymes, poetry, and dance to engage our children.	We will talk about all the things we do each day. We will find at least one short poem to learn and repeat a few times and enunciate clearly.	
Technique Six: Track	Helping your child track is a process whereby children follow an object with their eyes, stimulating vision, relaxation, memory, emotion, thought, creativity, motivation, and creative intuition. Exercises prepare their eyes for the speed, focus, and peripheral intake needed for photographic memory and speed reading.	We will use a wand to give Louise exercises for her eyes to follow up and down, side to side. We will also take a few minutes each night before sleeping to visualize something she desires: a happy day at the park, a harmonious next day playing with her sister.	
Technique Seven: Move	Move, with your child. Jump, walk, and run. Movement helps the brain. Help them touch their left hands to right knees, and right hands to left knees. This helps them integrate information they are learning. Brain circuitry works best when we coordinate the right and left sides of the body. Jump to the rhythm of flashcard flips. We can use finger plays, hands-on activities, and hand movements with songs.	We will sing songs together with hand movements. We will do cross-crawls (tapping right hand on left knee, and left hand on right knee, alternating a few times.)	
Left Brain Builders # Eight-Eleven	From approximately nineteen months – six years (when the left brain starts to be more active)	We will not use the rest of these techniques because she is seventeen months and developmentally needs more time above.	

Technique Eight: Think	Help your children create order out of their worlds, which is their need. This technique, "Think," gives the mind the basic skills to pull and organize information. As we introduce concepts, we then provide hands-on activities to anchor the child's experience and learning. We progress through four types of hands-on lessons that increase in complexity: matching, sorting, counting, and sequencing.		
Technique Nine: Draw	Instill joy in your child with artistic early writing and drawing of shapes, pictures, numbers, and letters. As soon as an infant can hold a pencil, he can begin connecting lines and dots, graduating to shapes and pictures, he will soon be able to recreate images from the world around him and place them on paper—or any other medium at his disposal.		
Technique Ten: Do	Provide purposeful work through practical life lessons, arts and crafts (discussed in Chapter Three), and imaginative play for your children. They can use household and arts and crafts materials to explore and create. Selfdirected activities provide an outlet for a child's imagination and sense of accomplishment through real and imagined projects. It can nurture their strengths and interests.		
Technique Eleven: Read	Encourage your developing children to learn to read when they show a lengthening attention span, readiness, and eagerness. Emphasize and point out words as you read stories together. Hands-on reading materials will help them identify sounds, build and blend words, and launch into reading. Please refer back to Chapter three of the reading sequence in the Language Area for more detail and resources.		
Whole Brain Harmony #Twelve	For children between four and six years old (when the left brain has integrated with the right brain)		
Technique Twelve: Fly	Continue nurturing your children whose right hemispheres have been nourished, successfully connected with the left, and have developed a strong "bridge" between them. When the emerging left brain has become brightened with purposeful play, continue to nurture your child's right brain abilities for higher creativity. Photographic memory games, memory linking, and speed reading are examples you can use.		

The Twelve TweedleWink Techniques Table

You can find a blank version of this template as part of a downloadable set of templates on my website. See the QR code on the inside cover of this book, front and back, to download the set from my website.

Hickein's Tweedlewink program for children under six uses the twelve techniques listed above and I want to remind you that you can take your time and choose what is doable for you to focus on now, and what you will leave for another day. The above techniques are used to teach eight categories of lessons, as shown in the following sample table. When we teach basic subjects with a right brain approach, the children playfully learn the material, sparking curiosity and making learning a fun adventure, unlike traditional educational settings. These lessons nurture the left brain and do not include left brain drills. When children between four and six show evidence of bridging, some activities are used to work with both the right and left brain, such as using hands-on reading materials and readers, but there is still a strong emphasis on abundant right brain activities.

Not all twelve accelerated learning techniques are used from the beginning. You will use more techniques as your infant develops cognitive and physical skills. Right Brain Kids is also careful not to use all the techniques at one time or all in one day. Children will also have their favorites, and it is essential to be flexible if you are doing a home program that works for your children. Even little by little is a good philosophy. By the time they are three or older, you will have many activities to choose from. The following table defines each of these curriculum categories. You will use the techniques above to share information with your child in these curriculum categories and nurture the right brain, too.The parts of the right brain curriculum here are facilitated with Right Brain techniques described in the table above.

Table 4.4 Tweedlewink Curriculum Elements

Tweedlewink Curriculum Elements	
1. Vision	Eye exercises strengthen children's eyes to follow a wand in all directions. Black and white flashcards stimulate a baby's vision and support right brain development.
2. Vocabulary	Activities that help children associate words with pictures and objects in fun ways from their immediate environment and other locations, rhymes, poetry, songs, and fingerplays
3. World	Right brain inspirations with the globe, maps, people from other cultures, languages, music, and foods, matching flags, tracing country outlines, matching continent outlines.
4. Music	Playing classical music for right brain development of composition, tone, rhythm, and perfect pitch with tuning forks, introduction of instruments and sounds, composer stories.
5. Reading	Right brain reading flashcards, sound and letter activities, poetry, and songs. Hands-on phonics and games introduced when children bridge with left brain between four and six.
6. Math	Right brain absorption of math quantities as flashcards, counting, mental math visualizing concepts, measurement as sorting weights, sizes, time, quantities, and skip counting songs.
7. Science	Pictures and words of scientific concepts: atomic structure, the water cycle, human anatomy, cultivation of imaginary journeys into these elements, science songs.
8. Art & Practical Life	Mommy models the movement first, slowly, mindfully, pasting, pouring or scooping. Child watches. Mommy and child work together. Child gets to do it independently.

After three years old, children want to use their hands, make decisions, and move while learning. For this reason, it is recommended that parents continue the Right Brain Kids program with whole-word reading, and also add a hands-on phonics program. You can refer back to Chapter Three in the Language area to understand how to implement a phonics program if English is your language. This will help your children to develop reading and spelling skills as the right brain continues to be nourished.

It is easy to inspire and share all the exciting things in your children's worlds with them with a right brain approach. Picture books, songs, and games are desirable. Be creative. Foster your children's imagination. You will include lots of human interaction. Help your children visualize. They can paint, draw, and dance according to their inspirations. Do all you can to keep their learning experience a joyful and passionate adventure. This means that parents also need to experience that passion for life. When we teach with games, don't we also experience joy and excitement? Children raised in a heart-based environment become sensitive, curious, and loving human beings. Teach to every sense possible.

Here is a sample template I created for you to use for organizing your right brain weekly lesson overview. You can find a blank version

T4.2 Right Brain Weekly Lesson Plan: Sample Template

	Monday	Tuesday	Wednesday	Thursday	Friday
Art					
Science	Solar System		Solar System		Solar System
World Cultures		Mexico		Mexico	
Music	C		C		C
Vocabulary		Oceans and Continents		Oceans and Continents	
Math	1-10, in order		1-10, in order		1-10, in order
Reading: Phonics	Present: Alphabet symbols, pictures	Match symbol to symbol, a-d	Match symbol to symbol, a-d	Match picture to word (below)	
Matching	...and corresponding word cards			Apple, boat, carrot, chick, doll	Match word to word
Speed Reading		My		my	
Positive Affirmations	I am loved. Mommy and Daddy love you so much.				

Used with permission from Pamela Sue Hickein's book, *Right Brain Education Ebook*. (Content revised.)

of this template as part of a downloadable set of templates on my website. See the QR code on the inside cover of this book, front and back, to download the set from my website.

You can use this lesson plan with your online *Right Brain Kids* video segments, or if you are doing your whole program on your own.

Doing an Online Tweedlewink Session
with my Granddaughter

Welcome to our home! I am Sophia's grandma. Sophia is twenty-two months old, and we love to do Tweedlewink lessons together. Come and join us as we share how to do an online session with your child.

Sophia and I like to do our Tweedlewink lessons on the floor. Today, when she is finished playing and seems ready for something to do, I ring a little bell and sing "Good morning to you." Sophia looks at me and smiles. "Good morning, Sophia! It's time for us to start our lessons. Are you ready?" I ask.

"Yes, Gramma," she says and runs over to me.

I invite her to sit on my lap and she jumps on. I tell her that we will watch a short video about the artist Claude Monet, see pictures of the golden ratio triangle, and the country of Japan. We can see the TV screen where our Tweedlewink lesson is all cued up. I ask her to close her eyes, take a deep breath, and blow it out with me twice. We do that together to help us relax.

In the beginning, there is a beautiful song we can sing to tell our children and grandchildren about how much we appreciate them. It goes like this:

> You are my child.
> I love you so.
> Just look in my eyes and you will know.
> You make me smile.
> You make me sing.
> I know, with love, we can do anything.
> -Used with Permission from Pamela Hickein.

When I sing this to Sophia, her eyes get big, and she looks up at me intently. The song helps me remember to tell her how important she is to me. I hug her so she knows that I mean what I say, "Sophia, you are beautiful and I so enjoy being with you." She smiles.

Next, we hear some positive character-building affirmations. I like to say the affirmations aloud, speaking right to Sophia. She watches the beautiful images and listens to the lovely child's voice as he responds in the video. These are positive affirmations our children can learn to say to themselves. Sometimes Sophia also repeats the child's responses. Because we have heard these often, Sophia smiles as I say them again.

Parent: "You are wonderful."
Child's Response: "I am wonderful."
Parent: "You are loved."
Child's Response: "I am loved."
Parent: "You can do anything."
Child's Response: "I can do it!"

Sophia responds with the child's "I can do it!"
I ask, "Did you like that, Sophia?"
Sometimes she says, "Yes!!" Sometimes she says nothing but always smiles when she hears the child's voice.

Sophia is attentive and sitting in my lap as the next section plays. The screen images change second by second. Colorful flashcards of Claude Monet's artwork come on the screen. The soft, gentle colors capture light in natural settings. Then, images of the golden ratio flash on the screen. The golden ratio's spiral is reflected in plant life and architecture with amazing symmetry. "Sophia, wasn't that sunflower beautiful?" I ask.

She squeals, "Triangles, Gramma, I saw triangles!" She is responding accurately to my enthusiasm.

When we do world studies, we see Japan's maps, pictures of the country, pieces of clothing, and celebrations. Today's music perfect pitch lesson on the video is the note D. Sophia listens intently as the piano key lights up in color, and she hears the D note played on the piano.

If Sophia starts squirming, I will invite her to stand and march in place with me while we finish the short eight-minute video. The speed-reading flashcards are a series of words, growing with each slide, interspersed with pictures of a specific teddy bear. The first slide is "bear." The next slide is the picture of the bear, and the next slide is a phrase about the bear. The fourth slide is the picture of the bear, and the next is more information about the bear. They proceed this way with more information gradually accumulating. The children's eyes and brain become accustomed to seeing and absorbing more and more of the content.

"The bear!" she squeals.

The picture helps her focus as she takes in the words at the same time. I encourage her to look for the word "bear," which she can pick out of each slide. Sophia loves the bear and waits for it to appear on the screen. "Yes, you are right," I say. Because the flashcards go so fast, she stays attentive.

When the vocabulary lesson comes on, we see pictures of furniture and common items most people have in their homes. We also see the words that go with them. She loves to point them out. Today, she says, "It's like Sophia's bed."

I say, "Yes, Sophia, there is a bed like yours!" She wants to touch the bed on the screen, and I let her gently touch it. I can tell she is thinking about all of this.

Our math lesson shows quick-moving quantities of identical fish flashing on the screen as their quantities are read aloud. Flashing and using beautiful colors stimulate the right brain. Sophia likes watching the fish that show quantities of fish, one to twenty. For the phonics lesson, we watch the letters flash on the screen and hear the sounds of /j/, /k/, /l/, /m/, and /n/ and see pictures with associated sounds. Sophia's face is still and concentrating.

I feel so happy to do these lessons with Sophia. She really seems to enjoy them. Sometimes, Sophia is active and has a short attention span. If this is the case, and she needs to play, that's what we do. We go outside to play or take a walk. Sophia gets excited, pointing out the flowers and leaves, and picking up rocks outside.

Sometimes, she needs to move during the lesson, even though she seems in a good space to do the lesson with me. If so, I use the *Move and Play DVD Routine* found in the Tweedlewink lesson guide. It is in the *Before You Begin* section, at the end of a tab called, *How to Give a TweedleWink Lesson*. It has great ideas for engaging busy children and helping them to enjoy the lessons.

After our video lessons, I follow up on the presentations later that day or another day. I download the matching cards from the Tweedlewink monthly lesson curriculum. You can print and cut these to be ready for the week. As she is interested, I try to do these follow-up lessons a few times a week.

To follow up, Sophia and I look at the globe of the world. I say, "Sophia, we studied Japan today. Here it is. It is a group of islands in the Pacific Ocean."

I point it out on the globe. "Japan!" Sophia says as she touches the spot.

"We saw pictures of Japan in the Tweedlewink video, and here are some pictures of Japan that we can match," I say as I lay the matching cards out on the mat.

She is now starting to match them by herself, and I help if needed. When she doesn't know, I hold one card next to its match and nod, saying, "Yes, I think that is the match!"

Or, if it is next to the wrong card, I show her that I shake my head back and forth as if to say, "No, I don't think that is it." She absorbs what I do and will grow in her perception.

To review the phonics sounds from the video, I say the sounds /j/, /k/, /l/, /m/, and /n/, enunciating clearly as I hold up each letter card. I try to bring my face close to hers so she can see and hear me saying the sounds. She watches with interest as I do that and can tell me the sounds of some letters. I take her hand and put it on my cheek so she can also feel what it is like to say those sounds. Similarly, when I show her a note and play the note on the piano or keyboard, she can sometimes play the same note with my help and is very happy! ✒

The activities take just a few minutes. Having spent years making flashcards, I greatly appreciate Right Brain Kids' succinct, beautifully crafted program that gives such great value with such little preparation on my part. It is an amazing program, and I highly recommend it!

Flashcards

Flashcards is one important part of right brain learning that stimulates brain development. When my children were babies and toddlers, I made hundreds of physical flashcards from posters, books, and calendars, and also bought some. I did not know that it stimulated the right brain. It was a wonderful experience that enriched our lives. Later we learned about right brain learning activities and pursued these with our children.

If you are a stay-at-home parent, homeschooler, or grandparent who would like to make or purchase physical flashcards and do developmental activities, you can find instructions for doing this in Hickein's book, *Right Brain Education: Changing the World, One Heart at a Time.* Another recommended resource is the Gentle Revolution.com. You can teach your children to read, do math, and learn more about life from books and resources by Glen Doman. His books explain and give instructions for making and using flashcards with children, including: *How To Give Your Baby Encyclopedic Knowledge, How To Teach Your Baby to Read,* and *How To Teach Your Baby Math.* Please see my website for more information: Montessorifamilies.com. Creating physical flashcards can take a great deal of time and work. It can also be a creative and enjoyable lifestyle to engage wholeheartedly with your children.

Right Brain Kids online programs incorporate many flashcards and other activities. I appreciate that I can share flashcards with my grandchildren with Right Brain Kids, as I did with my children, but without the hours of preparation. I feel I am providing something worthwhile and much more than possible for my family because making materials takes so much time. And, my grandchildren enjoy them. I also recommend their programs because the short video lessons are educational and enjoyable, and they have calm, relaxing music that benefits everyone. If the cost is more than your family can budget, Right Brain Kids suggests that families create a co-op and share Right Brain Kids' lessons.

If you begin working with your child after six, please look at Right Brain Kids' Wink program. The right brain can be further developed at any time, it's just easiest in the first six years. When I started practicing these activities with my children, I personally experienced changes in my brain in my forties.

How Do We Integrate Montessori Education with Right Brain Learning?

In my mind, both Montessori education and right brain learning are incredibly helpful, and both inspire the development of the inner genius. While we stimulate the child's right brain, we also structure the physical Montessori environment to nurture the child's sense of order and the development of the heart, the head, and the hand.

Right Brain Kids Videos are Established with the Montessori Curriculum

Right Brain Kids online lessons are essentially Montessori curriculum with right brain learning techniques. If you're considering using Montessori at home, I recommend using the Tweedlewink eight-minute online videos a few times a week. You can then add physical math, language, and cultural materials related to the online lesson. (see Chapter Three) The convenience of the Tweedlewink programs that provide downloadable follow-up activities makes this process easier. Additionally, you can incorporate practical life and sensorial materials to help your children develop their physical and sensorial skills, as a well-rounded Montessori curriculum.

Observe Your Children's Openness to Learning

Before calling my own children to a lesson, I tried to be sensitive to their timing and energy levels. Rather than only following my agenda, I needed to see if they were interested in working with me and relaxed. I needed to reflect on whether I was ready and check myself to see if anxiety was driving my schedule with my children. If it was, I learned to pause and do the lesson later because there was no need for pressure. I encourage you to listen with your heart, be open and flexible, and follow your children's timing. If you realize it is not a good time, sit quietly. Envision how the lesson will go in its ideal way and time. Feel peaceful and happy. This can prepare the way for the best outcome. Respecting our children is an invaluable Montessori concept.

It is also important not to test our children's knowledge, especially when they are under three. Testing children can sometimes discourage them from wanting to learn. Give them fun activities and have faith that they are learning. You will also observe their knowledge as you work with them.

As parents, to protect the receptive right brain, you may want to limit your children's exposure to anything that isn't positive and helpful on the screen and in person. We enhance their lives by keeping their environments and interactions positive because what they experience, they become. Right brain learning is such an amazing opportunity in our hands.

Please note that I have been graciously given permission by Pamela Hickein to use all of the information and tables in her book, *Right Brain Education: Changing the World, One Heart at a Time*. I am deeply grateful for this significant contribution to my book, and grateful to be able to share the message of right brain learning with the world.

T4.3 Observation Practice Four: Sample Template

What qualities do you see your child exhibiting from the left or right hemisphere?
• I see Laura loves to talk with people. She is outgoing and loves to express herself well with specific words. This may be the left brain developing. • She also is sensitive and realizes how she feels about things. Mireya is creative when she imagines wonderful stories. She also loves nature which is the sensitivity of the right brain to plant and animal life. These things show the right brain activity.
What pictures, picture books, or other resources can you get to nurture one of your child's interests?
• Laura loves animals, especially horses. I can find pictures and picture books to help her learn more about animals, their habitats, diet, and characteristics.
How might your child appreciate being invited to a lesson if they are working on something?
• I think Laura likes to finish whatever she works on. I will be patient and allow her to do so and just watch for a good time. I will have my materials ready and then ask if she is open to learning something new and fun. If she does, I will go forward. If not, I will be at peace thinking that I am building our relationship by accepting her decision at the moment.

Table 4.5 Chapter Four Takeaways

Chapter Four Takeaways
• Children live in the right brain from conception through age three and then gradually integrate with the conscious left brain by age six. Nurture the right brain with unconditional love and joy during these early years.
• During these first three years and until this integration, the right brain is highly impressionable. All input goes straight into the subconscious mind, so we want only positives. There's no limit to what you can teach your children and you can do it in ten to fifteen minutes daily with little stress.
• Different program options ensure that your child can have right brain learning opportunities. Choose one!

Fostering Wholeness in Your Child

"When our children have strong physical bodies, sharp minds,
calm emotions, and vibrant spirits, they are whole and free.
They are unfettered, exhilarated, and able to fulfill
their reasons for being."
—TERESA ANGELES

In their innocence, children can give us a picture of wholeness. On a day when they are delighted, they may show us what this wholeness looks like spiritually, mentally, emotionally, and physically. The following story elaborates on this point.

Wholeness in a Child's Spirit, Mind, Emotions, and Physical Body

Spirituality is naturally reflected in children who feel associated with something greater than themselves. Some sense of a connection with the universe. I often saw this in our son, David, when he would look up at the stars at night and tell me with the biggest smile, "Mommy, those stars are so big and bright. I like looking at them. There must be billions!"

"Yes, David, they are magnificent, and I agree that there must be billions!"

When our children have strong minds and are curious, they are open to learning about everything around them. When they are at their best, they reflect this. I remember Frederick, who was always passionate about nature and asked interesting questions. He once inquired, "Mommy, I wonder where the snail goes when it is nighttime? Does it have a place to sleep?"

His wonder touched me, and I replied, "I like how you think about the snails, Frederick. Can you see his shell? That is his home, and he curls up into it when he wants to sleep. It's convenient to have a house like that."

His eyes widened and his face lit up in deep contemplation. "Wow," he said quietly, and that was it, as he kept his gaze on the snail. His observant mind gave him many ideas that he often shared. He was constantly learning, and his beautiful, absorbent mind showed this.

When our children have peaceful emotions, they will want to be kind. They will be sensitive to nature and will like to collaborate with others. Our son Francis would often be the first to introduce himself and talk to people, even when he was three or four. He was also quiet and peaceful when he fished. "Daddy, see that fish over there? I have been watching him. He is just waiting. I think he likes waiting. Do you think so?"

Daddy said, "Yes, I think you are right, Francis. He is watching us!"

"I love you, Daddy!" he said, quietly returning to his fishing.

A strong, healthy physical body allows our children to enjoy movement and to feel good.

It helps their brains, their emotions, and their spirits. I remember our daughters, Elizabeth, Clare, and Marie, who loved to jump and swing. "Mommy, higher! I want to go higher!" I can still hear Elizabeth saying.

The girls would do cartwheels across the lawn. I loved their determination and their feelings of poise and freedom as they did this. I loved watching them have so much fun!

The principles of Montessori can help you create a way of life that supports who your children are and observe what wholeness looks like for them. This chapter will share some ideas of how and explore less-known approaches to nurturing your children spiritually, mentally, emotionally, and physically.

When these four parts work well together, our children are whole. Let me explain. It is easier for them to be calm and make good behavior choices when their bodies are nourished, and they can concentrate and enjoy learning. When children don't have nutritional balance and are missing certain nutrients in their diets, they may feel moody, insecure, or angry. They may not seem in control of themselves and may lash out or be lethargic. They may not feel valued or inspired about life. Inadequate nutrition, chemicals, family behavior patterns, and many other things can disrupt their natural balance. How can parents help them?

My search to help children has been a lifelong goal. This chapter will share some approaches to creating this wholeness that helped our family. I am excited to share resources that may help your children, too.

A Circle of Wholeness

This circle represents your children, who are a combination of spiritual, mental, emotional, and physical elements and reflect the potential wholeness in each area. The following chart describes each of these elements, and you can think about your own children when you look at it, perceiving where they are strong and where they may need support.

Because we all want our children to be whole, we can use a chart like this to see at a glance where most of our children's energies are focused. The concepts in Chapter One on the Montessori method inspired the design of this chart, and you can see how they work together here. She touched the whole child, inspired them to think independently, and raised their sense of responsibility to respect each other and care for the environment. Attractive lessons nurtured their curiosity and exploration. Immersing them in the natural world, she cultivated their spiritual appreciation.

You can observe and write notes about your children and then look at the chart to complete your understanding. You see where they have mastery and where they do not. You can then know what areas may need support.

Table 5.1 The Circle of Wholeness

Physical

Healthy constitution and immune system

Physical strength and coordination

Physical stamina that provides drive, motivation, vitality

Physical energy to make things happen

Spiritual

Having meaning and purpose in life

A belief that life can be extraordinary

Feelings of interconnectedness with life

Appreciation for life

Emotional

Emotionally intelligent, resilient

Understands own feelings and can self-soothe

Strives to patiently understand others

Can be sensitive, caring, and protective

Is compassionate, optimistic, and enthusiastic

Mental

Thinks clearly, concentrates, learns easily

Is imaginative, pioneering, adaptable

Knows his own mind and strives to also understand others

Is expressive and communicates well

My husband and I wanted our children to be resilient. Understanding Montessori's view expanded our vision and guided our way. Inspired, we challenged them with reading and math, science projects, nature studies, and sensorial activities. We ran around the block together and took bikes, scooters, and skates to school tracks and parks, spending hours there to give them physical exercise. We made an effort to use compassionate communication. We did different kinds of meditation and spent time enjoying nature. We loved them in the best ways we knew and hoped that a sense of belonging would cultivate their connection with us. Life was not without challenges, but we kept on and celebrated our victories.

Nurturing your Child's Spiritual Wholeness

Spirituality is a natural part of the child, as it is a part of all of us. It translates as a need to feel connected to something greater than ourselves. We have described spirituality as having a sense of purpose in life and a belief that life can be extraordinary. Montessori observed the zero to six-year-old period, when a child is especially sensitive to spirit. When a child is spiritual, it may be an awareness of the "inner teacher" or that still small voice in the heart guiding them, as Chapter One mentions. This spirituality champions freedom for the self and others, is spontaneous in children, and can grow as they mature. We can cultivate it by creating experiences that allow our children to feel awe, such as when we watch a sunrise, count the petals on a beautiful flower, or climb a mountain together. Fire can sometimes inspire mystical feelings. We may sense spirituality when we look at a candle burning or sit around a campfire. A little bit of regular alone time for children can benefit them. Naptime or another "quiet time" where they can play peacefully in their rooms or another very safe place allows children to connect with a calm presence. Instead of trying to teach spirituality, we can simply create opportunities for them to feel the spirit.

Modeling faith in a happy life can start with parents making an effort toward harmony. It isn't always easy in a marriage and family day-to-day relationships, but it is something to be aspired to. We can learn to control our reactions and give others the benefit of the doubt. Breathing deeply and moving slowly when things are tense can significantly impact family life.

Teaching children to meditate can cultivate a calm spiritual experience. I have a very vivid image of our two-year-old daughter, Marie, in our room one evening. She sat cross-legged on the floor, trying to meditate. Her little eyes were shut tight as she tried to focus, and she breathed deeply. Then, for a full minute, she became peaceful and quiet. When she opened her eyes, she seemed very relaxed. She still remembers a family activity when everyone lay on the floor and closed their eyes to relax. Here is what we did: we invited our children to relax their toes and then the pads of their feet. Gradually, we led them to settle every part of their bodies. It was a powerful way to release tension and sense the spirit.

You can teach your children to do affirmations or make a prayer such as:

1.   Today, I am grateful.

2.   Today, I am well and kind.

3.   Today, I am peaceful

Then they can visualize love, compassion, and peace going from their hearts to others, saying:

1. Today, may you be blessed.

2. Today, may you be well, happy, and kind.

3. Today, may you be peaceful.

A peaceful spirit can lead to a calm mind. A calm mind allows the child to concentrate and be still. Such a mind can hear the inner voice of wisdom and develop needed life skills.

Nurturing Your Child's Mental Wholeness

In some children, we see creative and critical thinking skills, problem-solving abilities, and resilience to bounce back from challenges. The presence of these skills leads to focus, self-confidence, and a passion for learning. When they they have empathy and respect respect firm boundaries, they will be sensitive to others and create positive relationships. They will hold positive images about life and figure out what they need for themselves. They will inspire others.

The freedom to make choices develops executive functioning skills, a popular scientific term today. Many of these skills are nurtured even for toddlers in the Montessori environment as they are encouraged to choose their work and gradually reflect on the outcome of their choices. This builds a model of self-sufficiency. Other skills of executive functioning include thinking outside the box and being able to adjust to unexpected changes. This reflects cognitive flexibility to solve problems with sound reasoning and respond rather than react. The ability to stay focused and resist temptations and distractions also involves self-control, self-discipline, and selective attention.

Children with Montessori experience are often known to concentrate for long periods. The more intense children's interest in some activity, the more deeply they can focus. The environment and the adult act as guides to protect and aid the child in making constructive choices. The children may repeat the simple task of pouring rice from one pitcher to another, and back and forth, for many minutes. Then, they may decide to sit quietly and observe another child working. They may opt to do a counting exercise for two minutes or longer. There are no time requirements or outer pressures to perform, only the expectation that they will respect others and the environment. They focus on what they are drawn to as the inner teacher inspires them. Parents can introduce many of these ideas to their children in their own homes and support the development of their children's executive functioning.

Dr. Adele Diamond, a neuroscientist at the University of British Columbia, studied children and learning. She suggested that children were more successful in increasing their executive function skills when they did a variety of activities rather than trying to focus exclusively on academics. As you try to raise your children's academic abilities, you can also take her recommendations to provide martial arts, sports, and social-emotional or creative activities, as well. She says this will increase your child's overall cognitive skills.

Another aspect of mental wholeness is helping our children to hold positive images about their lives. They can learn to use affirmations to succeed at their goals. We can see that our children have people around them who cultivate healthy self-esteem in them.

Nurturing Your Child's Emotional Wholeness

As parents, we can take time to quiet our minds and be present with our children. The demands and responsibilities of daily life can keep us so busy. Taking time alone for a few minutes is valuable because our calmness will affect our children and our home lives. We can also help our children learn strategies to be calm when they have big emotions.

To keep my composure as a parent, I have found breathing exercises to be calming. One type of breathing that can be helpful is called box breathing. Box Breathing heightens performance, concentration, and relieves stress. It is simple and effective, and you can do it anywhere. This is how to do it:

1. Sit or lie in a quiet place and close your eyes.

2. Breathe out for four counts, keeping your lungs empty for four, and then inhale at the same pace for four counts.

3. Hold this air in your lungs for four more counts, and then prepare to exhale again through your mouth and start the cycle anew. You can imagine the air filling your abdomen and removing any stress as you blow out.

You can repeat it a few times or many times. You can also read more about these techniques if you search online for box breathing.

Box breathing is good for older children and adults but may be complex for younger children. We can teach young children some techniques that are simple to do and easy to understand. Diaphragmatic breathing directs your breath into your abdomen rather than your chest, so your breathing is more profound and you take in more oxygen. You can show them how to sit comfortably and close their eyes. They can put a hand on their bellies to feel how they rise and fall as they follow your instructions to breathe this way. We can tell them they can do this whenever they feel afraid, sad, or mad.

To help our children handle their emotions, we can be present by relaxing and listening to them. We can hear their needs and wants. Checking our emotional reactions and maintaining harmony in the environment is important because many children are now dealing with anxiety and depression. Listening to them wholeheartedly and teaching them about breathing can help them feel more secure.

We also used strategies with our children from the HeartMath Institute (https://www.heartmath.org). This organization has done in-depth research about heart rhythms. Their scientific evidence reveals an intelligence residing within the heart. Their studies show that the heart and brain must be harmonious for the mind, emotions, and body to perform at their best. We can do this by visualizing ourselves feeling peaceful and resolving any challenges. One activity like this that can help children is to suggest that they first visualize a color they love. As they breathe in, they can imagine that color filling their minds and bodies, bringing happiness, calm, or whatever emotion they may need. Many of the HeartMath exercises are simple for parents to teach and for children to use.

Once, my six-year-old daughter Marie used an activity from HeartMath. As we drove, I realized she had a problem with a friend. I encouraged her first to say what she thought might resolve the situation. She responded that she thought she could resolve it by walking away and not talking to her friend again. I encouraged her to put the situation aside for a few minutes and to take a few minutes to breathe deeply with her hand on her heart. Then, I suggested she think of something that brought her joy and connect with that feeling of joy, sitting calmly, relaxing, and then feeling a warmth around her heart. After a few minutes, she then contemplated the situation again and quietly listened to the wisdom of her heart. After a minute, she thought of a new solution. She said she could respectfully share her feelings without blaming or expressing anger and help her friend understand how the experience had affected her. After this, her friend heard her and talked respectfully about their difficulty. My daughter felt happy to continue the friendship.

This activity allowed her to shift away from negative feelings and return with a more objective approach to the situation. It nurtured her heart's intuition and her ability to trust herself. This activity, Freeze Frame, can easily be accessed from the HeartMath website under Resources.

Nurturing Your Child's Physical Wholeness

We know that our physical bodies are not isolated from our other parts. Research has shown how nutrition, exercise, pure water, and plenty of rest help in every area of our lives. Before we have children, caring for our bodies prepares us to be foundationally healthy and strong enough to pass on vibrant genes, vitamins, and minerals.

Mothers can't pass these on to their developing babies if their bodies are not nourished with vital foods and nutrients.

Creating routines that keep our families healthy is also important such as adequate sleep and daily exercise in the fresh air, especially in the busyness of life. Establishing these consistent routines before we have children helps to nurture whole children in the long run. Researching water quality will advise us when alternatives to tap water are needed. Making sure our children get plenty of water is important.

There is a vast array of opinions and philosophies about nutrition in the world today. More and more, it appears that each individual's needs may be unique. Eating as many fresh, nutrient-dense, whole foods as possible is a good idea. Checking with a practitioner about food sensitivities can be helpful if there seem to be problems.

DHA to Build a Child's Brain

My family has benefitted from the recommendations of my friend, Ed Dratz, Ph.D. and Professor of Biochemistry at Montana State University. He has been studying DHA for forty years with major National Institute of Health support. He says that one nutrient that many pregnant/nursing women and young children need more of is DHA, often called the Queen of Fats, and the most important omega-three fatty acid. He says that DHA is essential for brain development in children from conception through age eighteen and is often overlooked or undersupplied. Dratz recommends *Nordic Naturals 'Omega-Three Fishies,'* which has a significant dose for young children, rather than gummies. *Nordic Naturals* purifies away all mercury, PCBs, and other impurities from the DHA supplements. Dratz encourages elementary students to take DHA if they are having concentration problems, to support neurological development. Dratz has many success stories about children who, after supplementing with DHA, were able to improve focus and concentrate on tasks they previously had not been able to do. He says, "If a child has learning or focus difficulties, hyperactivity, anxiety, rage, tantrums, depression, or similar issues, I encourage parents to try DHA supplements."

He goes on to say, "DHA makes up about 50 percent of the membranes in brain synaptic endings. Our current diets tend to be flooded with pro-inflammatory omega-6 fatty acids and are way too low in omega-3 fatty acids. This interferes with our synthesis of DHA and leads to fatty acids being put in the synaptic membranes that do not function properly. It is by *far* the best to use the purified DHA rather than commercial fish oil, since the DHA is a brain-active substance, and the pills are smaller and easier to take."

He has given college students DHA, done cognitive testing before and after a three-month supplementation, and found improvements in cognitive function.

Minerals to Build the Body

There are many important nutrients, but minerals, and most often trace minerals, are missing in many children's diets. Minerals facilitate thousands of enzyme functions in the body, support every body system, and are often overlooked in our diets. Ensuring your child gets adequate minerals from a good source is also crucial. Another friend once said to me, "If your kids are getting sick all the time, it's a good idea to look at where they are getting their minerals." I got minerals for them, and it got better.

Physical Activity Helps Organize the Brain

In my teaching and tutoring experience, I have encountered many children who have struggled with learning. During this time, I came in contact with a woman who is a *Handle* practitioner who has shared the philosophy with me and even helped many of my students. She says that the *Handle Organization* (https://handle.org/) perceives that children need lots of movement. From infancy through childhood, and even some of us into adulthood, use movement to develop and maintain neural pathways in the brain. These developed pathways help us work and do everything in life, including learning to read, write, do math, spell, and think in imaginative and creative ways. These pathways also help us live a balanced life. It is helpful for children to have sensory-motor systems integrated through lots of movement before they embrace serious academics so their brains and systems are ready. For this reason, providing abundant exercise opportunities for young children is important. Some examples include those that cross over the mid-line of the body such as crawling, creeping, walking, running, catching a ball, and jumping rope. Other activities such as cutting with scissors, kneading dough, weeding and digging in soil, beading, drawing, and other activities that exercise the muscles of the hands develop fine motor activities. Montessori encouraged many of these in her curriculum, and we can make sure our children have lots of opportunities for these in our homes every day. Sitting at a desk for hours at a time is especially limiting for children because they are in a prime time for development, and it is vital that they have movement.

Research now shows that physical activity is key to the organization of the brain, and that the brain grows by use. It is recommended that babies spend significant time in a place where they are free to move all of their limbs and trunk. The Institutes for the Achievement of Human Potential, and its founder, Glen Doman, are known for their groundbreaking work in brain research and child development. The books *What To Do About Your Brain Injured Child* and *How Smart is Your Baby?* describe Doman's findings about how movement affects the brain in detail. We don't have to have a child with a brain injury to benefit from his findings. Instead, we can be awed at how the brain works and apply it to our growing children. He spoke about how vitally important all stages of development are and recommended that babies spend abundant time on the floor where they can move. From his work with brain-injured children, he found that the brain needs movement to get organized, and when this is supplied, even hurt children can recover. So, likewise, normal children need movement to develop their brains, and if they don't have it, sometimes there are deficiencies in their abilities. He recommends letting infants be on a firm, clean, warm surface early in infancy. A very clean floor for an older baby, and a blanket on the floor or a crawling track for a younger baby of a few months old, are some recommendations. He spoke about how vital it is to let a baby develop freely without being in restrictive devices such as infant seats or jumpers, except for when necessary, such as in a car, because as these limit an infant's mobility, they also limit development. He emphasized the importance of all the stages of movement for their impact on the brain.

Movement Simulates Brain Development

A crawl track is a padded wooden track big enough for babies to lie in but with padded sides that let them plant their arms and legs and get traction by pushing against the sides to propel themselves forward. If you decide to use a crawl track, I have a suggestion: start early so they can develop their muscle strength for moving. When babies get heavier, they may not be able to move and may not enjoy it. You can search the internet for many examples and building directions for a crawling track.

This freedom to move helps babies to develop. It is beneficial if parents get down on the floor with their babies to interact, touch, and play. I did this and encouraged our children's movement, trying to give them time to develop their strength. Allowing them to resolve and work through challenges for a few minutes is healthy. Being free to move, even very early in their lives, is helpful to their development.

Babies crawling

Our daughter, Clare, loved to move from her earliest days and, by twenty months, had done lots of crawling, walking, running, and swinging. She could swing very high on a swinging teeter-totter and could handle it.

Helping our Children with Developmental Delays or Learning Challenges

If our children are not where they should be developmentally or have learning problems, observing early and taking notes is a good idea. Many different types of therapy and healing today can help us assess their issues and get them help. Finding the best avenue to get help may require some research. Getting information and assessments can help us navigate this time, which can feel confusing and overwhelming. We can find answers if we are diligent and take the time to research and talk to experts.

When we know our children have missed certain physical developmental stages—maybe they walked and never crawled—we may find crawling helpful for them afterward, even if they are five or any age. If you decide to encourage your older child to do this, I encourage you to do it in the privacy of your home. Help them understand why it may be helpful, make it a game, and join them on the floor. You can put pads on your knees. I worked in a school that had all of their elementary-aged children crawl like this on gym mats daily together. The truth is that even we adults can benefit from crawling to use our whole brain better. One note: toddlers may be reluctant to backtrack to crawling when they first start walking. You may need to wait a while before they will crawl again.

If your child has a developmental delay or learning challenge, different programs offer help. Most families experience some challenges with their children's development sometime in their lives, and we should feel encouraged by our communities rather than ashamed or alone. Children are very resilient, and with help, they can often improve quickly. Some exercises can help if your children miss crawling. I encourage you to research the organizations I suggest here, as my family or other friends and colleagues have seen results with them. I know there are many helpful resources available.

An excellent resource I have used with several students is again the Handle Institute (handle.org) mentioned at the beginning of this section. This organization will evaluate your children and people of all ages to give specific, simple follow-up exercises that will address developmental and learning challenges by strengthening areas of the brain. Some of the children I worked with had significant issues resolved when we did exercises for about two months, as recommended by a *Handle* practitioner. These exercises were fun and easy to do, with playful materials that took about fifteen to twenty minutes daily. You can start here with any concerns, and Handle.org can help you determine a plan for resolving them. It is very freeing for me to understand their philosophy that the brain needs strengthening for anyone at any age to be able to develop the necessary skills for life, rather than there is just something "wrong" with him. Parents can go to their website to find out about their programs.

The Institutes for the Achievement of Human Potential, mentioned above has other helpful resources. On their Home page at https://iahp.org, there are two valuable free forty-minute masterclass videos for parents addressing childhood development and how to approach developmental delays. They offer free thirty-minute introductory phone consultations where you can talk with a clinician about your child. If you work with the Institute, they will design a home exercise program to help you with periodic re-evaluations. The exercise programs are pretty extensive.

The National Association of Child Development, founded by Robert Doman, is a different organization. It also has important resources for children with developmental delays or problems. Their home page will change your thinking about working with children with neurological issues or learning or behavior problems (https://www.nacd.org/). If theywork with your child, an individual exercise program will be developed for them.

Other methods of brain integration are now becoming popular. Many teachers use simple classroom exercises to help their students perform better. Brain Gym is a method that has been around for a few decades. Parents can use it to help their children in some academic regions where they may struggle, such as math or language. It can also help with behavioral issues. Some of the exercises they use are cross-crawl activities that connect the two sides of the brain, such as marching and bringing your right elbow to your left knee and then reversing. The exercises they recommend made a difference with my children. You can read the book titled *Brain Gym* by Dennison, explore the exercises, and then try them at home with your children. These exercises are great for everyone.

Infant and Child Massage

I have often noted that families from India take special care to touch and do daily oil massages with their babies and children. This is becoming more popular worldwide. It makes sense that it would stimulate so many parts of the little child's being. Deep massage can relax and calm. It seems that touch would awaken the invisible energies for growth and health. It seems that being touched and caressed daily with warm oil would give the child a sensorial, comforting feeling of attachment to her parents. And, as Daniel Siegel talks about, attachment to parents creates emotional stability and prepares us to embrace our world. In our home, we used massage and oils often, and it seems our children loved it.

Activities to Cultivate Your Children's Wholeness

You can observe your children to see if any areas need attention, spiritually, mentally, emotionally, or physically. If you observe your children throughout their growing years and respond this way, you will make a difference in their lives.

T5.1 Observation Practice Four: Sample Template
Child: Jen   Age: Six   Date: July fifth

Physical: Coordinated, flexible, strong, with physical balance	Spiritual: Has a sense of something greater than himself or herself is inspired by sunsets, nature, and miraculous little things that happen.
Jen is strong, and flexible. She loves to run, jump, roll, and do anything physical. She could be stronger though and a little better coordinated	Jen is loving and kind, observant and loves nature. She ais passionate about music and seems very inspired by it. She is sensitive toward all life.

Emotional: Able to Self-soothe, have compassion for self and for others, stay calm and centered in the face of turbulence	Mental: Able to concentrate, focus, make decisions, make a simple plan, and communicate appropriately for age.
Jen is extremely sensitive and gets emotional very easily. She has a hard time self-soothing and needs to find a way to calm down and be at peace.	Jen concentrates well. She is a strong decision-maker and can make a game or activity plan and get other people involved. She communicates her feelings and needs well.

Here is a sample observation template I created for you to think about the four aspects of your child: physical, mental, emotional, and spiritual, to see where they are doing well, and where they may need support. You can find this template as part of a downloadable set of templates on my website. See the QR code on the inside cover of this book. We must realize that we may set goals, but children attain abilities at different ages in the developmental process. If you keep observation notes every few months or so, over time you might see patterns and know what might help them. You can ask your child to help you decide on activities without mentioning that you think there is a problem.

Helping your children to strengthen the different areas can bring balance. Observation has always helped me better understand my children, and I hope it will help you. You can highlight and make notes in this chart about challenges and choices for activities that might help.

T5.2 Activities for My Child's Four Areas of Wholeness: Sample

Highlight and add your plan for your child:	Child: Age: Date:
Physical: Involve them in:	**Spiritual:**

• Exercise and sports
• All kinds of physical play
• Healthy food and clean water
• Adequate rest and outside time
• Aerobics, martial arts, or yoga
Montessori practical life activities:
  • Care of the environment
  • Dishwashing, raking, dusting, sweeping, gardening
  • Food preparation
  • Care of Self: washing, dressing
  • Crafts and physical creativity: Painting, sewing, drawing
	• Look at the stars together
	• Breathe
	• Help them appreciate beauty in nature
	• Celebrate the seasons
	• Celebrate family rituals and traditions
	• Voice appreciation for blessings
	• Teach them and model meditation
	• Teach them to listen to the heart, the still small voice, the inner teacher
	• Experience a storm together from inside the house
	• Walk silently in nature and share

Emotions: Help them learn to:	**Mental: Teach them how to:**
• Self-soothe • Think of how others may feel • Consider doing an act of kindness • Listen and share compassionately • Laugh often • Collaborate on a task • Narrate a situation to make sense of it • Translate their feelings into words • Do Siegel's exercises for calming	• Use positive affirmations and self-talk • Use Compassionate communication • Strategize through challenges • Set goals and plan • Think through a project • Use logic and do math activities • Play non-computerized games • Read with phonics (see my website) • Read sentences and books

Table 5.2 Chapter Five Takeaways

Chapter Five Takeaways
• Our children have four aspects we can observe for balance: spiritual, mental, emotional and physical
• We can choose activities in these areas to help them create greater wholeness.
• Observing for red flags is important
• Seeking professional help is recommended if we are concerned about some aspect that is not responding to gentle support.

Enhancing the Montessori Method with the Multiple Intelligences

"All of our children have undeveloped gifts and magnificent potential. If we hope for a new world based on responsibility and true freedom, our goal must be to kindle and develop these special treasures in our children."

–Teresa Angeles

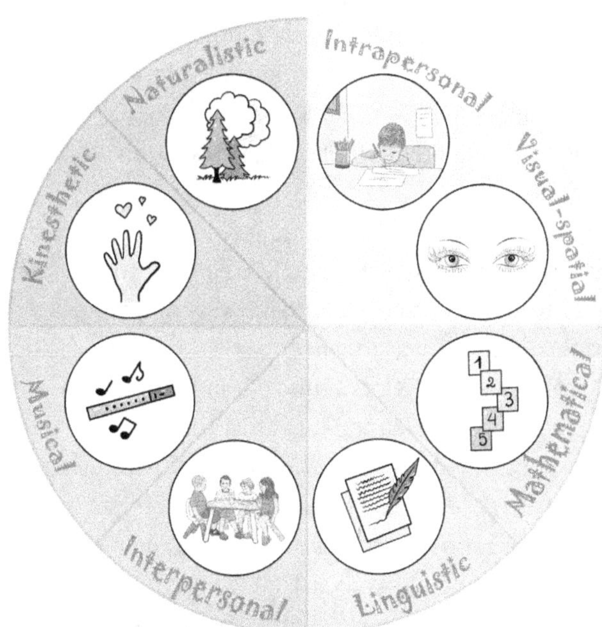

Frederick and the Baby Bird

One weekday afternoon in early May of 1994, I was making dinner in our little rambler. My husband was napping after a long day at the hospital where he was a recovery room nurse. The kids were quiet in different areas of the house. This time of year is supremely beautiful and peaceful in Washington state, as the buds come out and flowers are everywhere. The weather grows warm, and there are more sunny days than rainy ones.

I felt peaceful going about my daily tasks. Suddenly, through the back screen door, I heard our five-year-old son Frederick's little voice calling quietly, "Daddy, Mommy, can you come quick?"

I put down my utensils, turned off the stove, and ran to the door. There stood Frederick, clutching something very tenderly to his chest. He whispered, "Mommy, I found a baby chickadee on the ground. I think we should put it back up into the nest. It must have fallen out."

He bent down slowly to show me a tiny bird with black and white feathers, clearly not fully grown, clutched tenderly within his hands. His tenderness touched me. I put my hand on Frederick's back and smiled, whispering, "I will!"

Motioning that I would be right back, I closed the door, got my shoes, and woke up his daddy.

Outside, Frederick continued cradling his precious find and walking gently across the yard toward the apple tree. The pocket-sized creature was probably terrified in that little hand! Soon, Frederick's dad, Victor, was out with us. He, too, was touched to see the little bird and smiled at Frederick. Victor had spent a lot of time out in nature and loved birds. He brought over a ladder and leaned it against the tree. I wondered if Frederick wanted to put the bird up in the tree, or if my husband should do it. And then I saw Frederick leaning over to give the bird to his dad. Both of their faces were serious about saving this fragile life. Victor carefully took the baby in his cupped hands so that it wouldn't fall or jump out, and then stepped onto the ladder. He climbed as high as he felt was safe but couldn't reach the nest. The mother bird continued circling, clearly frightened. Victor put the tiny bird down in a hollow area protected by branches and leaves. The mother bird would be able to reach the baby from there. So, not feeling sure that everything was okay, but resigned to the feeling that we had done all we could, we backed away from the tree to watch. The mother bird did come to attend to her baby.

Soon, we realized that there were two more little birds on the ground and decided we should leave them alone! This mother bird was trying to do something that we didn't understand, and we might be interfering.

We continued to watch with Frederick and realized that the parents were purposely making the young leave their nest. This was puzzling as they couldn't yet fly, but we decided we should let nature take its course. The mother was watching and attentive.

The three of us standing outside on the cool spring evening, hoping to help this part of life, is a powerful memory for me. Our family has encountered animals in different situations over the years. I am always grateful for the wildlife that has touched us, drawing us into their worlds and out of ours. I always felt that these coincidences were God-inspired to nurture our sense of care for life and strengthen our connection with the natural world. In this way, our children develop naturalistic intelligence or familiarity with nature.

Frederick was really good at connecting with people and living beings. He has always cared for helpless animals like stranded baby possums. Our backyard provided many opportunities for his connection with nature. He had learned about types of birds, trees, and flowers, and he knew this was a chickadee. He was also reflective, able to listen to that still small voice in his heart to make good decisions. I believe that taking responsibility for this little life nurtured his self-esteem and his sense of responsibility.

I observed these gifts in Frederick and wanted to nurture them, although I didn't know how to do it at that time. We did our best and did provide lots of experiences. Since then, I have learned much about identifying what children love and are good at. I encourage you to observe your child's gifts and design your learning around these. When you know what they are curious about and what their talents are, guiding them becomes easier and more rewarding. Ultimately, this nurtures your children's innate potential. You will understand more as you read this chapter about the multiple intelligences. It is a simple approach that can bring great rewards.

Howard Gardner and His Discovery

In 1983, Howard Gardner, an American developmental psychologist and professor of cognition and education at Harvard Graduate School, proposed the theory of multiple intelligences in his book Frames of Mind. The concept maintains that we are not born with one kind of static intelligence but eight different possible kinds of intelligence. He named these eight kinds of intelligences Intrapersonal (knowing the self), Visual-Spatial (sensitivity to images), Linguistic (sensitivity to words and communication), Mathematical (sensitivity to math), Musical (connections with music), Interpersonal (connecting with people), Kinesthetic (connecting through movement), and Naturalistic (sensitivity to the natural world). He says that usually, we are born with an aptitude for the mastery of a few specific ones and revealed that intelligence is an extensive array of skills and knowledge built together by genes and the environment. This concept is a frame of reference that you can use to identify strengths and interests in your children and develop a plan to nurture them. I believe that focusing on these can make life wonderful and fulfilling for them, as well as for you, the parent.

Gardner and Montessori

With different cultures and at different times, Montessori and Gardner both came up with similar conclusions about human development. They arrived there from daily, personal, firsthand observation and experiences with people who were normal, gifted, and brain-damaged. Their philosophies support and complement one another. Both Montessori and Gardner's approaches nurture children's cognitive, social, physical, and spiritual development. Gardner reinforced Montessori's idea that individual differences within children arise in the early years of life. He identified that these natural tendencies require very different types of assistance, one from the other, in order to be developed. (Vardin, 2003).

In this chapter, I provide a section with a snapshot of each of the eight intelligences. You will find examples and related stories. My goal is to help you get a clear picture of each intelligence so you can identify which ones flourish in your children. I also aim to help you make a plan to encourage their development. The purpose of cultivating these intelligences is to enhance an innate gift in your child that can grow exponentially into something really wonderful. You can also foster skill competency in certain areas when you realize there is a need.

The best way to use the information in this chapter is to read through it with your children in mind. Look for them in the descriptions, envisioning what they love as well as what they struggle with. Next, you can go to my website (Montessorifamilies.com) and use my multiple intelligences questionnaire as you observe your children. When you have a clear idea of what your children's strengths and areas for growth are, make a plan of action.

Your Children's Areas of Strength

What your children are attracted to probably correlates with their natural gifts. Do they like to be outside, enjoying nature (naturalistic), singing everywhere they go (musical), or speaking and acting in front of a group (linguistic or interpersonal)? Helping your children identify and develop their strengths will open doors of service for them in fulfilling ways. It will help them to develop confidence and self-esteem and help you to understand their learning style. Knowing their gifts can help you structure exciting activities and lessons. As Montessori mentioned, your children may be aware of a purpose or calling in life, even beginning in the pre-school years. You can envision gifts they can develop.

Taking time to evaluate our children's areas for growth is just as important, especially when they are young. This can put us ahead of any potential issues. They will need certain vital skills to live in society, such as reading, writing, and math. Identifying any areas of need will help you help them. This is not to label, limit, or criticize, but to liberate them. You can use games, learning activities, and classes, or hire tutors. Emphasizing that almost everyone has some area of need can encourage them to even turn these weaknesses into strengths. See Chapter Five for professional help references if needed.

Intrapersonal Intelligence

Intrapersonal Intelligence is the capacity for children to reflect and understand themselves. It means having emotional intelligence to appreciate one's feelings, fears, and motivations. Children with this strength are often good at setting goals for themselves and knowing what they want to do. They are able to work alone productively and can make good choices. They appreciate positive feelings in the environment as they are sensitive.

I have observed that giving young children time to learn to

entertain themselves and enjoy the quiet is useful. Intense social atmospheres and busy households or schedules can keep children moving so fast that they never have time just to be. This is especially true if the child is constantly busy and used to peers being around every minute. Constant interaction and stimulation can be overwhelming. A friend once asked, "When will these children have the time to contemplate the universe's great mysteries and where will our great philosophers come from?" And this is truly an important question.

As parents, if we model using our intrapersonal skills with a positive attitude towards rest, yoga, or other types of contemplation, chances are that our children will, too. We can teach our children to breathe deeply, be still, and listen to the needs of their bodies and hearts. This nurtures their ability to connect and know themselves, a skill we hope they will learn. It builds intrapersonal intelligence. It can help them know their own interests and even what work they might like to do. We can sometimes observe these tendencies in our children by five or six if we are observant.

Gardner's view of this intelligence included children who love to daydream, plan, set goals, and reflect. They love creativity and self-paced projects. They may need to find a way to incorporate their own feelings, associations, and experiences into what they do with others. This skill helps them personalize their activities even as a part of a group.

Our family tended to have intrapersonal (knowing the self) and interpersonal (understanding people) tendencies. Our home was either tranquil while everyone read and studied, or very noisy with our children running through the house with their friends. I worked with them on their writing skills. Our boys loved working with coin and stamp collections that my father introduced to them, and they all loved drawing. Clare wrote poetry, illustrating her entries, and

Marie and Elizabeth loved to draw and work with flowers, as did Clare. We tried to help them establish hobbies they could enjoy and things that would develop their own sense of identity. This is what intrapersonal intelligence is all about: understanding the self. You might help your children make choices and ask, "Do you want to wear green or blue pants?" You can involve them in planning activities and ask what they want to know about.

Visual-Spatial Intelligence

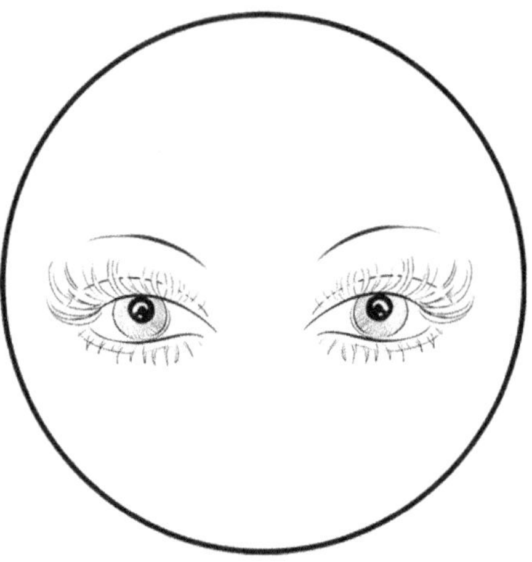

Visual-Spatial Intelligence is the ability to visualize and "think in pictures." It involves children's abilities to imagine and transform these pictures into physical drawings, photos, or three-dimensional representations. Sensitivity to line, shape, color, form, space, and the relationships existing among these elements is key. Perceiving patterns in everyday life, these children also have a good sense of direction and may work well with maps. They may remember landmarks, gauge distance and measurement, use a compass, and participate in simple orienteering activities. These help them to become aware of what is in their visual fields.

My granddaughters, Mireya and Louise, two and four, attend classes for creative arts to develop their artistic skills, and Mireya enjoys telling me about what she makes. I love to take Duke and Capri to the children's museum often so they can enjoy the inspiring art projects, and we also do art at home.

We can nurture our children's visual-spatial skills, which are stimulated by color and design, by using soft color themes in our room decoration. We can organize cupboards, closets, and drawers with containers and supplies in neat rows, as design and symmetry impact visual-spatial ability. Our children can learn by helping us do this. Helping your children visualize is another way. Encourage them to sit with you and close their eyes for one to two minutes to imagine walking in a peaceful field or garden. They can imagine seeing good things happen with their mind's eye. If they want to share and describe what they "see" with their imaginations, this may enhance their experiences. Classical music can help them relax and be inspired. Then they can draw or paint what they saw with their imaginations.

The impact of computers, cell phones, and TV screens on human life, especially on children, is not completely known. I encourage you to be cautious about how much you use screens with infants and young children. The internet is amazing, and yet screens are a relatively new technology. A *Psychology Today* (2014) article says that many hours of screen exposure per day changes the grey and white matter in children's keep alert even when our children are infants to see what is recommended and make decisions about limits. Our family did not have a television for many years because we found it difficult to monitor. This forced us to find other creative things to do. Watching movies as a family was fun. I believe that children who do not have a constant TV diet have stronger imaginations and are more able to visualize. If they stare at the TV all day, their brains do not have time to be creative and come up with images of their own. Having interesting things to do and projects to design with their hands helps children to develop visual-spatial intelligence.

Dr. Gordon Neufeld, a Vancouver-based developmental psychologist with over forty years of experience working with youth and author of *Hold onto Your Kids*, comments on screen time, questioning its value in helping children. He says that children need their attachment hunger fulfilled and that parents are the best bet for this. He believes that screen time can interfere. Parents should be sensitive to their children's needs. He says children will feel creative and spontaneously playful, and often choose creative solitude when they have a secure, warm connection with a parent. He said that this is when brains are built.

Our children enjoyed using tangram puzzles and loved to build structures. They learned directional skills in the forest with the Wilderness Awareness School (EN6.6), exploring the terrain and developing their observation of natural landmarks. For the boys, Legos were their life for many years, envisioning all the tiny pieces fitting together. I think this played a big part in developing their visual-spatial awareness. I believe this skill allowed them to pack our cars for vacations with amazing order and precision. They all loved drawing and lessons helped them create lifelike images.

Mathematical Intelligence

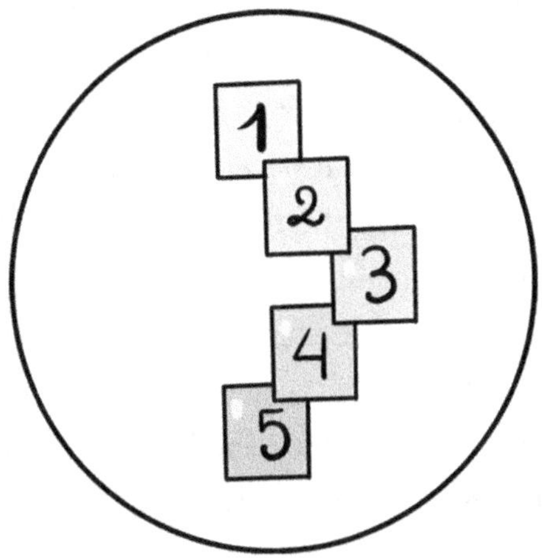

Mathematical Intelligence is the capacity to assess and analyze problems, categorize, and carry out mathematical operations. These children enjoy sequencing numbers and grasping scientific concepts. The Montessori materials are valuable because they help children touch and use their senses to develop the mathematical mind. Sometimes, this strength is called Logical-Mathematical.

You can look for math challenges in word problems, stories, and in limitless other places for your children. Take advantage of opportunities to observe scientific questions and processes, like, "How many utensils do we need for five people?"

Families can observe the four types of cloud formations, spend time observing the sky, and make a graph of what types of clouds they see. They can look at the moon and record its phases by taking turns drawing pictures of how it looked on the days of a large calendar. We sorted rocks and leaves and categorized them by their shapes, using large children's books as a reference. Our children took apart old machines to see how they were built. They worked with a Rubik's Cube (a three-D combination puzzle). We can also help children to observe the sequence of time: when we get up, when we sleep, when we eat. Sequences create predictability and structure. These things stimulate an orderly mind and scientific understanding.

Money is one aspect of math. When our children were young, we tried to share our appreciation for everything in life, including money. We did not have a lot when the first ones were little. We believed that we needed to take responsibility for saving a regular part of our income. We also shared our belief in the law of the tithe. From the ancient Israelites and many of the ancient cultures until churches of today, the law of the tithe has flourished. This law, which originated during the Old Testament times, stated that if people regularly gave one-tenth of all they received to God, it was multiplied back to take care of them, and they would never lack. When we did this, we found that life cared for us with prosperity, peace of mind, and financial plenty. We also believed that we needed to take responsibility for saving a regular part of our income, as well.

To help them manage their money as they got to be four or older, I made special envelopes where they could keep the money they received each week. Inside this bigger envelope, there were smaller ones. The inside envelopes were labeled: 1) At-Home-Savings, which was for a soon hoped-to-be acquired item or spending money; 2) Long Term Savings, for savings in a long-term bank account (bank deposit slips were enclosed for this purpose); and 3) Tithe ten percent of the total, which would be their choice to give to their church or a spiritual organization, which was like giving back to God. I helped them write their hoped-for goals and prepare their deposits. We told them stories about people who shared what they had of their wealth and their talents, and how more came back to them because of their generosity.

Other activities that might inspire Mathematical intelligence, depending on your child's age, might be to try to find mathematical challenges in daily life, such as adding two amounts for the grocery bill or counting the forks for dinner. Mathematical intelligence is important every day of our lives.

Linguistic Intelligence

Linguistic Intelligence is a sensitivity to written and spoken language and the capacity to learn different languages. This child might use writing as a way to remember information. They may love reading, listening to, and telling stories. Sometimes, this strength is also called verbal-linguistic, meaning a child may enjoy hearing himself or others voice opinions, writing, memorizing poems, brainstorming ideas with family, and then later reviewing them for a final opinion. Your child can keep a simple journal in the preschool years with words and/or drawings to express views and see them in print. He might enjoy word puzzles, vocabulary challenges, and spelling bees.

You may consider publishing your six-year-old child's poem, a simple story, or an illustration in a children's journal or magazine, such as *Cricket*. Some submissions earn monetary rewards. This is an amazing way to nurture a budding author. Children can publish even simple books on Amazon. You can have your children read and write about any topic of their interest develop these skills, and sharing their work in any way will further increase their enthusiasm for writing.

Children can write letters or even just draw pictures to communicate their thoughts. My granddaughter Mireya is four years old, and we are pen pals. We have a little journal that is blank inside, and we send letters, stories, pictures we draw, or leaves back and forth to each other. Mireya has always been very verbal, and I love sharing with her in this way. She draws what is on her mind and her parents write something for her.

Dr. Montessori used the linguistic skill of storytelling as well as songs and poetry to introduce many lessons. She captivated the children's interest and then provided information.

Reading together as a family sets a powerful foundation and inspires family bonding through shared experiences. We loved reading stories about great individuals, for example, Mother Teresa, Mahatma Gandhi, and Frederick Douglass. We thrived on their adventures and perceived their insights. Many individuals worked selflessly and courageously to accomplish noble goals with self-discipline and patience to see them through. These kinds of examples were powerful for our children, especially as the characters faced challenges and problem-solved. We observed as they made mistakes, learned from them, and finally triumphed. Together, we learned with them. In this way, our children developed a perspective about how these individuals thought. I could hardly wait for story time when we read together! These engrain virtue as the characters become our children's friends. Reading can also structure their minds with literary foundations and inspire creative ideas for their own writing. Reading the *authentic* writings of individuals is especially good.

Research has shown that reading to children is important, individually and as a family, and this includes to teens, as an important way of keeping them connected to family. Research has confirmed the importance of this. I didn't realize this once and was reading Harriett

Tubman to our young daughters, who were four, six, and eight at that time. I hadn't thought about inviting our older boys, ten to fourteen at the time, but I remember how they slowly found their way into the hallway to sit behind the doors to listen! They were captivated as Harriet freed her family from slavery. It was an amazing shared experience and a memory that has lasted for years.

Libraries were always important to us. My heart is full, even now, as I think of happy memories there and when our family came home to on the floor and read silently for thirty to sixty minutes. I loved to relax and watch them. A love of reading is a gift you can easily share with your children and family. This strength brings rich rewards for everyone!

Interpersonal Intelligence

Interpersonal intelligence means understanding people and working as a team player. It is about giving and receiving. Children with this strength can often read people, understand their intentions, be diplomatic, and influence others. As a teacher and parent, I have observed that some children are inherently good at talking to people, questioning, and leading discussions, even early on. They are often the ones who say hello first and seek out friends. They thrive with groups of children and enjoy group projects and setting goals together. My granddaughter Mireya has been greeting people by name since she was eighteen months old. She loves people and is always very interested in talking to them. I love that about her.

In the Montessori home, interpersonal intelligence is encouraged by using the "Peace Table" described in Chapter One, which helps children learn to express their feelings and needs, and then listen to others. When children can do this, they develop a compassionate heart for others, as well as being able to express their needs. Thinking of other people is important, and not always a developed skill. This is what makes for happy relationships in life. A compassionate heart can be the greatest development of your children's interpersonal skills and can lead them to be leaders in life. With these skills, they can build community and resolve challenges between people.

I wanted our children to experience the benefits of helping others, realizing that by helping others, we help ourselves, and lives are transformed. Children can see their problems as small compared to others, perceiving blessings in their lives and developing gifts and talents by serving.

Our family friends helped with us at a food bank, stocking and straightening shelves. We pitched in when friends needed help moving or working in their yards. Spaghetti dinners at our local church helped raise money for children in other countries and were a favorite. The best part was the bonding and deepening of friendships as we worked together. Staying until the end of events for cleanup was a great joy and became a way of life for us, as it was for me and my parents. It taught our children responsibility, and they loved the feeling of happiness and success at the end. This is how lifestyles get passed from one generation to another.

When some of our youngest children were under six, they helped their older siblings fundraise for a planned service project in Mexico, selling doughnuts and answering questions about the project almost as if they were teens. They took the money and gave change, with help. (Their money skills soared with no artificial lessons needed.) They also learned to share the vision and loved it! These little ones, now twenty years later, still love the idea of philanthropic businesses.

Deepening the greatest aspects of interpersonal relationships can happen if you want to serve together as a family. Think about what best suits your family's time, talents, and interests. Write down everyone's ideas. Consider situations in your community that allow children to give: raking leaves on a neighbor's lawn, making cards for seniors, baking cookies, or gathering wildflowers for someone who is sick, even those of your own family. Your child can sing, play a song, or read a short story. You can Google service organizations in your area that allow children. Veterinary hospitals are sometimes good places to serve. What your children contribute will empower them to interact positively with others and will grow their interpersonal intelligence.

Musical Intelligence

Musical Intelligence is a sensitivity to musical patterns, sounds, tones, and rhythms. Children with this intelligence love music and respond with an ability to sing and dance with music. They may learn to play and compose music. Music education gives them sensorial experiences and knowledge.

In his book, *Multiple Intelligences in the Classroom*, Thomas Armstrong, (2009) mentions a study written by Colin Rose (1987), who writes about students in a European study from the 1980s. These students memorized information more easily if they heard the instruction against a baroque or classical music background in four/four time, such as Pachelbel's Canon in D and largo movements of concertos by Handel, Bach, Telemann, and Corelli.

An article in the *Deutsches Arzteblatt International Journal* states that studies have found that listening to music by Strauss and or Mozart for at least 25 minutes produced lower blood pressure readings and heart rates compared with people who listened to a popular band, ABBA. If it does lower heart rates and blood pressure, it makes sense that this would mean that people would be calmer. I have seen children calm down when this music was played in our home and my Montessori classrooms. I try to play classical music quietly while the children work to keep the environment serene.

We shared what we knew and had our children take music lessons. We played Pachelbel and the music of Bach, Mozart, and other classical musicians. I have sung the notes of the scales while playing them on a guitar or piano to now help my grandchildren develop perfect pitch. At this time, they are infants and toddlers. This seems to help them internalize music principles, especially if they are exposed to it before age six, according to Montessori.

Families inspire their children's musical abilities bywhen singing songs and playing instruments. they have. I have heard that in Europe fifty years ago, families made their beds together every day while singing in three-part harmony. What a beautiful idea! We sang songs in the car, blessed our food with songs, often sang before the children slept, and when we went to church. You can sing any songs that you love or know from childhood. You can check out children's songbooks or find them online with YouTube videos. According to a *Time Magazine* article, "Singing Changes your Brain." Studies have shown that singing changes our physical bodies and our emotions. It has a calming yet energizing effect, soothing nerves as endorphins and happiness-stimulating hormones are released, lessening anxiety and enhancing feelings of trust and bonding.

Many music classes exist for young children who can attend with their parents. Kindermusik classes support powerful learning through musical play. My three-year-old granddaughter, Duke, has gone to Kindermusik for two years, and she has incorporated important concepts about rhythm, pitch, singing, and dancing into her mind. Most of all, she loves music. She will sit with me, do all the music lessons I can bring, and watch videos of children playing different instruments from the symphony orchestra. Her focus and concentration on these are very strong for her age.

Suzuki music lessons are a wonderful foundation for young children, encouraging their absorption of musical pieces through the right brain and the absorbent mind, rather than traditional left brain theory and rote memorization. Parents play specific simple melodies on their phones or CD players in the background for children to hear and later play by heart. Later, they learn theory.

We played the melodies recommended by Suzuki and had some Suzuki music training for our two oldest boys when we lived in Montana. David still loves to play and infrequently still composes today, thirty years later. All of our children learned piano or violin in the first six years, and some went on to play other instruments. They all enjoyed music. Later, some enjoyed choir, band, and musical theatre. We encouraged them to play for visitors at church and family gatherings, perfect or not. It gave them the confidence to share, even before they were six years old. Other activities you can do with your children include tapping the rhythm when you sing songs and playing any instruments. You can also take them to classical music concerts and performances.

Kinesthetic Intelligence

Kinesthetic Intelligence empowers children to use their bodies with precision and coordination, to solve problems and perform activities. They may create artistic things with their hands, use different mediums such as clay for sculpting, fabric for sewing, and other arts and crafts. They may manipulate age-appropriate tools and perform physically as athletes, dancers, martial artists, or mechanics-in-the-making. These children may love to take things apart in order to understand how they work. The skills involved include using balance, dexterity, flexibility, coordination, strength, and the awareness of their body's position in space. These children may feel good using their bodies, enjoying dramatization and sports.

As a teacher. I have used movement to help children understand botanical concepts, such as dramatizing how a tiny plant matures, using physical dance. In this way, parents may show diagrams and pictures, and talk about how plants grow from a seed. They may describe the process of sprouting and then observe the blossoms that open. The child may be encouraged (and maybe the parent, too) to model this with their bodies as if they were the flower unfolding (in a fetal position on the ground), and then how the root emerges first (one hand reaches out toward the ground) to drink in the water. Finally, a sprout (symbolized by the hand and arm) reaches up and gradually unfolds the early leaves. Music could be played in the background. A similar expression could be applied to almost any lesson, especially of science.

Children in the Montessori environment learn to use their bodies to develop strength and balance with outdoor play, running, and climbing. Yoga and other movement are also helpful. They learn to care for their environments, using tools to clean, often with great joy and pride. Correct body posture is encouraged, with precision while using tools. The children are shown where to put their hands and how to push a broom in the right way. Montessori observed that the children gained a lot from physical work, including fine and gross muscle development, increased concentration, and vitality. She encouraged teachers to focus on children's physical development normally, but also when they had difficulties concentrating. Attention to the children's physical balance and strength was an important priority to Montessori's. She saw this as the foundation for the development of the whole child.

We had our children clean and do chores and learned that it is important to encourage rather than force or struggle with them about this. This is something I learned and saw that doing so made them dislike helping. We did many outdoor activities and had an environment conducive to climbing, jumping, digging, and planting. Our children participated in different kinds of sports, such as track, cross-country, basketball, softball, baseball, soccer, swimming, tai-kwon-do, biking, ballet, and gymnastics. This is a compilation of all of our children's activities put together, and none did all. I believe that these opportunities increased their physical strength and sense of peace in their bodies. My perception is that bodily-kinesthetic intelligence gives children the feeling of being grounded, confident, and at ease with the physical world.

Naturalistic Intelligence

Naturalistic Intelligence is a love of and connection with the natural world. Children with this strength may love nature and pets and enjoy spending time in forests, climbing mountains, and planting a garden. It is the ability to identify, categorize, classify, and under-stand things in nature. It also involves being able to make practical items with natural products and maybe for survival.

Giving children hours of the day to play in nature, build forts, and romp in forests is regenerating. Spending time in nature can calm and heal. Some say nature is akin to spirit and has the power to quicken life. Many people live almost exclusively inside. Giving families time outside is powerful and nurtures naturalistic intelligence. It also nurtures health and relaxation.

Montessori often worked outside with children, both giving lessons and gardening. You can look at your outdoor environment to see what might inspire your children. Can you help them plant seeds, transplant, harvest, and watch the seasons change? Montessori urged adults to teach outside using live plants as much as possible and observing living animals for study. You can ask questions as James Audubon's father did of young James when they went on walks. You can ask, "How many petals does the tulip have?" "What shaped beak does that hummingbird have?" or "Why do you think the rabbit lives underground?" These questions can help your children to think. We can teach them to use herbs like chamomile tea when they cannot sleep and peppermint tea for stomach upsets. Experiences in the natural world can lead children toward becoming scientists, philosophers, naturalists, or even artists if they use art to depict what they see.

A news article published by the University of Cincinnati states that in a study of 20,000 people, those who spent at least 120 minutes, or two hours, a week in nature experienced a greater level of health and well-being. They recommended intentionally incorporating nature as medicine into your routine and using its healing power. We can do this regularly with family. Researchers are investigating the impact of nature as a supplement to current approaches for ADHD says Richard Louve, author of *Last Child in the Woods,* (2008) and founder of an organization called, *Children and Nature Network,* https://www.childrenandnature.org. He talks about how nature costs nothing and is free of side effects. He documents how powerful the natural world is in restoring peace and equilibrium, and how spending time in forests as a child helped him to focus. His books describe how children in the past spent their days running freely outdoors, but that life doesn't look like that anymore. But isn't it a choice? Can we create these opportunities again for our children to explore woods, fields, and gardens, to pick fresh fruit and herbs for free, and to have places to get "lost" (safely) for a while to play? These are not easily available for children today but are not luxuries. Children need these experiences. We can help our children return to a way of life that incorporates nature daily in very simple ways.

When our children were small, we spent lots of time in our backyard with forty-to-fifty-foot apple trees. Our five- and seven-year-old sons continuously climbed them. They spent hours and hours in the summer in those shady branches, bonding with nature and observing the life cycles of the apple trees without even realizing it. There was a sense of majesty! We enjoyed playing at the local school playgrounds on the monkey bars, swings, tires at varying heights to climb on, and bikes to ride to their delight. For our family, walking in nature and climbing mountains together has become important. It stimulates our senses and increases our sense of well-being, especially together. We didn't always have ideal surroundings and nature, but we tried our best to supply it with whatever we found around us.

I have heartwarming images in my mind of summer landscapes with our young family. I recall the sparkling water of the Puget Sound, the beaches, and the three inflatable kayaks that we splurged on, saying we just had to have them for our children. The bright blue sky and the perfect seventy-degree weather of the Pacific Northwest summers made life delightful. I recall the bowls of fresh fruit, the herbs, and fragrant bouquets of flowers from our neighborhood that we picked or were for sale at the farmer's markets. I remember our three-year-old Francis, who loved planting "lentos" and "onion balls" (lentils and onion starts) in our backyard. Most of our vacations revolved around camping at the ocean or in the mountains unless we were visiting family. The forests were amazing, and we loved them, enjoying swimming, building campfires and sandcastles, and exploring tide pools!

Our daughter, Marie, commented on her memories, "In the summertime at our home everyone was always doing something, but less scheduled out than during the school year. We had more time to play and be creative: playing *pretend* outside, sleeping on the trampoline, going everywhere barefoot, lemonade stands, campfires in the backyard, staying up past our bedtime . . . It was the best! And I could go on and on . . ."

To develop a relationship with the outdoors, we must spend time getting to know it, just like with people. Children are sensorial beings, and Montessori believed that it would benefit them to live naturally. If you give them time outside, they will appreciate it. Start when your children are zero to six years old to inspire a lifelong relationship with nature and develop naturalistic intelligence. You can include camping, backpacking, and eating natural elements in the woods. Take pictures of plant and animal life with your children. Borrow a pet to babysit just for the experience. Incorporate your child in its care. You can make a checklist with your child that they can follow for the care. Whatever ways you can find to incorporate nature into your child's life, it will be a blessing.

Understanding your children's strengths and areas FOR growth can help you design your educational approach and make life meaningful for them. Reflect on your child and consider his or her strengths, gifts, and areas for growth. The sections in this chapter relating to particular intelligences can give you clarity. Note your observations in the following template. You can also refer to the free questionnaire on my website, Montessorifamilies.org that can help you identify these. Take it for yourself, too! It is helpful for us all to know that we all have strengths as well as areas for growth. Finally, take some time to develop a plan to nurture these intelligences with games, activities, projects, or classes that might help them. Thomas Armstrong's book, Multiple Intelligences in the Classroom (2017) also has valuable assessments parents can use to identify their children's strengths and areas for growth.

Table 6.1 A Summary of the Multiple Intelligences

A Summary of the Multiple Intelligences	
Intrapersonal	This intelligence is seen in children who can work alone in peace and have a sense of who they are with their strengths and weaknesses. They can set goals. They like having space and enjoying hobbies.
Visual-Spatial	This intelligence is shown in children who love drawing, designing, building, and dreaming. Imagination and visualization are key to developing their mind's eye. They love looking at colors, pictures, and maps.
Logical-Mathematical	These children enjoy counting and love math. They like to solve number puzzles and word problems, and they like to experiment. Categorizing patterns of information and working with reasoning is also strong.
Linguistic	These children love to hear, write, and tell stories. They may enjoy speaking and writing, have a large vocabulary, and need to process things verbally. Facts, dates, and word puzzles may attract them.
Interpersonal	These children love people, can often read others' intentions, and are leaders. They may indirectly teach and help resolve conflicts. They may engage with clubs and teams and enjoy organizing and selling.
Musical	Musical intelligence reveals children who remember songs and love to sing. They may have good pitch and rhythm, tapping while they are working. They may want to play an instrument and compose songs.
Kinesthetic	This intelligence involves the ability of children to use their bodies to craft, fix things, or perform, such as in dance or sports. Often skilled with tools, they love manipulating objects to see how they work.
Naturalistic	These children may love to spend time outside, connecting with plants, animals, and the weather. They may be attracted to categorizing leaf shapes, animal types, and life cycles. They may love to explore living things and the wild.

Once you have clarified your children's strengths and areas of need you can use the following template to note these. You can find this template as part of a downloadable set of templates on my website. See the QR code on the inside cover of this book, front and back.

T6.1 My Child's Strengths and A Plan to Support: Sample Template

My child's Strengths: (Note all strengths like this.)	Description:	Activities to Support them:	Actions I need to take for these Activities:
1. Musical —	She loves music, taps, dances, and sings all the time. She wants to play the piano.	Sing with her and encourage her singing Listen and Play Suzuki piano music to stimulate ear and brain • Follow Suzuki to familiarize her with keyboard Create a routine	Download and play Suzuki music pieces from my phone every day. Hum these pieces with her. Find a little keyboard to start playing these simple melodies on a keyboard. Buy tickets to Seattle Symphony Tiny Tots (children's) Concerts to expose her to live, highquality music. Read about the childhoods of famous composers (Bach)
My child's Areas of Need: (Note all areas of need.)			
1. Kinesthetic —	She loves moving, riding bikes, dancing, and doing gymnastics but movements are not coordinated and she falls often. Using pencils and art tools, such as paint brushes, is difficult and messy.	Do stretching and jumping at home. Go outside and walk and run daily. Take gym classes. Play on bars at playgrounds regularly. Exercises will increase her body awareness, balance beam, climbing through a hula hoop	Research good parks in my area that have bars children can hang on and work out on Get balls, and find an obstacle course to visit frequently, hula hoop/jump ropes. Research Handle.org for suggested exercises to increase her body awareness.

Table 6.2 Multiple Intelligence Table of
Left Brain/Right Brain Dominance

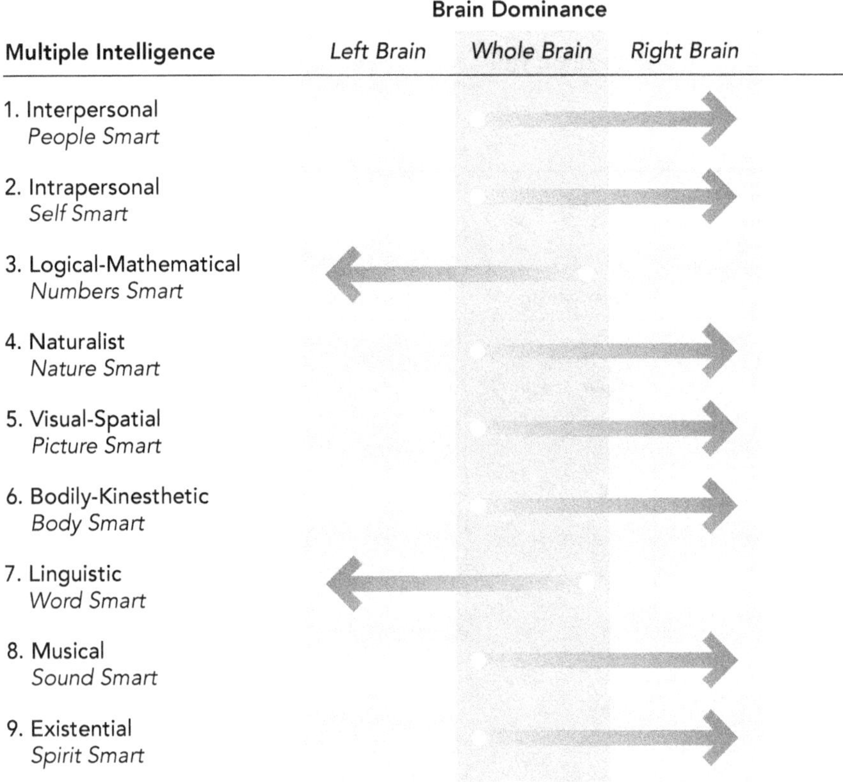

Your Child Can Help Others

Our children may be destined to discover something important, lead nations, or become magnificent artists. They may be a Madame Curie or Mahatma Gandhi. We can wonder what the parents of these great leaders and teachers were like. How did they help their children become both creative and practical? What can we do to cultivate greatness in our children as they did and help their children's genius shine? Isn't it love that fills a person with compassion to perform extraordinary work or a mission? Love will draw out your children's gifts and set their hearts on fire for their passions in life. Be a gardener, tending the flowers of your child's heart!

Table 6.3 Chapter Six Takeaways

Chapter Six Takeaways
• There are eight different types of intelligence identified by Howard Gardner, summarized in the table above.
• You can consider how you can provide opportunities for your children's growth in these areas.
• Your children may exhibit specific inherent gifts and talents related to these intelligences, which can be nurtured and developed with your help.
• Your children may also engage to strengthen areas where they need growth.

Developing Your Family Relationships

"All your strength is in your union,
All your danger is in discord;
Therefore, be at peace henceforward,
And as brothers live together."
– *The* Song *of Hiawatha* (1855)
Henry Wadsworth Longfellow

Elizabeth Felt My Presence, a Story

It was one late afternoon in the summer of 1999 at Five Mile Lake in Federal Way, Washington. The sun was hot and brilliant in the sky, and the lake glistened. Our family often came here to play on the swings, run on the beach, and romp in the little forest. It was a secret place only a five—to ten-minute drive from our home.

I was teaching in a Montessori preschool, completing my practicum, and wanted to spend time with my youngest daughter, Elizabeth, who was four years old. Usually, her siblings were with us, but it was just Elizabeth today. She was a peaceful child. Her round face and dark eyes twinkled in the sun and at the prospect of playing here.

She climbed onto the swings. "I want to go high, Mommy," she told me.

So, I pushed her up. After a few minutes, I sat on a yellow wooden bench to rest and watch her climb. It had been a long day. The other children on the playground were a little older than her, and Elizabeth was excited to see them.

"I'm going to go play with them, Mommy," she said as she ran their way.

"Ok, sweet girl," I said, "but ask them first if that's okay."

"I will," she said. Enthusiastically, she asked, "Can I play, too?"

"No, this is our game," they said and ran away from her.

Elizabeth was so disappointed and came running to me, crying. She jumped into my lap and buried her face in my shirt. "They didn't want to play with me! They don't like me!" she said.

I responded, "That hurts when you feel that someone doesn't like you and doesn't want to play with you. We want to be friends, but they have other plans. It doesn't mean they don't like you . . . I love you so much, Elizabeth."

And then we were quiet while her sobs subsided. I had seen what had happened and didn't know how to intervene. I would have liked to have spoken to these girls, but today, somehow, I couldn't do it. Even with my training and experience, I couldn't talk to them. It was their choice to play or not, but they could have been nicer about it. I felt like a terrible mother. Sometimes the kids at school got disrespectful, and I struggled to work with them, too. I was still learning and felt frozen. She sat on my lap and I could feel her tears.

After a while, she turned around to face the playground with her back against me. Those girls were way off, running and playing, while we watched. I could feel her sobs subside slightly, and I sat with her on my lap, breathing and being. Her hair was in my face as I peered out, and her little hands lay on mine. For five minutes, we sat there in silence, us together.

After what seemed like a long time, she looked up at me with her tear-stained face, a big smile, and a twinkle in her eye, and said, "Mommy, I want to slide down that slide. Can I?"

I said, "Yes, of course, Elizabeth."

I watched her jump down and run across the playground to the giant slide as I stood to go stand by her.

I was in awe of how she could so quickly and easily free herself of bad feelings to the point of forgetting about the whole incident. Our children can bounce back from challenges like this when they feel our love and support. A straightforward way parents can help them is by just being "present," as was illustrated in this story. We do this when we listen with our whole heart, with concentration and eye contact, letting them know we are completely with them. The power of our presence can bring composure and centeredness to our children and enfold them in a beautiful love that heals. ✐

This chapter is about the importance of family relationships. We will discuss most specifically how our presence can help our children, even neurobiologically. Our presence is a powerful force that helps them feel secure and whole. These perceptions can change the way we see our roles with our families.

Being in a family is what brings us great love and comfort. Throughout our lives, we are grateful for these relationships, which we can rely on when we need to find solace, share victories, and request guidance. Therefore, parents can intentionally form a family where their children will feel that way all their lives. Loving care, attention, and enthusiasm toward our families are key to generating the kind of family experience that leads to fulfillment.

Finding respect and peace within ourselves as parents is fundamental to creating a family with compassionate relationships. Teaching children how to find a calm place within their own hearts will also help them find serenity with others and will positively impact the family.

Bond with Your Spouse or Partner First

Before you have a family is time to come together with your spouse or partner to establish a secure connection that will stand the test of time. The entire family and home are built on this foundation of connectedness. Traditional parenting recommendations have put the parents' relationship before the children, in line with priority. This is so parents or guardians can unite *for* the children. As we all know, in an airplane, parents and guardians must fasten their seatbelts before assisting their children. The same concept holds true for families. It is essential to build a strong foundation so that the structure will be solid and reliable.

As parents, we can look at how we organize our lives before our children are born, or even after we have children. It is still important to consider. What do we value, and how do we lovingly approach challenges together? How are we present for each other, and for the others in our lives? How do we honor and collaborate in deciding approaches for raising and interacting with our children? For many families, caregivers who spend much time with children may also need important consideration as a part of this team. A healthy relationship with our spouse or partner sets us up for a successful family life.

Healing Our Psychology *for* Our Children

Dr. Daniel Siegel, clinical professor of psychiatry at the UCLA School of Medicine and parenting expert, encourages us, parents and parents-to-be, to observe and resolve our own past issues. Our emotional health, and the memories that we have or have not dealt with, can profoundly impact our children. In his book, *Parenting from the Inside Out*, he describes how the best gift parents can give their children is to try to make sense of their own lives. Siegel gives us the image that our communication with our children has a powerful impact on their development. In *Parenting from the Inside Out*, he says, "Learning to communicate and listen empathetically is a vital part of parenting. At the heart of this openness is parental presence–the receptive state in which we take in the signals from others and have compassion and kindness in our interactions."

He shares that doing this creates trust in our relationships and helps our children flourish in many areas of their lives. He says that when parents can create trust, children develop security, and this happens most when parents can make sense of the issues in their early lives. Healing the issues of our psychology allows us to keep unwanted patterns and behaviors from being perpetuated through future generations. Consequently, it will create a more peaceful emotional environment in our home and encourage our children to learn to make good behavior choices.

Many avenues for self-healing can change our lives and help us to be less reactive and more present with children. Some of these can include breathing techniques, such as the box breathing I shared in Chapter Five of this book. We can use journaling to contemplate our needs, do inner-child work, pursue counseling, and meditate. When we see the impact of our attitudes and momentums to influence not only ourselves and our children but generations multiplying beyond us, we realize our responsibility.

Children will bring to light those things about us that are not peaceful. Although it may not always be easy, realizing what needs to be healed in our thoughts and emotions when we are with children is good. We can ask ourselves what needs to change and how to accomplish this. We can create new attitudes if we look at ourselves without judgment and embrace these issues honestly. Only if we are willing to look at ourselves can things improve. We can then work on these areas and grow. Perceiving ourselves as lifelong learners helps develop humility, an essential quality for a parent aspiring to raise a happy family.

Developing compassion for ourselves as well as for our children is crucial. Our families are a great reason for us to change our psychology, which makes parenting ultimately transformative. We change because we love so much. We want to be the best for children. We also want to have a dream for our family and see it fulfilled.

Listening authentically and compassionately, in a non-judgmental way, was something that my husband and I pursued. It was a life-affirming skill that we could learn. With it, we increased our self-understanding and connection with each other. We learned how to hear and respect each other and our needs. One of the most valuable skills we learned was identifying and asking for what we needed rather than only complaining about what we weren't getting. With this mental framework, we could focus on finding solutions and see ourselves united rather than allowing issues to divide us.

Taking Time to Talk as Parents

When we have children, it is still vital that we nourish the relationship with our spouse/partner. We can observe our communication as a parent/guardian team. Does our relationship with our spouse or partner reflect peace? Do we have compassionate communication skills, access to support groups, or counseling, if needed? We can ask ourselves questions and strategize about how to keep ourselves healthy and balanced amidst a busy schedule. Do we have time to talk and plan as a couple? Can there be consistent help with our children from grandparents, extended family, or close community so we can have time as a couple? If not, what can we do to ensure that we get this much-needed time together?

Throughout our children's growing years, my husband and I tried to have routine times to talk about our children, ourselves, and what we all needed. We discussed and made written observations about our family and referred to these notes frequently. Taking one- to two-day trips, or even a date night away, helped us reflect on our relationship and family.

We sometimes went away for Marriage Encounters. These retreats lasted for two and half days and were times when we contemplated our lives with our children. The Marriage Encounter was held over a weekend where seven to eight couples gathered to think about their marriages. The structure included six presentations from experienced couples discussing a topic related to their marriages. They told us all what they did to meet the challenge. After this, all of the participating couples were encouraged to respond to a related topic question in their notebooks, writing for ten minutes. After this, they exchanged their books with their partners to see what each other had to say and then discussed their responses. It was a great way to really hear each other. The website for Worldwide Marriage Encounter is https://wwme.org/. Although it is Christian-based, the organization says that people of other faiths, or no faith at all, can find that it works well for them. They do ask that only couples who have been married more than one year (or have at least one previously married spouse) attend a Marriage Encounter weekend. There are other sites online for other kinds of retreats. At other times, we could take a short weekend trip or even an evening to think and talk about our lives together. These times made a difference and allowed us to renew our vision for our family and make our life's work together more enjoyable. Learning to love ourselves and strengthen a loving relationship with our spouse or partner is worth whatever it takes. When we can do this, we can also be there more fully *for* our children and establish a healthy and happy family.

You can create your own marriage retreat/partner retreat to check in with each other and create a vision of your life together. There are

many online sources and templates for creating a home-based retreat that can support you and your spouse/partner. You can simply Google "marriage retreat" to find a variety of options. It seems that too often couples wait a long time before they decide to get help when they have a problem. It is better to act early. That is why it is great to retreat for the purpose of building a positive relationship from the beginning when things are going well, and then you can build on that.

I have heard good things about the Gottman Institute at the University of Washington. This organization is a husband-wife team of psychologists who, for thirty years, have studied what makes marriages work, have authored books, and lead programs for couples worldwide. On his website, Gottman encourages couples to concentrate on their relationship, to put time and effort into it to make it work in order to make it happy. Their programs can help people who may be struggling in their marriages. *Eight Dates* is a book by the Gottmans for couples. My adult daughter has found it very helpful in her marriage. I agree that a marriage can be wonderful if a couple makes it a priority. Even difficult times can be the seeds for regeneration and new opportunities.

We found these kinds of experiences enriching our communication and marriage for many years. For varying reasons, we became focused in different directions. I realized later that the connections made during marriage encounters need to be engaged in regularly so that not too much time passes before couples take that opportunity to reconnect. Unfortunately, my husband, Victor, is no longer a part of our family picture, and he and I are no longer together. Unforeseen and difficult events transpired during our children's early adulthood; however, we forged an even stronger bond and helped each other make it through because we had love. Victor and I had been loving and nurturing throughout our children's lives, so this challenge did not destroy them. They had solid identities and self-esteem. They survived and even thrived, moving on to pursue their dreams in life. Our bond as a family allowed my children and me to be resilient as well as forgiving. Couples, as well as family members, need to maintain connectedness. For couples, establishing an annual goal of engaging in a Marriage Encounter or a retreat is a powerful investment in your marriage. Taking time for every relationship that you hold dear is essential.

Strengthening the Spiritual Bond as Couples Prepare to Conceive Children

Continuing to build the bond of love that prepares the way for children, we might consider that couples in some cultures have a spiritual ritual they follow before they engage intimately to conceive a child. They may practice prayer and meditation, or even fast for some time, as a way of elevating their minds and cleansing their hearts and bodies. This also connects them with God. They refresh their lives for new opportunities, strengthen their spiritual bond as a couple, and pray to bring a soul of love and spirituality into their lives. This is a wonderful and holy concept that couples can choose to make their own, determining what spiritual rituals are important to them in this process. In this way, the most intimate beginning of life with children comes with the greatest love for God and each other.

Nurturing Relationships with Our Children

Dr. Ross Campbell, M.D., psychiatrist and the author of several books on parenting and child development, wrote in his book, *How to Really Love Your Child*, what he believed were the keys to loving effectively. I really loved my children when I read this, and I still found that his humble encouragement along specific lines made a difference in our lives. I saw a change in myself and my children. In essence, his suggestion was to make sure that our children feel loved. There are many philosophies about nurturing or disciplining children, but in the end, if the children don't feel loved, there is no point.

Campbell suggests that we assess our hearts to perceive how strong a feeling of love we have for our children. He says parents need a passionate commitment to making whatever sacrifice is necessary to fill their children's hearts. If our love for our children is not strong and somewhat vague, we can contemplate what we need to do to feel that shift. He advises that we must frequently use eye contact, physical contact, focused attention, appropriate love, and loving discipline. Filling up and keeping our children's hearts full is vital to nurturing their self-esteem and hopes for the future.

Siegel talked about the importance of being present and aware when we are with our children. He says we need a receptivity that allows us to take in our children's cues about what is happening with them. If we are perceptive and understand that they need our full attention, we can respond with being rather than doing. We may not know what they need other than that they are disturbed. Our emotional connection with them can stimulate their bodies to secrete soothing neurotransmitters, calming down their neurological systems, which is astounding to me.

Attachment Theory

Siegel says that our closeness with our children is known as attachment. Children especially need predictable, loving experiences with parents or caregivers when they are newborns. Parents engage with their children to soothe distress, and these experiences promote the healthy development of the mind and nervous system in the baby.

This security impacts the brain to support children's learning potential and to support cooperative behavior. Children want and need to be close to their mothers or primary caregivers. It is vital for children, especially during times of emotional need. These experiences convey a sense that they are cared for and heard. It gives them the crucial connection to know that they are safe. These feelings and experiences in children create a secure attachment. John Bowlby, the attachment theory pioneer, described this connection in his article "The Origins of Attachment Theory." Bowlby reported that **this security is vital for children of all ages**. Ainsworth's contribution described the attachment figure as a safe place from which the child can move out to explore his world. He also formulated the idea that when mothers are sensitive to their infant's signals, it helps develop attachment patterns between the mother and child.

Siegel shares his views about how our children's well-being in relationships and resilience in facing challenges will demonstrate their beliefs about themselves and how secure they feel. In Chapter Five of *Parenting from the Inside Out*, Siegel details the possible problems related to insecure attachments and how this can affect a child's life.

Siegel elaborates further on his research that a child's personality develops from their genetic temperaments, such as outgoingness, shyness, and moodiness. It also grows in conjunction with their experiences with family and peers. What we do and how we express our love and closeness with our children profoundly affects their lives forever. So, addressing the controversy of nature (genes) vs. nurture (experience), we understand that both are important in shaping the child.

Siegel's groundbreaking work in psychology and parenting has shed a profound light on how we can help our children. He describes a new kind of wholeness—an interconnectedness of all parts of the child: the mind, the emotions, the physical body, and the spirit. Each piece impacts the others. In two of his books, *The Whole Brain Child* and *The Whole Brain Child Workbook*, we find these helpful exercises we can use with our children to help facilitate this wholeness. The *Whole Brain Child* has much more theory and has some illustrations. *The Whole Brain Child Workbook* has more reflective fill-in-the-blank pages to help you think about your interaction with your children. The pages can help you contemplate and rethink your daily patterns with new ideas and information. You can design a new approach to help your children feel loved and supported so they can also respond differently. The workbook also has many more illustrations of physical exercises you can do to help your child find balance. Using the keys contained in these books can change behavior patterns of all kinds. Siegel says it is during daily crises that we can have the most significant impact. If we seize the moment to connect, empathize, and redirect, these can be the most potent times for our relationships and healing change.

Relationships Affect Brain Integration

Integration is the concept at the heart of Siegel's book, *The Whole Brain Child*. Understanding this will give you the power to transform how you think about parenting children. The first step is understanding that the brain has many parts with different jobs. Horizontal integration brings the left and right hemispheres of the brain to work together in a better flow. Vertical integration involves creating a healthy relationship between the upstairs thinking or logical brain and the downstairs primal emotions brain concerned with instinct, gut reactions, intense emotions, and survival. The integration process involves learning to make good decisions in highly emotional situations. This integration is one of the most important skills that we can teach our children. They can learn to pause and consider the consequences and the feelings of others before acting. It also means determining appropriate behavior. Young children under three do not have a fully developed upstairs brain and so can't always be expected to be rational and make good decisions. They may not be able to think before acting and often do their best with what they have. They have not developed the ability to use logic and may not be able to use words to express feelings. Living entirely in the moment, reason, responsibilities, and time don't exist for them. So, when they feel big emotions, the brain can shift into overdrive. If we connect with their feelings and help them calm down, we can help them make sense of the experience by bringing in logic. We can put the events in order. Assigning words to their feelings and helping them remember how things happened, in what order, and how things worked out can be helpful for integration. We can say, "Yes, is it true that you fell off the swing? I'll bet that was scary. Daddy ran over and sat with you. Your knee was hurting, and you cried. He gave you a big hug. Then you went with him and got a Band-Aid. Did it feel better after that? Is that what happened?"

Helping your children remember what happened and how it happened can help them make logical sense of the scenario.

We can ask ourselves throughout the day which brain we are appealing to: the upstairs logical brain or the downstairs emotional brain. We can help them think logically about the best way to respond to a situation, helping to develop their upstairs brain. And Siegel encourages us *not to enrage our children but to engage them.* Let's help them discuss

logically how things evolved and also appeal to their emotions with love and calmness. When we do this, we will have a better chance of helping them find resolution during a difficult emotional situation.

If there is no integration in the upstairs/downstairs brain, it's easy to see. The child is overwhelmed by emotions, confused, and chaotic. He can't respond calmly and capably to the situations at hand, so he has tantrums and meltdowns and gets aggressive. Most of life's challenging experiences result from loss of integration, also known as disintegration. Siegel says that emotion is the key integrating force of our brains. When we put forth the effort to truly love, this emotion acts as an integrating factor for balance in our beings, which is an amazing fact.

Brain scans tell us that the brain is moldable and has plasticity. It is hopeful news to know that the brain can change throughout life, and especially children's brains can heal.

Discipline as an Opportunity to Learn

I didn't know about Siegel's findings when our children were small, but I can now see the value of this wisdom. Our family had challenges, as most families do, such as fighting and hitting. I can remember how our children would all try to talk at the same time to get a word in edgewise, and creating order was not always easy. We wanted to help them all feel included and that they would have their time if they were patient.

Sometimes our children were naughty, but most of the time it was very innocent, and we just needed to look for what was causing the problem. Maybe they were over-tired or hungry and their blood sugar was low. They may have felt sad or lonely and needed a little attention. If we identified the problem and met their needs, they would often be happy and able to move on. We could help them redirect rather than locking horns with them.

At times, usually regarding cleaning up at home and when they were getting older, I found myself in a gridlock of a power struggle. They wouldn't clean up their toys. I had tried everything, and they refused. And then I would dole out consequences until I was so frustrated. A couple of times, I remember giving them consequences where they couldn't join their friends or some other activity that, in the end, hurt my heart probably more than theirs. I learned that discipline worked better when I could disconnect emotionally from the situation and take a lighthearted approach. If it was a task that we could approach together from the beginning, it would have been easier, and I wouldn't have developed an attitude of self-righteousness, such as "I am right and you are wrong," then it all worked out better. And it was always more effective to focus on a solution rather than the problem, and if they were willing to help come up with a solution, it was even easier.

Our families do need boundaries, and everyone has to contribute to maintaining a home. But we can also take the high road, assuming the best of our children. We can stay positive and firm at the same time. That was the real trick for me. If I could say, "I love you, and I see you victorious," and "I love myself enough to be firm at the same time," it worked out best. If I could stay kind and firm, we all won in the end. This was better than a power struggle where one of us won because, in that case, both of us actually lost, as the relationships then suffered. Discipline can also create a situation where a child feels labeled by us or someone else and then starts to identify with that label. The best way to prevent this is to always believe the best about our children and do all we can to bring that best out while respecting ourselves, too.

Ultimately, for me, it was about self-image. I needed to feel worthy of being listened to and followed. I needed confidence in myself as a parent to lead. I had to believe I could create the world and the relationships I wanted with and for my children. Sometimes, as I looked around at my home when it seemed messy, I would feel exhausted, the days felt hard, and we just had to get through them. Yet, in spite of that feeling, there was an even more powerful sense of peace in me that I was with my children, sharing my life with them. When I read Dr. Montessori's books and journaled, talked with counselors, prayed, and affirmed my innate strengths, all of these together helped me. Dr. Montessori's philosophy showed me that we must teach our children how to behave positively because discipline is about learning, not punishing. They needed to know what good behavior was before they could demonstrate it. We had to be examples, which included loving ourselves in healthy ways.

Children make us grow in so many ways. If we are willing to be honest, they bring out all kinds of psychological discoveries in ourselves. These can include both the positives and negatives, and we can grow from seeing them. But we have to love our children and ourselves and be willing to go through the process. We may realize that we get impatient or irritated if our children refuse to clean up their toys, and we may want to yell or punish them. Or, we might feel angry if they get jealous and defiant when a sibling needs attention, and lash out. We can write down our observations and take time out to think about why we feel and act the way we do. We can even comfort ourselves, reflecting on our good intentions. This always helped me get out of the gridlock of feeling like a bad mom. When I was able to love myself, in spite of my shortcomings, it was easier to rethink the situation. I felt free to explore new ideas to support our children, so they might feel loved and make better behavior choices, as well.

In Daniel Siegel's *No Drama Discipline Workbook*, he shares many ideas on ways to approach discipline with our children. One example is proactive parenting. He says that if you regularly have the same discipline issue coming up again and again in your family, you can learn how to get ahead of it. You can watch for signs that one of your children may be on their way to a meltdown or conflict. When you can see it coming, you can think of ways to intervene before it happens, helping them to connect with something positive and name their feelings. His book outlines many options you can use to intervene in such instances.

Seigel encourages parents to connect with their children even when they seem to have messed up. When we have compassion for them and show it, especially when they are angry or out of sorts, this communicates unconditional love. Our children will feel understood, valued, and accepted when we do this. In doing this, Siegel says that we impact how their brains develop and who they will become. We may not be used to responding this way and may need to think about how to change so we can be supportive. We can list ways to connect with our children at these times to circumvent problems. Using these ways of connecting, not only when they are happy but also when they are not, will change our relationships permanently.

Siegel explains how we can set limits and kindly help our children follow them. For most of us, setting limits feels like we have to get stern, but it can look different from this. We can gently remind our children that we let everyone take a turn on the slide and keep reinforcing this rather than demanding with a loud voice that they need to share or go home. If we reach their eye level, put a hand on their shoulders, and speak respectfully, we have a better chance of touching their hearts and not triggering anger. All of these examples come down in part to us being the ones who control our emotions and show them the way. If we approach our children with kindness and model how we would like to be treated, we will have a better opportunity to connect.

I did not know of Dr. Siegel when my children were young, but I energetically experienced this dynamic in my own life as I evolved with our children. I started to see that just being with them, quietly observing, and being present impacted them the most. When I used this approach, it was more powerful than trying to fix situations or talk things through. Sometimes, when I just sat quietly while holding them or being nearby, it had a calming and comforting impact.

Understanding the needs of children in their different stages of development helps us to know how to interact with them. Children are most benefitted and appreciative when we address their needs and when those close to them care enough to recognize and attend to those needs. I am grateful for permission from Daniel Siegel to use the quotes and contents contained in this chapter.

Family Meetings

Author and parenting expert Steven Covey spoke extensively about a tangible love that must be present for a family to thrive. In his book, *Seven Habits for Highly Effective Families*, he gave ideas about how to nurture this love in our family relationships. He recommended that parents have regular "one-on-ones" with each of their children to support a more profound connection. During these times, children may talk to a parent about a difficulty they may not share at any other time. They may also express something they would like to change in their lives. This one-on-one time is when we can get our children's thoughts and ideas about our family plans. It is a powerful way to support them with our love one by one, and impact our whole family.

I remember one time when I took one of our sons out for a meal. He was nine, and our lives were very busy. After this time together, he downloaded a poem about love from the internet and sent it to me, thanking me for taking him out. I realized his amazing sensitivity and tenderness, which didn't always show then. I also saw how much he appreciated our time alone together and how important it was. It is valuable for our children to know that we deeply connect with them.

I have found it helpful to jot down notes about my meetings or times with my husband and children so I could remember what was said, what I thought about certain issues, and things that needed action or resolution. Below is a sample template for this purpose that you can use with anyone.

Journal Notes from Meetings with Spouse (Partner) or Child

You can find a blank version of this template as part of a download-able set of templates on my website. See the QR code on the inside cover of this book, front and back, to download the set from my website.

T7.1 Meeting Journal Sample Template:
Date: 8/26/23

Significant Discussion:	Follow-up Goals:

Jenna(8) and Mom, out for tea and a walk.
Key Communication: She doesn't feel she is heard at home.
	Plan to meet once each week for a walk around the block for 30 minutes or to get tea. Put it on the calendar.
	We will write down things she wants to see happen, her hopes and dreams for her own life, and brainstorm how to make them happen each week. We can check in on the most important ones:
	  1) Would like to start gymnastics
	  2) Wants to be on a swim team
	  3) Wants to be able to talk at family meetings

Significant Discussion:	Follow-up Goals:
Dad and Mom Took a walk around the lake to talk about how things are going with family night. It seems like the older kids don't feel engaged, and don't feel that they really can have a say in the process. They felt that our activity wasn't really fun.	Plan to have a discussion with the older ones ahead of time to help them know how important their thoughts and opinions are in our process of bonding as a family and creating a Family Mission Statement. We will ask them to lead the questioning of everyone to find out what they want to contribute. We will ask them to take turns thinking of an activity our family will do together, and make sure we create the opportunity for that to happen.

A Family Mission Statement

We can also embrace our family as a whole. What do you want your family to look like and feel like? What principles do you want to pass on to your children? Families can design a mission statement together, giving clarity and direction to life. My family took time to write goals for ourselves and create a vision, although we never made a family mission statement. It would have brought many elements of our lives together if we had, and I would encourage you to consider creating one.

A family mission statement is your family's stated purpose and declaration of how you want to live with each other. It can be phrases, sentences, paragraphs, or even symbols, depending on what you want it to be. Our children need to be included in the creation process. You can also create a mission statement with extended family to create a greater bond and identity. This can also help blended families get on the same track.

Each person's dreams, goals, values, and aspirations can all be incorporated. Regardless of age, everyone gets to contribute their thoughts and have them honored without judgment. Sharing these priorities can help empower our children to express themselves as they realize what is important to them. At the same time, this process will help to create family guidelines. Empowered parents can reinforce what everyone decides rather than feeling responsible for making all the decisions. They also will feel free of the need to please everyone. This was huge for me when my children were young. It always felt that my husband and I were responsible for making and enforcing the rules, whereas, here, the family can establish the guidelines together. Focus on the Family (focusonthefamily.com), a ministry that supports families worldwide, says a family mission statement is key to helping you identify what your family is all about. We may not always feel like great parents or family, but with a mission statement to clarify our purpose and goals, we can realign and stay on course.

Couples can create a family mission statement even before they have children. It can help them rise above conflicting role expectations and differing problem-solving approaches. Clarifying communication goals and committing to live life how you both want it to be can be especially helpful for a couple. Covey and his wife kept their mission statement all of their lives, even though they made another mission statement later with their whole family. He shared how it gave him and his wife a vision together. When they had issues, they referred to this statement to remember how they wanted to treat each other and resolve problems.

In his book, Covey discusses comments from younger teens whose families had made a mission statement. One teen shared how he felt more secure after their family created a mission statement. Another teen felt that her parents really had their act together, and she liked it.

Many online sites have free templates to learn more about making a family mission statement. There is no right or wrong way to do it; whatever you create will be valuable. Make sure you pursue the process in a way your kids will enjoy and include fun and a little celebration. Here is a sample of a simple family mission statement. You can find a blank version of this template as part of a downloadable set of templates on my website. See the QR code on the inside cover of this book, front and back, to download the set from my website.

T7.2 Our Family Mission Statement: Sample Template

Our Angeles Family Mission Statement	Date:

Our family mission is to love and support one another unconditionally, making an effort to develop close bonds and celebrate our uniqueness. We make sure that everyone's voice is heard when we make decisions. We value all of our family and seek to celebrate our history and future together with warm, joyful traditions. Education is important to us, and we seek to draw out each other's gifts and curiosity about life in a way that makes life wonderful. The exciting spirit of adventure beckons our family to explore what the world has to offer and to develop our gifts to make the world a better place. Our mission is love.

Written and signed by: David, Francis, Frederick, Clare, Marie, Elizabeth, Dad, and Mom (Family Members)

We can do things together as a way of building a family culture. One helpful plan is to have weekly family meetings, prioritize them, and schedule everything around them. This is when we can pass our values on to our children. Having a template for these meetings makes it easier. We can establish an agenda and plan to start and end on time using the template each week. Including a hands-on project is often a good idea. Some other options include beginning and ending with a song and having someone read our family mission statement aloud. A short presentation, under fifteen minutes, about something meaningful and pertinent to our children's lives can also be great. We can share many things with our children, such as information about our service, our faith, or character building. We can teach basic life skills, such as building a fire or doing a simple science experiment. Following up with a discussion about our topic allows children to ask questions and share their thoughts. Trying to make it engaging for everyone is important, although often, our children will learn even when they don't appear to be learning. Younger children may need to move while we are talking and can still absorb the essence of our meeting as they move.

After this, having time for play and laughter is also essential. We can choose something fun to do, like a game either inside or outside, along with a special treat. Playing with all of our children when we don't have to focus on learning or rules is also so valuable. It is like telling them, "We enjoy being with you." When we do it as a family, this message can resonate within us all that it is a pleasure to be together and happy. The daily routines of life become more enjoyable. When challenges arise, looking forward to family time can lift our spirits as we anticipate heartwarming connections and laughter. It will nurture our children's relationships with us and with each other. There are online templates for family meeting albums to keep memories.

I think that fun equals hope for children. A friend and psychologist told me this once, and I can't say enough about it. Relaxing a little is something that I had to learn when life seemed overly serious with six children, and I felt beset by responsibilities. I had to let go a little; having fun would round things out. Everything I needed to do still got done and in a more enjoyable way. It is easy to see that our children reflect our love and attitudes as parents. They will then reflect back to us on the love and attitudes we share.

Supporting the Role of Parent

I want to share the views of Dr. Gordon Neufeld, who we studied when our children were young. He really helped us. His perspective is that parents need to matter in the daily lives of their children of all ages. He says that time spent together is vital for creating attachment and is important to create a healthy relationship that can last a lifetime. His book, *Hold on To Your Kids,* helped me to realize how valuable we are as parents in our children's lives, especially as teens. Your decisions about spending time with them are pivotal in how your relationships unfold and how secure your children will be. Take confidence in your abilities as a parent and invest in your family in the best ways possible. I encourage you to listen to your inner teacher and follow your heart.

Gratitude and Visualization

Thinking about what is going well and giving gratitude to God will help us to be more positive and aware of our blessings. Gratitude is powerful. We can pray for help in areas with problems and let spirit guide our thoughts. During my quiet times when my children were small, I had amazing insights that helped me change situations. I wrote pages in my journal about what I hoped and prayed would happen for our family and envisioned what that would look like. By contemplating what we wanted and needed, we opened our hearts to the inspiration of the spirit. This invited abundance into our lives in the way that it was meant to be. I asked God to overshadow our days and bring joyous outcomes, even amid challenges.

When our family had needs beyond our budget, we taught our children to believe that God would care for us, and he always did. When we closed our eyes and thanked him for what we already had, things began to change. We refused to allow fear or worry to control our thoughts. Instead, miracles happened when we filled our minds with positive affirmations and hopeful expectations. The power of prayer with a grateful heart made the difference for us.

We asked God to protect us, our children, and the world each morning as we prepared for our day. We taught them that God's light surrounds us and goes before us. We can ask for his help in every detail. We tried to be positive role models.

Vision boards were helpful to us in making visual our hopes and dreams. We found pictures of things we wanted and glued them on card stock with statements of faith in the abundant life. We put these boards in a place where we could see them often to remind us of our goals. They really seemed to help us. We also helped our children make their own. You can now find many resources to help you create vision boards where you can place pictures of things you want and need for your family. A book I recommend is called *Dream It, Pin It, Live It*. This book was very helpful to me in learning to use this wonderful tool of vision boards further and bolstering my faith in myself to write this book.

In her book *The Spiritual Laws of Prosperity*, Catherine Ponder shares the idea of how powerful it is to have the whole family work together on ideas and goals. The payoff comes when you all help manifest the vision. She contributed much to my view of keeping faith with an expectant attitude toward life when my children were small and in her encouragement to nurture children and spouses with faith in them and a commitment to hold only the most positive outcomes for their lives.

Parenting from around the World

I looked at cultures worldwide and gleaned some beautiful images of how families live. Many parents prioritize having routines and spending time with their children. An abundance of games can be found in bookcases of families around the world. This creates a lovely image of all those families playing together for hours, laughing and talking, and just having fun. Often now, moms and dads share in the care of children and opt for part-time work or fewer days for this purpose. Fathers choose to spend dedicated time each week with their children. Grandparents can take their grandchildren for one day each week, giving parents time for greater life balance. This is incredibly enriching, especially if it means that cousins regularly spend time together at their grandparents' homes. It encourages intergenerational connections, the passing on of family culture, and the creation of family identity. The whole family can eat breakfast together regularly, ensuring that children are nourished for school or work at home, and also have bonding time with parents and siblings. Eating breakfast is also associated with better learning outcomes and fewer behavior problems. We can work together on household chores, such as chopping wood, cooking, and cleaning. Bonding happens in the simple activities of our lives and enriches us, as our children can also learn so much with us.

Integrating the Generations in Your Family

Support from extended family and friends can enrich our lives with love and joy, bring new ideas, and create bonding. The influence and wisdom of our elders is invaluable. Ann Buchanan, a British social worker and researcher at the University of Oxford found that a high level of grandparent involvement helps children in many different ways, increasing a sense of well-being, with children demonstrating better behavior with fewer behavioral and emotional challenges overall. We sense the strength of the family as relatives, neighbors, and close community members live and work together, which is a great blessing.

My parents came to help every time one of our babies was born. They took over all the household chores and cared for the older children. They made meals, cooked and cleaned, took walks with the children, went to parks, and had picnics. They visited train stations, museums, and observatories, opening up the world for our children. For our children, time spent with their grandparents was precious, and those connections lasted throughout my parents' lives. My parents were nurtured by these relationships as much as our children were. They were an integral part of our lives, and we appreciated the blessing they were to us. Even today, their ways and opinions still matter to us and guide our thinking and planning. They had strong, clear values, and we can still hear their words and ideas. Our children counted on their regular twenty-to-thirty-dollar birthday gifts every year, and they were received with great anticipation and appreciation. We are eternally grateful for how our parents helped to shape our family.

Our family traveled several times to visit my husband's family in the Philippines. We spent time with his parents and cousins, learning about the Tagalog language and the family history, which built bonds when we spent quality time with them. My husband's family had a strong, culturally rich foundation in the Philippines, and we experienced this when we visited, adding greatly to our children's feelings about our family's roots.

The family is important because those who care for children build society. The home environment shapes family relationships and lives. Ultimately, it is there that we can bring the world to a higher place founded on love, selfless giving, and caring.

T7.3 Observation Practice Chapter Seven

Observation Practice	Date:
1. How does your family spend time together regularly? • Our family enjoys going to the beach to walk or camp, walking in the forest, and going out for dinner.	
2. What in your life needs healing so you can better support your family emotionally? • I need to give myself quiet time daily so I can be more aware of what is happening inside me, and feel more connected to perceive what my children really need so I can respond lovingly.	
3. What is your dream for your family? • My dream for my family is to find and nurture each of my children's and grandchildren's gifts and strengths, to help them flourish, as well as my own. I also want us all to be close over the years, helping each other, and working together on many projects and aspects of our lives.	

Table 7.1 Chapter Seven Takeaways

Chapter Seven Takeaways
• Nurture self-acceptance and heal the issues of your life so you can support your children.
• Maintain a loving connection with your spouse/partner as the foundation for family life.
• Secure an attachment bond with each child through one-on-one time, eye contact, physical contact, focused attention, appropriate love, and loving discipline.
• Integrate the generations/extended family to bond and build a family identity.

There is a blank template like this available for you on my website if you use the QR code in the front and back cover of the book.

Cultivating Your Family Culture

"Family culture, with its traditions and rituals, can give your children a sense of identity and belonging, continuity with the past, a framework for lasting memories, and hopes for a positive future. It can reinforce values and bond your whole family together. And your family can choose the elements of your family culture."
— TERESA ANGELES

Marie and the Christmas Gifts

Right before Christmas one year, when our youngest children were still preschoolers, our whole family piled into our van and headed to a dollar store, nearby. All eight of us. Everyone was excited. We had given each of our children five dollars and fifty cents to buy gifts for each sibling, plus fifty cents for tax.

This event happened before dollar stores had become common. We knew of only two of these stores that sold everything for a dollar then, and we were amazed. One store was in Oregon, and we always stopped there on our way to Uncle Mike's. The other was fifteen minutes from our home, and it was exceptional. It was tiny but had marvelous things that piqued our children's interest.

Marie was five or six then and wanted to stay with me and hold my hand. She was pleased to have money to buy everyone a present and said, "Mommy, what do you think I can get for Clare? I want to get her something pretty, like a doll or a ring, and Elizabeth too . . . maybe a pretty star. Do you think they will have those here?" she asked.

"I'll bet they do, Marie. And, if they don't, I am sure that you can find something else that they will love!" I said, "I think it is so nice that you are excited to get something for everyone."

Her eyes twinkled with excitement as we slowly walked down the aisles, peering at the trinkets and ornaments. Our children found unique gifts for their brothers and sisters, such as beautiful candle holders with little mirrors and ribbons, small dolls, tools, and baseball card holders. They were all so excited to get something for everyone and to pay all by themselves. It was quite a process to get everyone through the line, and everything paid for and bagged without their siblings seeing what they had selected!

After going home, Marie asked, "How do we do the wrapping, Mommy? I want to make them look really pretty!"

I was touched by Marie's thoughtfulness. She always wanted to make things beautiful and give to others. These are qualities she still has today.

"I will show you, sweet girl!" I said, "Your presents will look lovely. Which one would you like to start with, and what paper do you want?"

"Oh, Mommy, I will wrap this candle holder with that paper with the Christmas trees on it. Can I cut the paper?" she asked.

"Yes, of course.," I replied. "Please get the tape on the crafts shelf. We have scissors and ribbon here, so we are set."

Marie returned with the tape and I demonstrated how to wrap my gift first so she could see how I did it. I told her, "First, I lay the wrapping paper out flat, then cut a long strip wide enough for the present and more than twice as long. I put the gift in the middle and then fold the paper over and secure the sides with tape. Lastly, I cut a long ribbon and tie it around the gift like this. You can see how to curl the ribbon here, at the end. You can do it, and I will help you."

Then, I organized the materials so she could do it by herself, but I stayed there to support her and help if needed. After wrapping them all, she said, "I am so excited, Mommy! I am glad I have presents for everybody, and I wrapped them all myself!" said Marie. "Let's put them under the tree!" And we did.

Pulling her up on my lap, I hugged her. We sat together, looking at all of our beautiful gifts. Marie had a big smile on her face. I could always count on her to be enthusiastic about anything you shared with her. Sitting there with her in the light of our peaceful home was a joy. "Mommy, do you think that everybody will like my presents?" Marie asked.

"You carefully picked out gifts for everyone, Marie. I think they will love them." I responded.

A few days later, on Christmas morning, Marie suddenly jumped up from the breakfast table, ran to me, and putting tiny, sticky hands around my ear, whispered a short urgent message. "Mommy, I forgot to get Frederick a present! I will see what I can find to give him."

"Good idea, Marie. Do you need help?" I asked.

But she was gone quickly and back again soon. She had a Snoopy Beanie Baby dog in a bag in her hands to hide it. It was from her collection that still looked like new. She asked me to help wrap it quickly so he wouldn't see. We did, and soon it was under the tree, as beautiful as all the other gifts. Her worried face turned jubilant as she sat with our family, opening Christmas gifts that morning. And Frederick loved her dog and treasured it for many years. My heart was full of the joy of celebration and satisfaction that Christmas, knowing we had helped our children give to each other and keep traditions together. 🖋

Defining and Fostering Family Culture

Family culture is the essence of how we embrace life with one another, how we feel about being together, and what we value. Feelings of love that we share can be very tangible, as can our love for our Faith, our country, or other cultural traditions. The rituals and celebrations we establish instill meaning in our lives together. They structure a framework for us to reflect on our family blessings, mark the passage of time, and navigate change.

When we celebrate traditions with each other, we find joy and bonding. Shared experiences strengthen trust and connection in relationships that build a solid family foundation. Enjoying rituals together helps us feel that we each have a place and are known, ensuring our sense of loving and being loved. They also help children know what to expect from life. Daily routines may bring joy to our children's lives, such as reading, praying before bed, or taking a regular Saturday morning bike ride together. There may be more significant celebrations and family reunions that connect our generations. Traditions establish set times for interactions for bonding, even amidst busy schedules, and they bring comfort. We can relax as we hear each other's stories. We can take in the vibrancy and smells of the seasons together year after year, as people have done since the beginning of time. Participating in family vacations regularly teaches our children that our people are a priority, creating a colorful fabric of continuity that nourishes the heart.

Our values and the rituals we tie to them deeply affect our children. As parents, we are empowered to help shape their understanding and life experiences. Rituals can be a key to our children developing a sense of who they are. When we decide with our families which rituals are important, we can use joyful traditions to celebrate them. Montessori believed traditions were valuable and demonstrated delightful ways to help children understand them at their developmental levels. You can do the same and create a framework for celebrations that give your children's lives meaning.

This chapter discusses why traditions, rituals, and celebrations are important and describes how Montessori approached them. I share how our family celebrated and learned about our favorite holidays. Lastly, I will provide templates to help you create a framework for the family occasions that are the most meaningful to you.

Use Storytelling and Scientific Knowledge

Dr. Montessori used storytelling, lessons, and activities to make cultural traditions come alive, demonstrating that focusing on these brought knowledge and joy to the children. For example, by helping children understand the earth's rotation around the sun and scientifically observing the change of seasons, she helped them deepen their connection to the universe. They enjoyed celebrating the solstice and equinox, enjoying activities that brought light and festivity to dark winter months. Montessori also believed that exposing children to the holidays of diverse nations allowed children to develop compassion and cultural acceptance.

Understanding Family History Increases a Child's Well-Being

According to psychologists Marshall Duke, Ph.D. and Robyn Fisvush, Ph.D. who studied fifty families and published an article in HuffPost, children who have a clear understanding of their family history demonstrate greater resilience in the face of stress, a heightened sense of self-worth, and perceived control over their lives. They also view their immediate families as more successful, highlighting the positive outcomes of this knowledge. The article gives twenty questions parents can ask and discuss with their children to increase their knowledge. In addition, when children learn where parents and relatives have come from they learn history and geography. We can use maps, atlases, and other resources to help our children learn about them. Better yet, traveling to these places can create warm connections and relationships that inspire.

Many Montessori communities today provide cultural experiences for children. Families can learn how to do the same at home, helping their children develop celebrations and traditions. They can help prepare special foods, decorations, or songs, or do other contributing projects. Because children are still in the absorbent mind from zero to six years old, it is the sensorial aspects of these celebrations that really touch and impact them. Remembering colorful costumes, tastes, festive music, and dance can quicken their imaginations. They anticipate seeing grandparents, cousins, and friends who regularly come for certain holidays and are excited to play and talk with them. All of this deepens relationships, nurturing emotional security, social skills, and designing a vision of a positive future filled with joy. Taking advantage of these opportunities is priceless.

A Child's Birthday Ritual Around the Sun

One example we can follow is the unique Montessori ritual of celebrating a child's birthday and incorporating a meaningful understanding of the solar system. You can share with your children what happens to the Earth in relation to the sun when the seasons change, providing very simple explanations. Because the Earth is on its axis and rotates around the sun, it is angled toward or away from the sun at different times of the year, and this is what creates the seasons. Children can celebrate their birthdays with this wonderful ritual where they hold a globe and walk around the sun for every year of their lives. Your family can talk about the unique things about their lives and the events of each year. You can sing a song about the Earth going around the sun, which it does each year, and then sing Happy Birthday at the end.

Prepare for the Birthday Ritual

- ✧ Place a mat in the middle of the circle or gathering space.
- ✧ Place an object to represent the sun in the middle of the mat. This can be a fake or real candle, a three-D paper sun, a drawing, or whatever you choose.
- ✧ Find a globe that your child will hold as they go around the sun.
- ✧ Place two-by four-inch cards with the names of the months on them in a circle around the sun, moving counterclockwise.
- ✧ Appropriately place similar cards with the seasons' names around the months in which they occur. For example, spring is placed beside May, between March and June, and so forth.
- ✧ Make some notes of what your child was like at that age, what they liked to do, your family events, etc.
- ✧ Gather at least one picture or more to represent every year of his or her life.

Conducting the Birthday Ritual

Your family and friends can sit around your circle in chairs or on the floor. At the beginning of this ritual, place whatever object you have chosen to represent the sun in the center of this space. You might start the ritual by telling your family or guests how excited you were that your son or daughter was soon to be born, sharing your feelings of joy and hope. You might take two to three minutes to do this and then show pictures from when your child was first born.

Next, if your sun is a candle, help your child to safely light it with a long lighter or taper. (She may put her hand on yours as you light it.) Then, have her take the globe and stand on her birth month (example, May or June if she was born then) on the circle and walk counterclockwise around the sun once. This will represent her first year of life. Everyone sings a song about the Earth going around the sun as she walks. When she stops, you can show pictures of her at age one and two the second time around, etc., and talk about what she was like and what she enjoyed. Mention where your family lived and the significant family events of that year. Repeat this activity for every year of your child's life, and then sing Happy Birthday! She can share a treat—fruit, a salty snack, or cake, and can help prepare the ritual and the snack ahead of time. This heartwarming activity can help her feel she has a special place and is loved by her family.

There are many Montessori birthday ritual songs, templates, and videos online to help you prepare. Although this ritual may seem daunting, once you understand it, it will be easy. Find a song that you like and make it your own. Search online for "Montessori Birthday Ritual."

Celebrations to Develop Multiple Intelligences

Celebrations can stimulate multiple intelligences in the sensitive child of six and under. We can give simple lessons about the history or purpose of rituals and follow up with activities. Children will remember it all! Seeing lit candles, symbols, and pictures at religious, spiritual, or patriotic events may increase the visual-spatial part of the child's brain that envisions inspiring colors, designs, and heartwarming images. Hearing music and singing songs may arouse musical intelligence. Dancing or using tools with crafts can develop kinesthetic strengths. Linguistic and interpersonal skills may increase with conversations, especially as they talk with people of different languages. Nature intelligence can be nurtured as children observe the change of seasons and cook apple cider with cinnamon sticks, cloves, and orange slices in the fall, or use nature elements to celebrate favorite holidays.

In the few weeks before a holiday, you can start to place books about that event on your child's bookshelf or corner. Share songs, stories, poems, and play games to honor the coming event or holiday. Be intentional about planning which traditions to celebrate and get their input about what they love. Fun family celebrations can change our children's lives. Being proactive in designing a plan now, you will reap great benefits for the future. We have choices to make, lessons to prepare, and celebrations to enjoy! Working together toward a celebration can make life really fun.

My Family Traditions

Our family loved to celebrate Christmas and the winter holidays. We embraced our faith by celebrating the four weeks of Advent in the Christian tradition, which commemorates the Israelites' waiting for the coming of Christ. We studied the scriptures, read Bible stories at dinner, watched movies, and discussed what it meant to develop a compassionate Christian heart.

Over the years, we have enjoyed many kinds of activities and celebrations, and I will share a compilation of some of what we did. They did not all happen at once, and our celebrations may be different from yours. Things also changed as our children got older. My hope in sharing what we did is to encourage you to find the magic in what your family loves to do together and what interests them. You can create beautiful activities to express and enhance those interests. Every family is different. Be bold, be creative, and resourceful to find what will be wonderful for you!

Decorating with Nature's Beauty

Decorating our home during Christmas time was very special. We tried to involve our children in every part of it, giving the little ones simple things to do and encouraging the older ones with patience when they were less inclined to help. Feeling capable and empowered, they often took on greater initiative and joy. The first thing of the season was the making of the Advent wreath from cedar branches in our yard. We placed it in the center of our dining table and lit the candles on each Sunday in December. We sang and prayed as we lit the candles. The circle and the evergreens symbolize eternal life because evergreen trees retain their needles through the winter rather than dying in the fall, as deciduous trees do. The circle shape also reflects this. We used the branches to frame the windows, doors, and fireplace mantel. As possible, we all went to purchase or cut a tree together and placed it in our front window, which was really tall and so exciting. We added Christmas lights to all of this, often taking days to get it all done. We covered oranges with cloves and gathered pinecones, which we hung in the kitchen. The essential oils emitted a wonderful scent. It was an amazing feeling to have all of this light, beauty, and almost a reverence in our home. Watching our children's faces was precious as they took in the scent of these natural oils and gazed at the festive lights of the mystical season.

Frederick and the Christmas Lights

I remember a funny story about our son, Frederick, who was about eight and was helping his dad and older brothers put up Christmas lights. It had become a tradition to make the lights as beautiful as possible. That year, it was Frederick's turn to engineer the process. He got help from his older brothers and friends to haul the boxes of lights down from the rafters to the family room. For a few hours, they worked to untangle the strands, and then began to wind the strings up the banisters and around the very large windows in our two-story house. The girls and I made snacks for the crew and worked on Sunday dinner.

Finally, when everything was done, it was time! In the kitchen, Frederick looked around in anticipation as everyone excitedly held their breath. All the lines were connected to one plug, and Frederick got ready. Biting his lip in anticipation, he and his dad plugged them in.

A fantastic display of lights lit up the house. It was magnificent. We all just stood and stared . . . And then, just as suddenly as it came on, everything went black—everything in our house and outside. Our lights had blown the electrical circuits in the whole neighborhood! It was very shocking, and no one could say a word at first. We stood there silently until we realized what had happened. And then, we all laughed hysterically. It was hilarious and memorable. I can't remember what happened after that, and I am sure it all got resolved, but it was a heartwarming memory that we will never forget.

Other Holiday Activities

Mid-December, we often went to *Holiday with Lights*, an annual event held at a water park about five minutes from our home. The park transforms its rides with thousands of Christmas lights and traditional music yearly. My husband got discounted tickets at the hospital where he worked, so we could also take the children of our friends and neighbors. It was exhilarating and set the tone for our holiday season. We also celebrated Francis' birthday. One wonderful Christmas, we went to Zoo Lights with cousins in Oakland, California, and that was so much fun!

The Spirit of Christmas

We believe that the Spirit of Christmas touches people's hearts and makes our world kinder. Santa, or Saint Nicholas, is the model of loving-kindness we can all emulate and celebrate. We can refuse to allow our image of this kind of personality to be tainted by commercialism or anything that would deprive us of the richness of love and joy at this time. It takes strong hearts with vision to focus on possibilities and refuse to give in to a culture that does not support it. That Spirit can move through our lives, making miracles happen for those who believe. Our children made drawings of Santa and the Christmas elves. At church, they participated in nativity pageants wearing handmade costumes with simple scripts, songs, and adorable hand movements. Sometimes, they played musical instruments, even imperfectly, for others. We went to local concerts of singers, dancers, artists, and per-formers focused on Christmas. Once, we enjoyed *Christmas and Winter Holidays from Around the World*, at the Seattle Center. Our entire family went free of charge. Costumed children in the performances shared the Mexican Posada, Swedish Saint Lucia Day, and Filippino dancing.

Serving Others During the Christmas Season

Christmas Eve was often a memorable day when we tried to do something special, such as gathering with our community to play music and sing at the VA Hospital or senior centers. The people loved seeing the children and hearing the old, familiar Christmas carols. Especially on this day, the Veterans appreciated our little troupe of families who could share some joy.

We also went to the *Forgotten Children's Fund*, a warehouse that gathered gifts for children in need. Volunteers could come to choose, wrap, and address gifts. It was a wonderful experience for everyone to feel so helpful. All of our children enjoyed doing this, and it took time and effort to help everyone, but it was worth it! Our children's friends and their parents came with us. It was an exciting time to think of others and share our love.

Celebrating Christmas

Our Christmas celebrations were simple and more about being together. We placed our gifts for each other under the tree, and with so many of us, it was often quite a sight as the children got older. We went to church, often with my parents, on Christmas morning. We enjoyed giving to each other, and opening gifts that each had prepared. When our children were young, we did not have a large income, but because of this, we all learned to appreciate giving in a more heartfelt, ingenious way, even as our children got older. As they grew, our children prioritized giving over receiving and appreciated spending time together to relax, talk, or play games. Sometimes, we had close family or friends for dinner and appreciated celebrating our life together.

My Children's Comments about Christmas:

Elizabeth's Memory

"My favorite celebration was always Christmas, with the lights all up. We would go get our tree, and the smell of the tree would waft through the house. Our house was always full of the noise and laughter of my brothers and sisters. We would have gingerbread competitions, and I can remember the smell of cider and mostly just laughter everywhere. Such a happy time!"

Marie's Memory

"Christmas night always held so much peace and magic in my memory. After all the presents were open and the food was eaten, I often snuggled on the couch contentedly. Sometimes, I read upstairs in my bedroom with the door open. I could hear the full house and all the merriment downstairs. I felt so happy, even if I wasn't in the middle of it all. We had the best time, and I could go on and on."

Celebrating Winter Solstice

Now, after teaching in Montessori classrooms, I recommend celebrating the winter solstice as part of the holidays. In our classroom, as I mentioned earlier, we talked about what caused the solstices and the equinoxes and used a globe and a flashlight to show how the Earth tilted its axis as it went around the sun. It also received different angles of the sun's rays as it rotated. This demonstrated how when the North Pole tilted away from the sun, it became winter in the Northern Hemisphere. In class one year, the children acted this out. A child held a globe representing the Earth and wore a sign that said "Earth." Another child held a ball with a flashlight over it like the sun directing its rays onto the Earth. The "Earth" child twirled continuously as she gradually made her way around the sun, representing how the Earth rotates every twenty-four hours, and circles the sun in 365 days. When the sun is positioned right over the Tropic of Capricorn and is twenty-three and a half degrees in the southern latitude, you will (notice that the southern hemisphere will receive direct sunlight. There will be long days there because the sun's angle is high in the sky.

Conversely, when there is little direct sunlight in the northern hemisphere, the days are very short. The winter solstice is the shortest day of the year. The children loved this activity. You can easily do this at home and give mini-lessons with your children to explore and discuss aspects of the solar system. A celebration of candles, songs, and refreshments can follow.

Continuing to Celebrate the Christmas Season as Our Family Grows

Even as our children have grown and married, we still observe rituals with our grandchildren. A few years ago, some of us went to the mountains to cut down Christmas trees. Here is a picture of the hot cider and candy canes that my daughter-in-law brought to celebrate our little party in the mountains. It was very special.

Hot Cider and Candy Canes in the Forest

A Culture of Faith

Dr. Montessori observed that children are naturally spiritual and love rituals. Spirituality helps us feel connected to and supported by something greater than ourselves. Experiencing this can give us inspiration, faith, and hope. Just as people of different faiths all over the world have prayer corners or altars where they pray or meditate, we can create a unique area of our home where our children can do the same. They can do yoga with us or hold beautiful things that inspire a peaceful feeling, such as a candle, a flower, or a seashell. If you have one, you can include something representing your family's spiritual faith. If you have a prayer corner, sharing in quiet rituals can touch your children's hearts and share peacefulness.

Helping our children contemplate spiritual concepts was important, so our family life was interwoven with rituals. We shared our view that life is a gift to be treasured and that our goal is to return to God the gift of ourselves with our talents multiplied. It is valuable for your children to hear your thoughts and spiritual beliefs, whatever they are. Children between zero and six are most sensitive to developing a spiritual relationship with God.

Exploring Religious Scriptures with Children

I have found that children love to hear stories, especially from religious scriptures—maybe because the stories are often miraculous and give us hope. Children love hearing how angels have helped people and have come when called. To many of us, these scriptures represent the word of God. Families can decide how to pass on their spiritual beliefs to their children through stories of spirituality and by having the children act them out with costumes, dolls, friends, and props. Your love for your children will guide you.

If you are Christian, there are many Bible story picture books that you can use to help familiarize your children with the stories from the Old and New Testaments. One beautifully illustrated recommendation is *The Bible Story* by Arthur S. Maxwell. It has a five-volume red set with select stories for very young children and a ten-volume more comprehensive blue set for older children, an overview of stories from Adam and Eve to the Apostles. In addition, there are CDs with recorded stories. My children loved and memorized the stories and the sound effects. Thirty-plus years later, they still remember them, almost word for word. These kinds of books contain a wealth of spiritual principles that they absorbed, and I encourage you to find the prize literature from your faith or spiritual calling.

Catechesis of the Good Shepherd

After my children were grown, I found a valuable resource I would like to share with you. Let me give you some background on it. As Montessori was Catholic, she viewed things from this perspective. Again, I encourage you to view her observations and make them work for your family's faith or spirituality.

Dr. Montessori and her assistant, Sophia Cavalletti, witnessed the children's spontaneous spirituality. They believed God was deeply present with the children who showed a profound capacity for religious life. Montessori and Cavalletti saw that the children could discover and develop a deep relationship with Jesus Christ, the Good Shepherd. For this reason, they worked together to develop a religious education program for children, allowing them to interact with religious hands-on materials, touching, moving, and handling them in order to connect more deeply with spiritual concepts.

In 1954, two years after Montessori's sudden passing, Cavalletti and another Montessori-trained teacher, Gianna Gobbi, developed the *Catechesis of the Good Shepherd* (https://www.cgsusa.org). It is a program that focuses on biblical stories with figurines and props to help children learn, act out, and retell the stories.

The Catechesis stories start with the Good Shepherd, who loves and cares for his sheep and will not let one get lost. Jesus is the Good Shepherd, but the children are not told this right away. They learn to love the Good Shepherd and experience his great love for his flock. Later, they come to realize that Jesus and the Good Shepherd are one, and that Jesus loves them as one of his own sheep. Parents can create stories and figurines for any scripture of any faith.

An important set of lessons in the *Catechesis of the Good Shepherd* is called the Infancy Narrative, a series of stories about Jesus' birth. The materials used for the birth story of Jesus are similar to the nativity scene often seen at Christmas in family homes and churches. It is a highly creative way to teach and definitely attracts young children. Materials that go with the story of Jesus's birth include a manger and small figures of Joseph, Mary, and baby Jesus. But there are many other scenes using miniature houses, temples, and outdoor environments to illustrate other stories.

Infancy Narratives from the Bible:

The Annunciation of Archangel Gabriel to Mary: Luke 1:25-38

The Visitation of Mary to her Cousin Elizabeth: Luke 1:39-56

The Birth of Jesus and the Adoration of the Shepherds: Luke 2:1-20

The Adoration of the Magi: Matthew 2:1-12

The Presentation in the Temple: Luke 2:21-33, 36-39

If you choose, make a shelf in your cultural area just for these materials. Your children can work with them on a rug or a table and re-enact the story as often as they want, internalizing the meaning. They can return the materials to the shelf each time they finish. This also extends the learning environment in your home to a spiritual one.

Lighting a candle signifies that reading these stories is a sacred time, and we honor the Spirit of God. Many of us believe God speaks to us through these scriptures. We can also read the Bible passage directly, explaining the more challenging vocabulary so the children can understand and even encouraging children who can read. After a story, we can follow up with spontaneous prayer, song, or even silence as we contemplate the story. Afterward, you can encourage your children to draw or paint pictures that go with the story and then use the picture to share the story with others.

The Catechesis of the Good Shepherd recommends that parents and teachers make their materials, if possible. It is quite moving to understand that the organization believes that when adults make the materials, they absorb the experience more deeply and do not seek to hurry. In a world where it is easy to engage in consumerism or excessive efficiency, making our own materials can help us slow down and pace ourselves more to the rhythm of our children and the Holy Spirit. They also believe that making physical materials can bring adults a greater integration of the heart, head, and hand and will cause this to nurture the same qualities in their children. You can make backdrops or buildings using a cardboard box that you paint. Even if parents or adults are not skilled artists, simple figurines can be created with clay, pipe cleaners, or paper mache. They may be only three to five inches tall and, again, may be handmade. There are many blogs to teach you how to do this, as well as vendor sites related to setting up this holy environment. You can also purchase ready-to-use materials, which are beautiful, online Etsy and otherwise. Google *Catechesis of the Good Shepherd* and religious education at home. You can create simple opportunities for your children to have spiritual experiences.

Catechesis of the Good Shepherd is a growing Catholic movement in communities and homes around the world. If your faith is different, I again, encourage you to witness what they are doing and apply it to your faith. See how this amazing approach touches children's innate spirituality.

Create Your Family Traditions

Before you start preparing for family traditions, I recommend creating a Why Traditions? statement. This statement will clarify what you hope your children will gain from these rituals and activities and help you remember why you are celebrating. Realizing all the benefits our families receive from these activities is helpful. You can keep this statement with your tradition plans so you will see it often. I recommend printing it on beautiful paper so your heart will leap every time you look at it!

One great way to launch into making a family tradition plan is to start reading and researching different holidays and events you think your family could be interested in. Children's books from the library can be beneficial. There are so many to choose from, and they will inspire you. Gather your resources, find a couple of hours to yourself, put your feet up, and get your favorite hot drink. Enjoy some time to yourself to contemplate and dream. Your ideas and inspiration from this will be your vision to inspire your family. Saturate yourself, enjoy the process, and relax! This quiet time will sink into your heart, and later, you can share your discoveries. Below are template samples to help you prepare for holidays, traditions, and celebrations. An excellent book for celebrating with children is *Simply Fun for Families* Design your dream for your family.

Plan your Family Culture Calendar

Some holidays and celebrations may be straightforward and short and take only a few hours. You will want to observe during the whole month or season for some traditions, but you can do this in small or large ways, as you choose. The wonderful thing is that it is all up to you! You might start out with just one or two traditions that you will celebrate in a bigger way and then a few really simple ones for the year. In subsequent years, you can determine to do more for some and less for others in that year, depending on what is happening in your life and schedules. Select the traditions you will follow and try to honor those every year, even simply–such as a family dinner or special dessert. This will deepen your family's experiences, and when they look back at pictures of these events, they will reconnect with the joy and enthusiasm they had at that time and rekindle it. Children will never forget, and it will be worth all the effort.

Organize your Information to Your Greatest Advantage

In addition to your calendar, you can organize a binder or an online tool to keep your plans and resources. You should note on your calendar when you will celebrate and when to start planning. Your family can be a part of the preparations. For more significant celebrations or seasonal observations, you may introduce little lessons and activities to your children a few weeks before an event, solstice, or equinox. You will want to note these lessons on your calendar, as well.

Next, create a section in your binder or online planner for every event you plan. With each section, you can keep a lesson template that includes a description of what you plan to do and how you hope your family will benefit. Finally, create a simple step-by-step lesson plan, listing activities and needed materials—this does not need to be complicated, but if you jot down your steps, it is more likely to happen, and be more organized. You can also keep research results and other information that might be helpful. I recommend keeping pictures from celebrations in each section to warm your family's hearts and help you remember the high points. It will make everyone happy, especially when you have kept traditions year after year.

When you have read and gathered lots of resources about a given event, I recommend you find some quiet time to sit down and plan out your lessons. Consider simplifying information and start with what your children already know about a topic. This will give them a feeling of security as well as curiosity. Show them pictures and help them see what is important about the event and what will be fun! For example: Will cousins and grandparents come? Will the children put on costumes? Or will you go to a special event downtown to learn more? You know your children best and can gauge what time might be best for a lesson or a series of a few simple lessons. Fifteen or twenty minutes may be short enough for little ones, and the more hands-on you make them, the better. If children don't want to sit still for the lesson, right-brain learning says that they can absorb it even if they are moving. Sitting together quietly creates a nice ambiance, but we also want to support our children's developmental needs and allow movement as needed. You can purposefully give them physical things to do or objects to hold.

In the lesson, you will want to identify a lesson's essential purpose. Plan to deliver certain specific facts (maybe three simple ones) so your children can ask questions. And then, couch all of this in an atmosphere of colorful images, stories, and fun. Showing books and very short documentaries or appropriate videos can extend the information. You may want to use maps and resources from history. Pictures of happy children celebrating these traditions can inspire your children with positive expectations.

Dr. Montessori said the way to the child's heart is through the hand. Following up your lesson with hands-on related activities allows the concepts to go deep. You can make crafts, bake, cook, use related puzzles, or make maps. You may put a tray of objects from the culture or celebration on your shelf with label cards, demonstrating how and why they are used. These could go on a shelf for children to touch and talk about. You might gather costumes, hats, or scarves to try on with your family. Making things to decorate the house is a favorite for children, is often easy to do, and makes the ambiance amazing—and you can keep the decorations for the future. Children love to display things they can feel proud of. Making a family timeline with pictures of everyone's births, graduations, marriages, and highlights can be a wonderful project, and if you have physical pictures, your children can help lay it out. (Number the backs of the pictures in order of their layout so others can help you.) This timeline can touch the hearts of everyone in your family because it is about everyone, together!

Logistics for Planned Events

The more you celebrate traditions, the more you will inspire others. The enthusiasm is contagious, and if people can share in the preparation tasks, that can make things easier. Grandparents, extended family, and even the children can help prepare, and everyone will grow closer. If you have extended family, you might consider taking a day in the fall to gather and have everyone interested in planning come together to propose a celebration plan for the year. (If there are young children, maybe someone can create a fun activity for them to do during this time.) Integrating family and community into your celebration planning will be more fun and more accessible for everyone. And, as your family members help year after year, it will create momentum.

Step-by-Step Organizing

Here is a series of sample templates I created to help you organize your traditions and celebrations. A blank version of these templates is available as part of a downloadable set on my website. See the QR code on the inside cover of this book, front and back, to download the set from my website.

1. Start off by writing your *Why Traditions* statement. This may be just you as the parents, or you may want to do it with your children to get the whole picture and include everyone's input.

T8.1 Why Traditions: Template

Why Traditions?
"Our family is choosing to celebrate traditions to increase our knowledge about our family history, to honor our sacred rituals, and to grow closer together. "The lights are my favorite part!" (Francis) We like the decorations and food that makes us feel happy. (Marie)" "And, we like Grandpa and Grandma and our friends to visit. (Frederick)" "It's just super fun." (David)." "I like to give and get presents." (Elizabeth) "I like that we get to have yummy food and do special things." (Clare)
Signed: Family Members David, Francis, Frederick, Clare, Marie, Elizabeth, Dad, and Mom Date: July, 1997

It may seem like a lot of work to organize and plan these activities, but the fun and joy of learning and celebrating together can be more valuable than you can imagine. If needed, keep things simple and set aside a little time each week to work on it, even a few minutes. Just getting things in motion is so motivating.

T8.2 A: Our Annual Family Celebrations and Dates:

Our Annual Family Celebrations and Dates	Date:
Birthdays:	
Anniversaries:	
Annual Family Reunions:	
Other Annual Dates:	
(Hannukah, Diwali, Christmas,) Celebration:	
(New Year's Eve or Other) Celebration:	
Celebration:	

2. Next, take time to discuss with your family and learn what celebrations and events are important to them. Consider choosing from different kinds of activities, like a travel trip for one, and honoring a religious celebration for another choice to round out your experiences. Start by jotting down notes here about your family's thoughts and choices before you launch into a bigger calendar. You might even want to make some tentative decisions, think about it for a few days or a week, and then bring these up for discussion again.

3. Checklist to Begin Tradition Research and Discussion with Family Template

4. Choose one or two events to add to the following template calendar schedule. This may be your preliminary calendar brainstorming session to let things develop.

T8.3 Checklist to Begin Tradition Research and Discussion with Family:

Check-off	Celebration or Event	Your Family's Comments and Notes
	Birthdays	
	Weddings	
	Family Reunions	
	Family Game Nights	
	National Holidays	
	Spiritual rituals: bar mitzvahs, baptisms, Diwali, Kwanzaa, Channukkah, Christmas, Easter. Or write your own:	
	The Solstices and Equinoxes	
	Other:	
	Lunar New Year, Cinco de Mayo, Cherry Blossom Festival/Other	
	Modern Holidays: Earth Day, International Day of Peace	
	Sunday Family Dinners	
	Sunday strolls extended family	
	Entertain friends of another culture	
	Camping trips (campfires, making bows, arrows, & whistles together)	
	Trips	
	Visits to extended family	
	Observatories	
	Science or Art Museum	
	Bike rides	
	Hike in the hills/mountains	
	Backpacking Trips	
	Boat trips	
	Another destination of your family's choice	

5. Plan Your Traditions and Celebrations for the Year

T8.4 Plan Your Family Traditions and Celebrations for this Year!

January	July
February	August
March	September
April	October
May	November
June	December

6. The next step is to write down *when each event planning needs to start*. This template will give you an overview of what the year might look and feel like. Make sure that you give yourself enough planning time for each event so you will enjoy the process and want to do it again next year. When you feel you have a nice plan, you can transfer this onto your main calendar.

7. Now, use the Event Planner Template for each event to get into the details. The more you use it, the easier and more detailed your thinking will be, and the more successful the outcomes! You may find you will be happier with your events when you plan the details ahead of time.

8. Event Planner Sample Template-

T8.5 Event Planner Sample Template

Name of the Event	Mark's Birthday
Envision this Event	A picture of a previous fun get-together of family on Mark's birthday or picture of him.
Purpose of this Event	To celebrate Mark and let him know how much he is cherished and supported by everyone. He will hear each person's appreciation and feel inspired. To create memories and enhance all family connections We will all feel more connected. It will enrich our lives. To have fun on the lake, swim, barbeque, talk, play games
What supplies will you need? (This could be anything and everything—decorations, ritual objects, food, games and activities, tickets for an activity, clothing, etc.)	1. Picture(s) of Mark's previous birthday party 2. Make a sign wishing him a happy birthday 3. Have sand toys for building a sand castle 4. 4-5 different games for kids and adults to play with prizes 5. Crepe streamers and balloons for canopy 6. Canopy from storage 7. Lunch items (See shopping list) 8. Cake and candles 9. Paper plates, disposable utensils 10. Someone to go early and reserve a spot at the beach
Steps to Get Ready for the Big Day	1. Decide on a date 2. Talk to Mark about details of what he wants for the day 3. Write down a plan 4. Delegate jobs (make food, shop, make signs… 5. Write down a plan 6. Delegate jobs (make food, shop, make signs… 7. Call all friends and family (or send invitations) 8. Talk to Mark about details of what he wants for the day? Activities or games? 9. What decorations? Cake? Food? Gifts? Party Favors for guests?

9. Set Up Your Binder or Online Planner (One Note works for some).

10. You can create organized sections and add positive images and phrases.

✧ Picture of your family

✧ Your Why Traditions statement

✧ Templates 2, 3, 4

✧ A calendar

✧ Tabs for each event of the year

✧ Liberal use of Event Planner Template (sample below)

✧ A section for celebrating multiple events (like birthdays) with an overall list of ideas and a separate template for each event.

✧ Add pictures showing happy past events or a generic picture to help you envision what you want.

Our Heritage Enriches Our Children's Lives

The richness of our family heritage on both sides of our family has enhanced our lives. We come from immigrants who worked and made their way to America from Ireland, Scotland, France, and the Philippines. We can study our ancestors' lives and celebrate our family heritage. Belonging is a need of every person. As a child, I had grandparents on my mom's side and a grandmother on my dad's side, both within walking distance of our home. I also enjoyed a large family of cousins, aunts, and uncles. I did not see them monthly, but I cherished the gatherings we had, the feelings of belonging this created, and I carry this hope for all families.

When I think carefully of the home I grew up in, I can recall every square inch of it. It is as if I remember it through my absorbent mind from when I was zero to six. There, I was an infant absorbing my world, and there I attached to my parents and brother, knowing the love and support that set the foundation for my life. I remember the feelings of the house, the projects, the discussions, and my spiritual experiences. It is all recorded in the weave of my being, as is every child's.

Dr. Montessori believed that we could nurture our children's strengths and abilities to lead our world to a new world. The heart of the Montessori home is a place of profound compassion and wisdom. It is the cradle that can nurture hidden possibilities in our children and allow them to lead us to a radiant future.

T8.6 Observation Practice for Chapter Eight: Sample Template

Observation Practice:

You can ask yourself:

1. **Does my family enjoy being together? If not, what can I do to nurture this?**

   Sometimes when we have family meetings, I am too focused on what I want to teach and find that our kids don't like them. I don't want our family meetings or our traditions to feel like that! Instead, I want to empower my children and let them know that they are important in the running of our home and the direction of our family. I want to involve them in the planning of our family nights.

2. **What would I like to teach my children about important traditions and holidays?**

   I would love for our children to have a connection with their Irish relatives. We would like to learn some of the old language and history and travel to Ireland again.

3. **How can my family create a deeper appreciation for our heritage?**

   We can interview family members from both sides of the family in person or online and write a little summary or notes. We can also study the geography and history of our ancestors or parents in Ireland and the Philippines, gather pictures and make a timeline or little book about our family tree. Our children and grandchildren can read and learn from this. We can also use it at family gatherings.

Table 8.1 Chapter Eight Takeaways

Chapter Eight Takeaways
• Family culture is the essence of how we embrace life with one another, how we feel about being together, and what we value.
• Traditions bond us through generations with our history and what we hold as important.
• Montessori enriched children's lives with stories, music, food, and art related to traditions, and families can do the same.
• Your family can choose and plan its traditions and create your desired future.

"Great Book, Teresa, But Where Do I Even Begin?"

I totally get it, gentle reader! If you are a working mom or dad, if your family is very busy, or you just feel overwhelmed, you may wonder, "How do I even begin to implement the suggestions in this book?"

Take a Breath!

Well, there was a time when I, too, had to work through fear and overwhelm. It was the early 90s when I was just getting into the game with four young children and had decided to focus on Montessori for their education. I was so easily excited with new ideas, and my friends and I gathered weekly to talk about how to teach our children at home. I wanted to try everything. It was stimulating to my mind, but the enormity of the task also overwhelmed me. I had accumulated so many resources, but I did not know where to start to get organized.

My head would spin, my heart raced, and I'm sure my face flushed. I can remember hearing myself saying, "How can I do all this? We have so many materials in our garage, but how do I organize them?" or, "We have children of four different ages, where do I start?" Sometimes in my anxiousness, I would just do the first thing that came to mind, rather than making a plan (even a simple one), and that only added to the feeling of chaos.

Ultimately, I found a helpful system. First, I would get my children into bed, clean the house up a little so I could think, and then find a quiet place to sit. Breathing to relax (such as the box breathing described in Chapter Five) allowed me to look at the big picture of what I was trying to do. As I took those deep breaths and thought about what we really wanted, I could then backtrack to see what steps were needed for now. And, then, the details would unfold. I had to learn to simplify my thoughts.

I also comforted my inner child with some soothing words. I would say things like, "Teresa, you love your children and are doing your best. Relax and let go of your fear. Take one step at a time and be gentle with yourself."

When I talked to myself like this I spoke as if I was talking to my children. By letting go of my fear, I could get off the roller coaster of racing anxious thoughts, which did nothing to move me forward. Instead, I could concentrate, and I then could decide what was practical for that moment and keep my dream visible. Keeping a journal was helpful, as was discussing the big questions with my husband. Both were vital, but it was helpful for me to get to a place of my own clarity first, and writing in my journal always helped me. Then, we would discuss our ideas and make a plan.

When our children became six and older I made a list of the big questions:

⬦ Would we have our kids in a Montessori school? Would we have our kids in a public school and use Montessori concepts to enrich their education at home? Would fifteen to thirty minutes a day on topics we were excited to share with them be enough?

⬦ Or should we homeschool everyone with Montessori? Would we homeschool on our own or find a homeschool community?

⬦ If we decided to homeschool, taking a Montessori parent training course would be a good idea. (At that time there were no parent traing courses, only full teacher certification, but it helped me set up a curriculum and a learning environment.)

For several years, we used the knowledge and materials I already had. Then, I took the Montessori teacher training course and used it with our children. We homeschooled for some years and also had years where we supplemented our children in school. Homeschooling was a lot of work overall, but so worth it. I believe it is a very special opportunity for families to learn to live together without the pressure of outside programs and to build the vision of who they really are.

With eight grandchildren, I've discovered the immense joy in sharing experiences with them, as I've detailed in this book. Even something as simple as planting and gardening becomes a delightful adventure. In the process of planning for them, I often find myself revisiting my own advice on staying organized. It's in these moments that I take a step back, breathe, and let my vision unfold. I sketch out a plan and move forward, ensuring I don't feel overwhelmed. I've found that returning to the templates and resources I've created also helps me immensely, and I'm confident they'll be just as beneficial for you.

I encourage you to see the process of doing what is recommended in this book as a journey. Let go of fear and overwhelming feelings and focus on your goal. Have faith that it is possible, mainly by keeping your eye on just one step at a time. I hope you have some ideas you consider implementing from this book that excite you and encourage you not to think it all must be done simultaneously. Instead, do some today and a little more tomorrow. When I saw what I wanted and how to do it, I became so excited that it wasn't difficult anymore. I did work hard, but the work became fun and took on a life of its own.

Deciding your bigger picture with your spouse or partner is important because then you can plan your next steps, together. It is really helpful to have both people on board, but it is not essential. Yes, there will be many steps to take, but starting with a few is best. That way, you can keep your sense of calm and model it for your children.

If you decide that you would like to take a Montessori parent course, the one I recommend is Authentic Institute of Montessori (https://aimmontessoriteachertraining.org). This organization offers virtual training for teaching children from infants and toddlers through upper elementary ages. They are located in Bozeman, Montana, and their programs are mostly online. AIM provides resources and a wonderful community to support and help you. If you take a parent training course, you will be able to focus on your children, get organized for them (rather than for a teaching career), and go full steam ahead. There is something so deeply wonderful and satisfying about investing time and energy like this for our families!

If you decide that you would like to teach your children and possibly homeschool them, take courage. There are so many resources to support you, now. Joining a homeschooling community with others can often make it more fun for you and your children, and you can get help from other, more experienced parents who can support you in every way. When I did this, I felt that it made the whole process more lighthearted. Sharing the joys and challenges of working with our children was so helpful and comforting. However, it's important to remember that homeschooling also requires a clear plan and dedicated time. Both aspects are crucial for a successful homeschooling journey. My intention is to continue developing valuable resources you can use to teach your children at home. Please see my website, Montessorifamilies.com.

If you decide to homeschool, I encourage you to contemplate the "why" first and write it down so you will always be clear about why you are doing it. When things get hard, you can return to your statement of "why" to remember why it is important to you and realize that you are accomplishing your goal. Building relationships with your family may be one of your top reasons, and I believe it is worth it for that alone.

Incorporate Dr. Montessori's respect and unconditional love to nurture your children, your spouse or partner, and yourself. Her timeless principles are key to developing a happy family and will guide you in creating a thriving home learning environment. Her curriculum will help you tap into your children's curiosity. Learn how right brain learning can foster your children's whole brain development, even in the womb. Assess your children's wholeness spiritually, physically, mentally, and emotionally so you can tune into what they each might need and identify and support their strengths as keys to their fulfillment in life. Lastly, perceive why traditions and celebrations can so deeply enrich your family culture.

Embracing the ideas in this book can powerfully impact your family and inspire new intentions and a new dream. Thank you for reading my book and being a part of this journey with me. I wish you well!

Sources

CHAPTER 1

"AMI Montessori." Association Montessori International USA. https://amiusa.org/families/childs-development/.

"Biography of Maria Montessori." Association Montessori Internationale, 2021. https://montessori-ami.org/resource-library/facts/biography-maria-montessori.

Bulletin #4356, "Children and Brain Development: What We Know About How Children Learn." Used with permission from The University of Maine.

Epstein, Paul. "Motivated to Grow: The Child's Passion for Work." *Tomorrow's Child Magazine*, February, 2024. The Montessori Foundation.

Maunz, Mary Ellen. Founder and Program Director. Authentic Institute of Montessori. https://aimmontessoriteachertraining.org/

Montessori, Maria. *From Childhood to Adolescence*. Delhi, Union Territory: Aakar, 2020.

Montessori, Maria. *The Absorbent Mind. Internet Archive.* Accessed 2022. http://archive.org/details/in.ernet.dki.2015.202650. P. 56.

"Erdkinder Virtual Tour." bluffviewmontessori.org. Accessed March 5, 2024. https://www.bluffviewmontessori.org/discover-bluffview/erdkinder-middle-school/erdkinder-virtual-tour/

NAMTA Journals: "North American Montessori Teachers Association – Support to Further Montessori Principles and Understanding for Schools, Teachers, and Parents." n.d. http://montessori-namta.org/.

Orem, Reginald Calvert. *Montessori: Her Method and the Movement*: *What You Need to Know*. New York: Putnam, 1974.

CHAPTER 2

Lillard, Paula Polk and Lynn Lillard Jessen. *Montessori from the Start*. New York: Schocken, 2008.

Montessori, Maria. *The Secret of Childhood*. Trans. Barbara Barclay Carter. New York: Frederick A. Stokes Company, 1939.

Orem, Reginald Calvert. *Montessori: Her Method and the Movement*: *What You Need to Know*. New York: Putnam, 1974.

CHAPTER 3

Klein, Randall. *The Klein Method of Early Reading Mastery*. Bozeman, MT: Early Reading Mastery, 2020.

Montessori, Maria, Anne E George, and June Gormley Goodrich. *The Montessori Method*. New York: Barnes & Noble, 2003.

Orem, Reginald Calvert. *Montessori*.

CHAPTER 4

Hickein, Pamela Sue. 2019. *Right Brain Education: Changing the World One Heart at a Time*. Bozeman, MT: The Soul Learning Comp., 2009. Used with permission.

"The Nobel Prize in Physiology or Medicine 1981." NobelPrize.org. 2019. https://www.nobelprize.org/prizes/medicine/1981/sperry/facts/.

Verny, Thomas R. and John Kelly. 1988. *The Secret Life of the Unborn Child*. New York: Dell, 1988.

CHAPTER 5

Dennison, Paul Ehrlich and Gail E Dennison. *Brain Gym*. Santa Barbara, CA: Edu Kinesthetics. 1986.

Doman, Glenn J. *What To Do About Your Brain-Injured Child: Or your brain-damaged, mentally retarded, mentally deficient, cerebral-palsied, spastic, flaccid, rigid, epileptic, autistic, athetoid, hyperactive child*. Philadelphia: Better Baby Press, 1986.

Doman, Glenn and Janet Doman. *How Smart is Your Baby?* Garden City Park, NY: Square One Publishing, 2006.

Robert Doman. "Review of National Association of Child Development." National Association of Child Development.

"Free Masterclass." The Institutes for the Achievment of Human Potential. Accessed September 18, 2023. https://iahp.org/htm-masterclass.

The Handle Institute. www.handle.org.

"HeartMath Institute." HeartMath Institute. https://www.heartmath.org/.

Stinson, Adrienne. "Box Breathing: How to Do It, Benefits, and Tips." www.medicalnewstoday.com. June 1, 2018. https://www.medicalnewstoday.com/articles/321805.

CHAPTER 6

Armstrong, Thomas. *Multiple Intelligences in the Classroom*. 4th ed. Alexandria, VA: ASCD, 2017.

"Classical Music and Your Health." n.d. Hylton Performing Arts Center. Accessed May 5, 2022. https://hyltoncenter.org/news/2020-01/classical-music-and-your-health.

Dunckley, Victoria L. "Gray Matters: Too Much Screen Time Damages the Brain." *Psychology Today*, February 27, 2014. https://www.psychologytoday.com/us/blog/mental-wealth/201402/gray-matters-too-much-screen-time-damages-the-brain.

Fleming, Emilie. "The Healing Power of Nature." UC News, August 3,2023. https://www.uc.edu/news/articles/2023/08/the-healing-power-of-nature.html

Gardner, Howard. *Frames of Mind: The Theory of Multiple Intelligences.* New York: Basic Books, 1983.

Jenkins, J S. 2001. "The Mozart Effect." Journal of the Royal Society of Medicine 94 (4) 2001, 170–72. https://www.ncbi.nlm.nih.gov/pmc/articles/PMC1281386.

Kinder Musik. https://www.kindermusik.com/.

Louv, Richard. *Last Child in the Woods.* Chapel Hill, NC: Algonquin Books, 2008.

Neufeld, Gordon and Gabor Maté. *Hold on to Your Kids: Why Parents Need to Matter More than Peers.* New York: Ballantine, 2014.

Rafiee, Marjan, Kramay Patel, David M. Groppe, Danielle M. Andrade, Eduard Bercovici, Esther Bui, Peter L. Carlen, et al. "Daily Listening to Mozart Reduces Seizures in Individuals with Epilepsy: A Randomized Control Study." *Epilepsia Open* 5 (2) 2020, 285–94. https://doi.org/10.1002/epi4.12400.

Rettig, Michael. "Using the Multiple Intelligences to Enhance Instruction for Young Children and Young Children with Disabilities." Early Childhood Education Journal 32 (4) 2005,

255–59. https://doi.org/10.1007/s10643-004-0865-2.

Rose, Colin. *Accelerated Learning*, as cited in Thomas Armstrong, *Multiple Intelligences in the Classroom.*

Suzuki Institute. https://suzukiinstitute.org/.

Wilderness Awareness School: wildernessawareness.org/.

CHAPTER 7

Bowlby, John Bowlby Mary Ainesworth. n.d. Review of "The Origins of Attachment." http://Www.psychology.sunysb.edu/Attachment/ Online/Inge_origins.pdf.

Campbell, D. Ross. *How to Really "Love" Your Child.* Colorado Springs, Co: David C. Cook, 1977.

Covey, Stephen R. *The 7 Habits of Highly Effective Families.* New York: St. Martin's Griffin, 1997.

"The Gottman Institute." 2015. The Gottman Institute. September 22, 2015. https://www.gottman.com/.

Gottman, John Mordechai, Julie Schwartz Gottman, Douglas Carlton Abrams, and Rachel Carlton Abrams. *Eight Dates: Essential Conversations for a Lifetime of Love.* New York: Workman Publishing, 2018.

Leinicke, Connie. "Worldwide Marriage Encounter – Experiences for Married Couples." *Worldwide Marriage Encounter.* Accessed September 17, 2023. http://www.wwme.org/.

Longfellow, H. W. https://www.hwlongfellow.org/poems_front.php.

"Neufeld`s Model of Attachment." n.d. https://neufeldinstitute.org/ course/neufelds-model-of-attachment/.

Neufeld, Gordon and Gabor Maté. *Hold on to Your Kids: Why Parents*

Need to Matter More than Peers. New York: Ballantine, 2014.

Ponder, Catherine. *The Dynamic Laws of Prosperity.* Camarillo, CA: Devorss Publications, 1997.

Savoy, Terri Savelle. *Dream It. Pin It. Live It.* https://www.audible.com/pd/*Dream-It-Pin-It-Live-It-*Audiobook/B0C5K6VWBW.

Siegel, Daniel J. and Mary Hartzell. 2014. *Parenting from the Inside Out: How a Deeper Self-Understanding Can Help You Raise Children Who Thrive.* New York: Jeremy P. Tarcher/Penguin, 2014. Used with permission.

Siegel, Daniel J. and Mary Hartzell. *The Whole-Brain Child: 12 Revolutionary Strategies to Nurture Your Child's Developing Mind.* New York: Random House, 2012.

Siegel, Daniel J. and Mary Hartzell. *The Whole-Brain Child Workbook: Practical Exercises, Worksheets, and Activities to Nurture Developing Minds.* Eau Claire, WI: Pesi Publishing & Media. 2015.

Siegel, Daniel J. and Mary Hartzell. *No-Drama Discipline: The Whole-Brain Way to Calm the Chaos and Nurture Your Child's Developing Mind.* New York: Bantam Books, 2016.

Staff. "Research Impact." University of Oxford. Accessed June 28, 2024. https://www.ox.ac.uk/research/research-impact.

CHAPTER 8

Catechesis of the Good Shepherd. https://www.cgsusa.org.

Duke, Marshall, and Robin Fivush. "The Stories the Bind Us: What Are the Twenty Questions?" *Huffpost* (blog), May 23, 2013.

Ellis, Gwen. 2005. *Simply Fun for Families.* Ada, MI: Fleming H. Revell Comp., 2005.

Photo and Art Credits

Picture 1.1 Partial cover art, Maria Bano on Fiverr.com 2024;

Picture 1.2 Maria Montessori, World Renowned Speaker, https://www.montessoricentenary.org/photos/;

Picture 1.3 The Beautiful Absorbent Mind of a Child, 1.muhammad-taha-ibrahim He6qW0KX24-unsplash (1)free; Picture 1.4 Adolescent Farm Work, https://www.montessoricentenary.org/photos/;

Picture 1.5 Nature Montessori Rope Bridge, https://www.montessoricentenary.org/photos/;

Picture 1.6 Siblings Brushing Teeth, Kathryn Angeles 2023;

Picture 2.1 Partial cover art, Maria Bano on Fiverr.com 2024;

Picture 2.2 Triangle of Child, Adult, and Environment, Teresa Angeles 2024;

Picture 2.3 Dishwashing Station, Teresa Angeles 2024;

Picture 2.4 A Learning Area, Teresa Angeles 2024;

Picture 2.5 A Cubicle Shelf Works for Five Areas, Teresa Angeles 2024;

Picture 2.6 An infant on a blanket, Depositphotos_289041464_XL;

Picture 2.7 Toddler Weaning Table, Hallie Lobough 2016;

Picture 3.1 Partial cover art, Maria Bano on Fiverr.com 2024;

Picture 3.2 Sponging Water, Jessica Chu 2016;

Picture 3.3 Spooning Beans, Teresa Angeles 2024;

Picture 3.4 Picking Tomatoes, Hallie Lobaugh 2016;

Picture 3.5 Children Making Dumplings in China, https://www.montessoricentenary.org/photos/;

Picture 3.6 Cutting Vegetables, Hallie Lobaugh 2016;

Picture 3.7 Scooping Veggie Burgers, Hallie Lobaugh 2016;

Picture 3.8 Child Using Cylinder Blocks, https://www.montessoricentenary.org/photos/;

Pictures 3.9 Boy with the Red Rods, https://www.montessoricentenary.org/photos/;

Picture 3.10 Child Working with Constructive Triangles, https://www.montessoricentenary.org/photos/;

Picture 3.11 Boy Reading, aaron-burden-6jYoil2GhVk-unsplash;

Picture 3.12 Matching Pictures to First Sounds, Teresa Angeles 2024;

Pictures 3.13-16 Three-Letter Word Work, Teresa Angels 2024;

Picture 3.17 Children Working with Math Materials, https://www.montessoricentenary.org/photos/;

Picture 7.1 Partial Cover Art, Maria Bano on Fiverr.com 2024;

Picture 7.1a Family Running on the beach, vecteezy_happy-young-family-have-fun-on-beach-at-sunset_12642135; Picture 7.2 Couple Biking, Free everton-vila-AsahNlC0VhQ-unsplash;

Picture 7.2a Father with Son, Laughing, pexels-dariaobymaha-1683975;

Picture 7.3 Father and Daughter, Free caleb-jones-rpPvrOQmR2s-unsplash (1);

Picture 7.4 Family, Free Adam-sherez-WMjqzYGoU5w-unsplash;

Picture 7.5 Children, Jumping with Joy, stockvault-the-joy-of-childhood-bw101868 (2) edwin s. loyola free;

Picture 8.1 Partial Cover Art; Maria Bano on Fiverr.com;

Picture 8.1a Candles burning, vecteezy_a-collection-of-colorful-candles-burning-in-front-of-a_48657124;

Picture 8.2 Hot Cider and Candy Canes in the Forest, Kathryn Angeles 2017;

Picture 8.3 Girl Closing Eyes in Prayer, Depositphotos_21134289_XL (1);

Picture 8.4 Girl Praying with Grandmother, Depositphotos_184707626_L;

Picture 8.5 The Good Shepherd Lesson 1 and 2, Constance Dratz 2018;

Picture 8.6 Nativity Figurines, Teresa Angeles 2024;

Picture 10.1Back Cover Maria Montessori, https://www.montessoricentenary.org/photos/;

Picture of Teresa Angeles, Lifetouch Photography 2016.

Picture of Maria Montessori, back cover, https://www.montessoricentenary.org/photos/;

Acknowledgments

I would like to express my heartfelt thanks to my friend and colleague, Christine Lapierre, whose gift of clarity helped me to shape and embellish this book with the ideas and love I truly wanted to share. Her knowledge of Montessori and commitment to excellence was a gift. This book would not have happened in the same way without her help.

My children and their spouses were an amazing support team who helped me make this book possible. They read, edited, advised, and rewrote. They consulted on stories, fonts, cover design, and illustrations. For the many hours of work with me on my Instagram account, other technology, and best business practices. Their continued gifts of love, encouragement, and expertise have been irreplaceable and appreciated.

I am so grateful for having grown up as part of a loving and supportive family, with grandparents from French Canada and Ireland. They believed sincerely in the importance of family and made everyone know it was a priority. Through my parents, aunts and uncles, cousins, and especially my brother, Mike, and sister, Debbie, this has continued and has set the course for our lives and our children. A vision of family as a foundation of love is a powerful place from which to raise children, and I am so grateful.

A very special thank you is due to my first readers, Ashly and Will Stukaloff, Christopher Angeles, Jaji Dhaliwal, Pearl Angeles, Marianne Molina, Valerie McBride, Linda Cruce Robin, and Jose Manuel Gonzales. Thank you for your significant time and commitment to give me feedback and answer so many questions. It helped me tremendously.

Thank you to those who took the time to review and endorse my work. It is much appreciated and a treasure to have your commendation: Nancy McNabb, Joye Bennett, Mary Ellen Maunz, James and Pamela Toole, Philip Gang, Carol Fisher, Tina Storti, and Hallie Lobaugh. Many of you also gave valuable feedback and editing recommendations, especially Mary Ellen Maunz, who gave hours of professional detail.

Thank you also to Lynn Wilton, who supported me in the earliest days of my writing and was a voice of confidence and encouragement.

A special thank you to Psychiatrist and author Daniel Siegel, who permitted me to quote and paraphrase his books *Parenting from the Inside Out* and *The Whole Child*. These books have added irreplaceable and heartwarming elements for parents to better understand themselves and their children.

I am deeply grateful to Pamela Hickein for permitting me to quote and paraphrase freely from her eBook, *Right Brain Education*. This, along with the continual support of her associate, Wennie Sun, has allowed me to delve deeply into right brain learning. I learned a tremendous amount as I integrated this material in my book, and then used it with my grandchildren where I learned even more. I genuinely hope everyone reading my book will use their wonderful programs.

Early on, I benefited from rich discussions with Candice Vann, nutritionist, homeschooler, friend, and ministry teacher, who shared her experiences with me about doing right brain learning activities with her children and others. It was very helpful.

I am so grateful to Hallie Lobaugh for the gift of her children's pictures which reveal her thoughtful approach to Montessori parenting. I appreciate the beauty and evidence they have contributed.

Thank you to Patricia Conant, who gifted me with her beautiful drawing of an infant which I have used in my book and so appreciate.

I am grateful to Ashok and Sambita Ghosh, with whom I have spent much time discussing family and cultural values and customs, which helped me clarify what I wanted to say here.

My students of all ages and times have taught me tremendously including my children, as well as students at school and in the homes where I have tutored. They were indeed my teachers, and I have been honored and blessed to support them.

I am grateful for all who welcomed me to teach in their schools and gave me the opportunity to practice Montessori principles. I learned so much about working with children and the community. I loved the outdoor programs we developed, the debris huts we built in the woods, and the gardening at every school, and I am grateful.

I thank my coworkers who collaborated with me. We often learned together. Our discussions and friendships helped me work through the challenges and demands of curriculum and classroom management. Marie Lynn, you were an angel. Pamela Fulton Thomas, your early support and joy fueled my fire to write this book, and I miss you. Sherrell Hayes, I learned much from you about structure as we worked with infants. Kim Adams and Becky Beirne, I appreciate your spirits and all you taught me. Kathy Swingle, Brianna Paznokas, Julie Cox, Shawna and Diana, and so many others at Saint Nicholas Montessori, thank you! Hallie Lobaugh, Clary Gasper, Chelsea Fields, and Azra Govani at Living Montessori; Alice Mcullen, Ms. Yoko, Ms. Bing, and Ms. Guererro at International Montessori, thank you. I am grateful for all we shared and the children's lives that we touched.

Thank you to my Montessori homeschooling moms and friends, Valerie McBride, Jennie Haley, Marietta Alas, Christine Lapierre, and Patricia Conant, for the years of collaboration in so many ways. We learned together and supported one another. Our friendships and vision have supported our families for decades and continue to do so.

Thank you to the Family and Youth Ministry Team who have contributed more to my awareness about children and my mission to support them than anything else in my life. I am eternally grateful to Peter and Tina Storti, Candice Vann, Annemarie Quinto, Mary Ellen Maunz, Joye Bennett, Kate Gordon, Mayela Koster, Anneli Rontallo, Joseph Angeles, and many others as we worked tirelessly together for years.

This acknowledgment would be remiss without deep gratitude for the help of many coaches at Steve Harrison's *Get Published Now* Program. These coaches helped me with every aspect of this book: Dr. Sarah Brown, your humor, wisdom, and experience as an author were invaluable. Your clear objectives kept me focused and balanced and helped me cut through challenges and confusion. Thank you so much for believing in me so I could believe in myself! Geoffrey Berwind, thank you for helping me make my stories the best they could be to express some of the tenderest moments of my life. I am so grateful for the feedback that these stories have made a big difference in my book. Valerie Costa, I appreciate the warmth and enthusiasm you shared about my writing as you edited, which made such a big difference. Cristina Smith, I loved the beauty surrounding your Zoom presence and your published books, and so appreciated your help. Debby Englander, thank you for the kind counsel regarding vital details of the editing process. Christy Day, thank you for your patience as I endured a very long process of assembling my front cover. Your counsel was invaluable, and your exceptional skills in putting the physical book together are astounding to me. Russ Weinzimmer, thank you for your kind and valuable legal counsel about writing my book. It made me feel safe to go forward. You have become friends, and I am grateful.

Thank you, Steve Harrison, for a truly excellent organization that has blessed and helped me accomplish a very important goal.

The excellent coaches and structure of *Get Published Now* saw me through one of the most significant challenges of my life, and I have no words to express my gratitude.

Thank you to Handle Practitioner Judy Russell, my friend, who has been an ongoing mentor, helping me understand how specific simple exercises can heal children's neurological issues. Your generosity has been an enormous blessing, deeply enriching my work with children in foundational ways, possibly more important than academics. It has become a part of my daily work for myself and my students.

Thank you to Kathryn Long and Ruth Chester Jones for your love and prayer support. It opened unimaginable doors, and I am so grateful.

Thank you to the Bellevue College Library librarians and student tech volunteers, especially Will, who helped me with many technical issues and questions about book credits.

And, last but not least, a special thank you to Lilian Alvarado, a friend and colleague who spoke confidence into my heart six years ago and suggested that I write this book. Thank you for holding the vision for me and sharing your passion for pursuing it! You are a true friend.

About the Author

Teresa Angeles is a mother of six, grandmother of eight, an experienced Montessori-certified teacher for children two to twelve years old, and a past homeschooler. She has a master's degree in education with an emphasis in Montessori from the TIES Institute at Endicott College. In the school setting, she has worked with hundreds of families with infants, toddlers, and children. For over twenty-five years, her work in family ministry led her to co-facilitate five-day overnight retreats for teens, assisting in wilderness adventures; and organize teen mission trips to Mexico with her children and others. Her passionate love for children, youth, and families has cultivated a mission of service and education. She continues to create resources to help parents navigate the challenging years of raising children based on the transformative principles of Montessori and other helpful approaches. She firmly advocates that parents believe in themselves and follow their dreams. Designing a home and lifestyle where families can flourish is invaluable, even if those dreams are out of the ordinary.

Residing in the picturesque Pacific Northwest, Teresa operates a Montessori tutoring business, focusing on reading and writing. She enjoys consulting with parents and conducting seminars on how to teach children to read the Montessori way. Her personal joys include spending time with family and community, hiking, singing, playing music, gardening, and celebrating cultural traditions. She desires to share her knowledge with parents around the world to improve children's lives everywhere.

FREE OFFER

If you want downloadable copies of the templates in this book, please go to my website at Montessorifamilies.com, or use the QR code below.

www.ingramcontent.com/pod-product-compliance
Lightning Source LLC
Chambersburg PA
CBHW071454140726
47997CB00005B/1723